S0-DHW-914

DISCARDED

EX LIBRIS

SOUTH ORANGE
PUBLIC LIBRARY

A WOMAN'S GUIDE TO WALL STREET

A WOMAN'S GUIDE TO WALL STREET

BY N. LEONARD JARVIS

Prentice-Hall, Inc., Englewood Cliffs, New Jersey

332.6
Ja

A Woman's Guide to Wall Street by N. Leonard Jarvis

© 1969 by N. Leonard Jarvis

All rights reserved. No part of this book may be
reproduced in any form or by any means, except for
the inclusion of brief quotations in a review,
without permission in writing from the publisher.

Library of Congress Catalog Card Number: 69–19108

Printed in the United States of America · T

13–962241–1

Prentice-Hall International, Inc., London
Prentice-Hall of Australia, Pty. Ltd., Sydney
Prentice-Hall of Canada, Ltd., Toronto
Prentice-Hall of India Private Ltd., New Delhi
Prentice-Hall of Japan, Inc., Tokyo

Acknowledgment is hereby made for quotations of material
from the following sources:

Social Technology by Olaf Helmer © 1966 by Olaf Helmer,
Basic Books, Inc., Publishers, New York.

Standard & Poor's Listed Stock Reports, Standard & Poor's
Corporation, New York.

TO
PEGGY MARJORIE JUPE JARVIS
WITH LOVE

ACKNOWLEDGMENTS

The author is indebted to Herman Klurfeld for his invaluable editorial assistance. He is also grateful for the cooperation offered by the New York Stock Exchange, the American Stock Exchange and the National Association of Securities Dealers, Inc. The author is further indebted to the following for their typing and other assistance: Mrs. Jeanette Klurfeld, Mrs. Norma Pilzer, Mr. George Hellman and Mr. Sam Klurfeld.

INTRODUCTION

Until recently, Wall Street was virtually a No-Woman's-Land. During the past decade, however, the unprecedented surge in stock market interest has been accompanied by a phenomenal increase in women investors. This progression is continuing at an accelerated pace, but women investors have unique problems and require special guidance. Entering the financial wilderness is easy. Emerging from it with profits requires a bit of planning. Hence we have compiled a guide that will throw light on the hidden recesses of the market and point the way toward successful investing.

This book is a map of the financial community. It charts the prosperous avenues, the forbidding by-ways, the short cuts to success or failure and the profitless deadends. We trust it will be useful to women who have ventured into this fascinating and complex area. It will prove especially helpful to those who intend to explore it.

It would be foolish to conclude that proper guidance guarantees profits; without such guidance, however, losses are inevitable. In dealing with the stock market, preconceptions and misconceptions abound. A proper understanding of the financial terrain will help the investor gain the know-how to safeguard new investments and put her intuition and judgment to the best possible use.

N. L. J.

CONTENTS

chapter one

Romance and Riches in Wall Street

Can a woman find happiness married to an IBM computer? The answer is an enthusiastic affirmative if the lady is the one we have in mind. In the thirties she put $6,000 of her hard-earned savings into the stock of International Business Machines. By the 1960's her investment was worth well over $1,000,000.

Back in 1938 a young lady fell in love with a company called Minnesota Mining and Manufacturing. She expressed her devotion by investing $4,000 in the company's stock. Her faith remained steadfast. In 1961 her shares had a market value of more than $500,000. How is that for a happy ending?

Then there's the lady investor who has been going steady with Xerox for sixteen years. It is the most satisfying relationship she's ever had.

Of course, not all Wall Street stories are of the Cinderella variety. Some end up more like Humpty-Dumpty. Nevertheless, to a greater or lesser degree, everybody in the stock market is driven by the desire to use money to make more money. And increasingly those people turn out to be women.

Even beyond Wall Street females are playing increasingly important roles in investment decisions. This reflects both the rising educational level of women and a growing awareness that the complexities of modern family finances require the interest and attention of both husband and wife.

An in-depth study conducted by the New York Stock Exchange in 1965 confirmed that seldom does the final decision to invest in a stock involve only one partner of a marriage. Togetherness dominates the buying and selling of stocks, although the extent of the wife's participation varies greatly. To be honest, in the majority of cases it was found that the wife's role amounts to no more than that of a silent partner. However, it should be stressed that regardless of how passive it was, her approval was frequently essential, even in cases where the husband had taken the initiative in acquiring the necessary background information and was strongly in favor of

1

the investment. Furthermore, the wives exercised veto power; the survey disclosed that a man rarely makes a stock investment decision when his wife is unwilling to invest.

On the other hand, one out of five new investors interviewed credited his wife with having initiated the family's interest in stock ownership. The wife had either looked into the situation herself or had encouraged her husband to investigate the opportunities in stock investing. One husband observed: "My wife always questioned if the best thing was to put our savings in a bank account —or whether we should be investing in stocks."

As a woman, then, you would be downright silly to feel that high finances were out of your line. Evidence has it that the times are indeed changing.

A recent issue of *Time* magazine carried a report about the popularity of television stations that devote the bulk of their programming to business and stock market news. The article noted: "So enthusiastic is the audience that country clubs now keep their sets tuned to the market action, as do bars, beauty salons and doctors' offices. The most ebullient response comes from businessmen's wives who suddenly find that they can talk intelligently about the market with their husbands. One overwhelmed Dallas woman wrote to a television station that 'your stock market show is the greatest thing that has happened to me since sex.' "

One has only to compare the average American woman with her counterpart of fifty years ago to note the change in the habits of living caused by the accelerated motions of the twentieth century. Little more than two generations ago even the right to vote was reserved as a purely masculine privilege. After dinner the sexes would separate so that the little lady would not be troubled with conversation that was "over her head." Today her television and radio tells her what is going on in the world; her car whisks her to town, and jets take her to places that once were touched only by her dreams. She and her children are protected far more adequately by modern medicine and modern hospitals. Her world is much broader than the world of her grandmother. Her folkway has changed; more important, it is still changing and will continue to change even more.

Wall Street offers a prime illustration of this transformation. Less than fifty years ago the financial realm was an all-male society understood only by a small group of men. This "men's club mystique" has now ended; women are growing more and more aware of Wall Street.

Certainly money knows no gender. As a woman, you have the same reasons for investing as any member of the Elks. Various surveys have categorized the motivations of stock market investors Can you find one that doesn't appeal to the distaff side?

1. Comfortable retirement
2. Security for family
3. Children's education
4. Home improvement and real estate
5. Long-term wealth
6. Inflation hedge
7. Increased income

Every investor shares a common objective: a desire to become that much richer.

As a woman, you actually have advantages over the male investor. You probably have more leisure time in which to read, learn, and make decisions. You have your feminine intuition and your basic knowledge of shopping and bargain hunting. Unfortunately, most investment guides do not take these female assets into account.

This book will show you why and how you should invest and help you to get richer quicker. It can even help you become a broker, should you want to.

Perhaps the easiest way to learn the basics is by watching someone else go through the motions. So let's take a case history, step by step.

Any woman whose heart beats faster while reading about a starlet's 33.19 carat, $305,000 diamond ring, or while scanning elegant mansions pictured in glossy periodicals, will concur that the richer the better. So did Elaine.

A Baltimore housewife, she was interested in increasing her income. She decided that she could afford to invest some of her savings in the stock market, so she talked to friends about their brokers and watched newspapers for advertisements of brokerage houses. Over the course of two weeks she visited several brokers. She opened an account with one of them who especially impressed her with his helpfulness and his knowledge about investing. He had given her materials to read, talked to her about some of the stocks and companies, and answered her questions.

She was shrewd enough to take several wise steps: (1) She took time to select a broker in whom she had confidence; (2) she studied several industries and stocks; (3) she got facts and expert opinions about the stock she intended to buy; (4) she tailored her investment to fit her particular needs.

Moreover, she spurned the seductive song of an enthusiastic promotor of hot tips. "Buy Geewhiz Electronics," he crooned, "and you can quadruple your investment in a month. The company will soon announce a new product that will cure cancer as well as athlete's foot. Get in on the ground floor, dearie." (However, she would have been a foolish girl indeed to have turned a deaf ear to his blandishments if it had turned out that his hot tips were *continually* as hot as advertised. Let's face it—a girl should be practical.)

Elaine decided to buy 100 shares of Upandaway Airlines, a company listed on the New York Stock Exchange. One day she phoned her broker and asked him to find out what Upandaway Airlines shares were selling for. Thus began a process that in technical terms might sound incredibly complex but which takes place with relative ease hundreds of thousands of times a day.

THE QUOTE

Over a wire to his New York office the broker asked for a "quote" on Upandaway. A clerk in the firm's New York office dialed a four-digit code. Within seconds a computer identified the stock, located the current quote, assembled the response from a recording drum vocabulary, and sent it back to the clerk in the New York office. He immediately reported to Baltimore that Upandaway was quoted at "twenty to a quarter, last at twenty and a quarter." This meant that at the moment the highest bidder was offering to buy Upandaway at $20 per share and that the last transaction in that stock had been at $20.25.

Elaine learned that 100 shares would cost her approximately $2,000, plus a commission based on the price rather than on the number of the shares she bought.

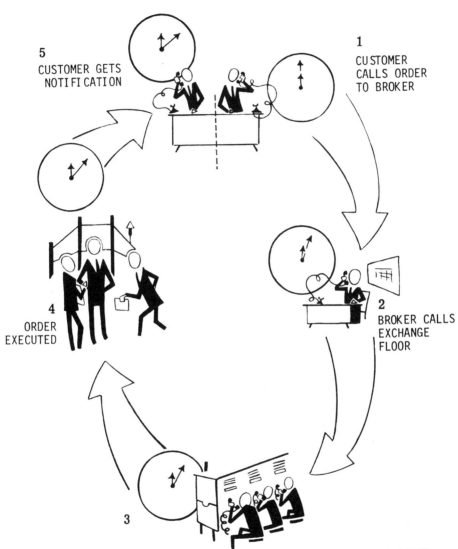

5 CUSTOMER GETS NOTIFICATION

1 CUSTOMER CALLS ORDER TO BROKER

2 BROKER CALLS EXCHANGE FLOOR

4 ORDER EXECUTED

3

CLERK ON FLOOR RECEIVES ORDER

She told her broker to go ahead. So he wrote out an order to buy 100 shares of UA (the symbol for "Upandaway Airlines") "at the market" (that is, at the best price possible at that time) and had it wired to his New York office, where it was phoned or wired to his firm's partner on the floor of the Exchange. Here's what the order, called a buy slip, looked like:

NY	NYSE • ASE • OTC • MFD • SYN • FGN • CMY • MUN
BO	BSE • OTC
LA	PCE • OTC
CH	MWSE • OTC • CMY • CDA • SYN • MUN

LONG	SELL		
QUANTITY	SECURITY	PRICE	GTC
100	*UA*	*20*	GOOD THRU

C. F. O.

ACCOUNT NO. *11 - 0010 - 3 - 304*	INSTRUCTIONS	
	HOLD FUNDS	
SPECIAL INSTRUCTIONS:	PAY PROCEEDS	
	PAY BALANCE	
	SPEC. INSTNS.	

HAYDEN, STONE INCORPORATED

Now, each stock is assigned a specific location at one of the eighteen trading posts on the floor of the Stock Exchange, and all bids and offers in the stock must take place at that location. The broker's floor partner hurried over to Post 14, where UA is traded.

THE SELLER

At the same time Norma, a Seattle saleswoman, decided she would sell her 100 shares of Upandaway to get funds for a long vacation in Europe. She called her broker, got a quote, and told him to sell. That order too was wired to the floor after the sell order was written. As you can see, the order is similar to a buy slip:

NY	NYSE	ASE	OTC	MFD	SYN	FGN	CMY	MUN
BO	BSE	OTC						
LA	PCE	OTC						
CH	MWSE	OTC	CMY	CDA	SYN	MUN		

B U Y

QUANTITY	SECURITY	PRICE	GTC
100	*UA*	*Market*	GOOD THRU

C. F. O.

ACCOUNT NO *17 − 3167 − 4 − 702*	INSTRUCTIONS:
	TRANSFER & SHIP CUST
SPECIAL INSTRUCTIONS	TRANSFER & SHIP OFFICE
	TRANSFER & HOLD
	HOLD STREET NAME
	SPECIAL INSTN

HAYDEN, STONE INCORPORATED

Of course, Norma's floor broker also hurried to Post 14. Just as he entered the UA "crowd," he heard Elaine's floor broker calling out, "How's Upandaway?" Someone answered, "twenty to a quarter."

This meant that Elaine's floor broker could, without further thought, buy the 100 shares offered at 20¼ and that Norma's floor broker could sell her 100 shares at 20. If the two brokers had done this and if Norma and Elaine had been able to look over the brokers' shoulders, the two ladies probably would have said, "Why didn't you try to get a better price for us?" They would have been right—that's what any broker is expected to do.

When he enters the crowd on the floor he is supposed to exercise his experience, knowledge, and brokerage skill to get the best price he can for his customer. Accordingly, he finds himself making some split-second decisions.

Here's how Norma's and Elaine's brokers might have been thinking as each sought the best price for his customer:

Elaine's broker: "I can't buy my hundred at twenty. Someone has already bid twenty, and no one's willing to sell at that price. They're waiting for a better offer. Guess I'd better bid twenty and one eighth."

Hearing Elaine's broker bid 20⅛, Norma's broker realized, "That's even better than twenty, but not as good as it could be. Still, the price might slip. I'd better compromise." Instantly he shouted, "Sold one hundred at twenty and one eighth." They agreed on the price and a transaction took place.

THE DEAL IS MADE

The two brokers completed their verbal agreement by noting each other's firm name and reporting the transaction back to their phone clerks so that both their customers could be notified.

In the meantime, an Exchange employee at Post 14 pencil-marked a special card to indicate the stock symbol, the number of shares, and the price and placed it in an optical card reader. The card reader then scanned the pencil marks with its photoelectric eyes and transmitted the information to the Market Data System computer. This computer recorded the information in its memory banks and in turn transmitted the details of the transaction to some five thousand tickers and display devices in the United States, Canada, Europe, etc. It appeared like this: UA 20⅛.

All this had taken place within a few minutes.

You may buy from or sell to the specialist if he wishes to bring the market quotations closer than outside bids and offers.

Over and over again this procedure is repeated on the floor of the Exchange. As the New York Stock Exchange's literature often notes, there are four considerations to keep in mind if you're an investor: (1) When you buy (as Elaine did) you buy from another person (Norma); (2) when you sell (as Norma did) you sell to another person (Elaine); (3) the Stock Exchange itself neither buys, sells, nor sets prices; (4) the Exchange merely provides the marketplace.

1. The abbreviated name of the company issuing the stock is given—in this case, American Potash & Chemical Corp. It is common stock unless

2. "pf" follows the name—indicating a preferred stock.

3. Columns showing the "highest" and "lowest" prices paid for a stock on the Exchange during the year—in this case, $43.25 and $29.37½.

4. Numbers following names show *the rate of annual dividend*—for this stock, $2.00. The amount may be changed but is an estimation based on the last quarterly or semi-annual payments. Letters following the dividend numbers indicate other information about the dividend. For instance,

5. The "b" indicates that in addition to the annual dividend rate shown ($.50 for this stock) a stock dividend was paid. Other symbols used are explained in a table appearing in each newspaper.

6. This column shows the number or shares reported traded for the day—expressed in hundreds, for this stock 31,700. This number does not include stocks bought and sold in odd-lot quantities, that is, in quantities less than 100 shares for most stocks. The "z" means the actual number of shares traded—for Anaconda Wire & Cable Co., 130 shares.

Yr High	Yr Low	Stock	Sales	Open	High	Low	Close	Chg
32-1/8	8-1/4	Am Photo .33	.. 144	13-1/4	13-3/8	13-1/8	13-1/8-	1/8
54-3/4	24	Am Potash 1.20	.. 45	32-5/8	33-3/4	32-5/8	32-3/4	..
30-7/8	14	Am Resrch .61e	. 9	19	19	18-1/2	18-1/2-	1/4
40-3/8	23-7/8	Am Seat 1.60	.. 27	28-1/8	28-1/2	28-1/8	28-1/2+	1/8
18 1/2	8-5/8	Am Ship	.. 11	13-1/4	13-1/4	12-1/2	12-7/8-	3/8
65	48-5/8	Am Smelt 2.40	.. 20	55-3/4	56	55-1/2	55-5/8+	3/8
152	142	Am Smelt pf 7.z	30	148-1/4	148-1/4	148-1/4	148-1/4	..
33-1/4	20-7/8	Am So Afr .40	.. 63	27-1/4	27-5/8	26-5/8	27-3/8+	7/8
18-1/4	12	Am Std .80	.. 69	13-1/8	13-1/4	13-1/8	13-1/4+	1/8
43-1/4	29-3/8	Am Sugar 1.60a	. 8	37-1/8	38	37-1/8	38 +	1/2
36-3/4	32	Am Sug pf 1.75	. 8	36-1/4	36-1/2	36-1/8	36-1/2	..
136-1/4	98-1/8	Am TelTel 3.60	. 32	115-1/8	115-1/2	114-1/2	114-5/8	..
44-3/8	25-1/8	Am Tob 1.50	.. 144	30	30-1/4	29-7/8	29-7/8-	1/8
134-3/8	123	Am Tob pf 6xd.z	270 128	128-1/4	128	128	..
61-5/8	42-1/2	Am Viscose 2	.. 97	60	60-1/2	59-1/4	59-3/8-	3/4
25-1/4	20	Am W Wks 1	.. 1	21-3/4	21-3/4	21-3/4	21-3/4+	3/8
24-3/4	22-1/2	Am WW pref 1.25	5	24	24	24	24	..
15-3/4	10	Am Zinc .50b	. 4	12-7/8	13	12-7/8	13	..
54	39	Ametek 160a xd	. 3	46-7/8	46-7/8	46-3/4	46-3/4	..
33-7/8	17	AMP Inc .36	.. 41	26-7/8	27-1/8	26-1/2	27 +	5/8
20-5/8	10	Ampex Cp	... 317	18-1/8	18-1/8	17-5/8	17-3/4-	3/8
37-1/2	16-3/4	Amph Borg .80	.. 48	22-7/8	22-7/8	22-1/4	22-1/4	..
37-5/8	23-1/4	Amsted 1.60	.. 29	30-1/4	30-3/8	30	30-1/4-	1/8
52-5/8	35-3/4	Anaconda 2.50e	.. 70	41-1/4	42-3/8	41-7/8	42-3/8+	3/4
37	23-1/2	Apac WC .50e	..z130	28-3/4	29	28-5/8	28-5/8-	5/8
37-3/8	25-3/4	Anch HG 1.40	.. 54	29-1/4	29-1/2	29	29-3/8+	1/4
49-7/8	34-3/4	Ander Clay 2	.. 2	38-1/2	38-1/2	38-1/2	38-1/2+	1/2
79	18-3/4	Anken Ch .20b	. 131	44	44-5/8	42-5/8	42-5/8- 1-1/8
24-5/8	11	Apco Oil	 68	15-7/8	17	15-7/8	17 + 1-1/8
39-7/8	33	Arch Dan 2	 5	39	39-1/2	39	39-1/2	..
38-7/8	23-1/2	Ariz P Sv .80	.. 99	30-1/8	30-1/8	29-7/8	30 +	1/8
71-3/4	40	Armco Stl 3	.. 52	53	53-1/4	52-3/4	53	..
57-1/4	32	Armour 1.40	.. 47	41-7/8	42-1/2	41-7/8	42 +	1/2
73-3/4	47-1/2	Armst Ck 1.60a	. 4	65	66	65	66 + 1-7/8
89-1/4	82-1/2	Ark Ck pf3.75.z	.130	88	88	87	87 - 1
47	25-1/2	Armst Rub 1.40	. 14	35	35-7/8	34-7/8	35-7/8+ 1-3/8
18	9-1/2	Arnold .50b xd.z	240	10-1/8	10-1/8	10	10 - 1/8
24-3/8	15-7/8	Aro Corp .80	... 4	17-3/4	18	17-5/8	18 + 1/4
33-1/2	20-1/2	Arvin Ind 1	.. 14	27-3/8	27-5/8	27-3/8	27-1/2+	1/2
28-5/8	19-3/4	Ashl Oil 1.20	.. 32	25	25-1/4	24-3/4	25-1/8-	1/8
3-7/8	2-1/4	Assd Brew	 3	2-3/8	2-1/2	2-3/8	2-1/2+	1/8
47-7/8	37-5/8	Assd DG 1.40	.. 37	46-1/2	47	46-1/2	47 + 1
110-1/2	105-1/4	As DG pf 5.25.z	. 10 108	108	108	108	..
80-1/2	52	Assoc Inv 2.60	.. 5	63-7/8	64	63-3/4	64 +	1/2
27-5/8	20-1/2	Atchison 1.20a	.. 89	25-1/2	25-1/2	25	25 - 1/2
10-5/8	9-3/4	Atchis pf .50	.. 37	10-1/2	10-5/8	10-1/2	10-5/8+	1/8
49-1/2	34-1/4	Atl City El 1.48	. 0	42-7/8	43	42-7/8	42-7/8	..

7. The opening price is given in this column; for Armour & Co. the first trade was at $41.87½ per share.

8. The highest price paid for this stock during the trading session was $25.25—the lowest, $24.75 per share.

9. The closing or last price on this stock was $64.00 per share—$.50 more than the closing for the previous day as indicated by the "+½."

OTHER ORDERS

You can purchase less than 100 shares; you can even buy a single share. The procedure is the same. An order for less than 100 shares is called an odd lot order. And these orders are serviced by members who act as dealers in odd lots on the trading floor.

A "limit" order is one which specifies a price. If an order is entered to buy UA at $19, it cannot be executed at a price higher than $19. If an order is entered to sell at $19, it cannot be executed below that price. Of course, if your broker can sell higher or buy lower, he is still free to do so.

If a customer wants his order to hold good indefinitely, he gives his broker a "good-till-canceled" order. This type of order is carried as an open order until the broker is able to execute it or until the customer cancels it.

BROKERS' COMMISSIONS

Here is the commission structure now in effect: Based on the current commission schedule a purchase or sale of 100 shares of stock at a price of $36 carries a minimum commission of $37. On a sale at $36, there would be additional charges of $5 for N.Y. State Transfer Tax, and 8 cents for SEC Fee. The State Tax ranges from 1¼ cent to 5 cents per share depending on the price of the stock.

The SEC Fee is charged on transactions made on any registered Exchange, and is at the rate of one cent for each $500 or fraction thereof of the principal amount of money involved in sales.

On December 5, 1968, a discount on Block Trading was initiated (see Exhibit A). This reduced rate of commission applies to that portion of an order that exceeds 1,000 shares.

Example: On a transaction of 2,000 shares of stock at $36, the commission on the first 1,000 shares would be at the rate of $37 per 100 shares. On the remaining 1,000 shares it would be at the rate of $21 per 100 shares.

EXHIBIT A

On that portion of an order which exceeds 1,000 shares, on stocks selling at $1.00 per share and above commissions shall be

*based upon the amount of money involved in a single transaction
and shall be not less than the rates hereinafter specified:*

*(i) Subject to the provisions of paragraphs 2(a)(2)(iii),
2(d), 2(f), and 2(g), on each single transaction not exceeding
100 shares, in a unit of trading; a combination of units of trading; or a combination of a unit or units of trading plus an odd lot.*

Money Involved	Commission
$100 to and including $2,800	*½% of money involved plus $4.00*
Above $2,800 to and including $3,000	*Compute as $2,800*
Above $3,000 to and including $9,000	*½% of money involved plus $3.00*
Above $9,000	*1/10% of money involved plus $39.00*

OTHER HIDDEN COSTS

Norma's profit from the sale of Upandaway was $1,100. She
had to pay a $27 commission to her broker. However, a villain was
lurking in the wings: Mr. Tax Collector.

Interest and dividends are taxable as ordinary income, except
income received from state and municipal bonds and similar obligations, which is tax-free.

If Norma had owned her stock for more than six months, it is considered a "long-term" capital gain. If not, her profit is considered a
"short-term" capital gain. For tax purposes short-term capital gains
and losses are merged (added together) to obtain the net short-
term capital gain or loss. Long-term capital gains and losses
are also merged to obtain net long-term capital gain or loss. If
your short-term net gain exceeds your long-term net loss, 100 percent of your profit has to be declared as income. But if your
long-term net gain exceeds your short-term net loss, then only 50
percent of the gravy has to be listed under income. In any case,
the maximum tax on capital gains is 25 percent.

In case you haven't been lucky at all, a net capital *loss* up to as
much as $1,000 in any one year and in each of the next five
years is deductible from ordinary income. Alternatively, previous
undeclared losses of as many as five years previously may be applied *at any time* to offset capital gains.

This complicated set of laws actually works to your advantage as an investor. Stock market losses are deductible and can put you in a lower tax bracket. Long-term gains, however, cannot be taxed more than 25 percent (plus 10 percent if the surtax is in effect) —although the rates for ordinary income can go as high as 70 percent! Thus, the higher your income, the more sense it makes to invest in stocks. And even if you're in the lower brackets, you can use deductions and lower tax rates to your personal advantage.

Obviously, though, your main objective is to *make* money. Norma made money when she sold her stock at 20—but only because she had bought it at around 9 dollars per share. Over a certain period of time bidding just like that which we have described was responsible for the fluctuation in price.

Multiply our description of a single stock transaction by millions of shares involving thousands of people and billions of dollars, and you have an idea of a stock exchange in action. It is this complexity that makes *when* to invest a pretty tricky business.

These billions of dollars are exchanged on the basis of opinions of investors all over the nation. The synthesis of opinions is rooted in myriad complicated and contradictory factors, generally categorized under the headings of economics and psychology. Many of these factors will be detailed in later chapters.

The prices of stocks, like hemlines, go up and down, and the reason for both fluctuations is the same—people. Investors' thoughts and emotions form the opinions which are reflected minute by minute, hour by hour, day by day, in the prices of all stocks. When people are optimistic ("bullish") and buy in hope of the market's rising, the general market will rise. When most people are pessimistic ("bearish") and sell, the market will decline. Individual stocks, however, can move independently of the main body of shares, and they frequently do, reflecting developments peculiar to that individual company or industry. News events, moreover, find a constant barometer on the exchange.

Thus money works in an effort to earn more money, and it is free to work wherever it can get the most pay for its services. The foregoing is simply an outline of the basics of our present economic apparatus. But in order to evolve to its present state, the system has undergone some revolutionary changes during the past century. And in the next chapter, we'll see exactly how.

chapter two

The Supermarkets

Wall Street is a community located at the exact center of the twentieth century's economic forces. Little in our world can be done without an effect on Wall Street; and very few things are done in Wall Street without careful appraisal of their effects on the rest of the world.

Wall Street is a paradox. Although it is the financial capital of the world, it is really only the headquarters. Actually Wall Street is present in every hamlet and city in the United States and in almost every foreign nation. Indeed, you can summon Wall Street to your doorstep with the price of a stamp or a phone call. The reasons for this small miracle are three major markets: The New York Stock Exchange, the American Exchange and the Over-the-Counter Market. These—and regional stock exchanges—act as the show-case for every stock and bond and offer a variety of services.

NEW YORK STOCK EXCHANGE: THE BIG BOARD

Basically this Exchange is a swirling marketplace for securities. During working hours its vast trading floor, in a building at the corner of Broad and Wall Streets in New York City, offers a scene of controlled frenzy. It is the nation's largest organized securities market, where hundreds of brokers buy and sell daily for thousands of clients the stocks and bonds of the majority of the nation's prime corporations.

This incredibly complex and remarkably efficient buying and selling apparatus had its origin in 1792. Congress had authorized an issue of $80,000,000 in stock to help pay for the costs of the Revolutionary War. There was a scattered market for this government stock as well as for the shares of banks and insurance companies then in their infancy. Trading was carried on in various coffeehouses, auction rooms, and offices, but it was generally casual and unorganized. People were reluctant to invest, since they had no assurance that they would be able to sell their securities.

Then, on May 17, a group of merchants and auctioneers convened in the hope of imposing some form of discipline on the shapeless market. They decided to meet at regular hours daily to buy and sell securities under an old buttonwood tree on Wall Street, only a short distance from the present site of the Stock Exchange.

These twenty-four men were the original members of the Exchange. They handled buy and sell orders on the new government stock and on the shares of insurance companies. Banks served as brokers for insurance companies—notably, Alexander Hamilton's First United States Bank, the Bank of North America and the Bank of New York. In 1793 the Tontine Coffee House was completed at the northwest corner of Wall and William Streets, and the brokers moved indoors. The War of 1812 checked private financial activity for a time, but peace brought the formation of new enterprises. New York State bonds, issued to pay for the Erie Canal, joined the issues traded on the new Exchange. Private enterprises began burgeoning. As a case in point, the cotton industry, which had been able to boast only a few mills in 1804, was operating half a million spindles by 1815. The tempo of business quickened to the tune of the postwar boom. By 1827 the stocks of twelve banks and nineteen marine and fire insurance companies plus the Delaware & Hudson Canal Co., the Merchants Exchange, and the New York Gas Light Company—the nation's first public utility—were also traded on the Exchange.

Soon after the turn of the century it became apparent that the Tontine Coffee House was too small to accommodate the volume of trading, and the stock brokers moved to a meeting room in what is now 40 Wall Street. Intensified activity spurred the need for a more formal organization than that created under the 1792 agreement. On March 8, 1817, the first formal constitution of the New York Stock Exchange and Exchange Board, as it called itself then, was adopted. One of the constitution's provisions stated that the president was to call out the names of stocks, fix commissions,

ORGANIZATION OF THE NEW YORK STOCK EXCHANGE
APRIL, 1967

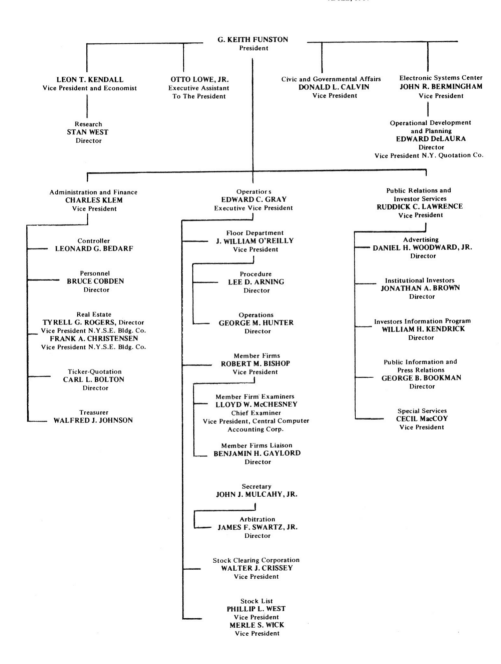

and set fines—from six to twenty-five cents—for violation of procedure or nonattendance at sessions "unless when sick or out of the city."

Each trading session consisted of an 11:30 A.M. roster of all stocks on the list. As the name of each stock was called, the brokers made their bids and offers.

From 1817 to 1827 the Board met in various offices. Thereafter it moved a dozen times or so before settling, in 1863, upon the site of the present Broad Street building. (Erected in 1903, this structure contains most of today's trading floor. The adjoining office building at the corner of Broad and Wall Streets was erected in 1922.) Although the passing years transformed the architecture and financial resources of the Exchange, its fundamental function remained the same. It still allows the individual to put his capital to work whenever he chooses.

In a free society, capital cannot be shackled. It must be free to move from one enterprise to another—entitled to profits when the venture succeeds, ready to absorb the losses when it fails.

The movement of free capital creates the need for additional capital, as well as the imperative demand for new skills. This is nothing more than saying that if new railroads are being run, there must be railroad specialists. It means that the new railroads need new materials, such as railroad ties, steel, and signal systems, all of which in turn require special skills and materials. The stagecoach driver must change if he wants to remain in the transportation business. If he cannot learn to handle the throttle instead of the whips, he is bypassed as completely as the roads over which he drove his horses.

CAPITAL POWER

The railroad industry is one illustration of the remarkable energy unleashed by free flow of capital. It took people to build the railroads and thousands more to run them as they expanded westward. It took thousands and thousands more to run the new threshing machines and make the new sewing machines. A young man from Cleveland named John D. Rockefeller saw potential uses for the newly discovered Pennsylvania oil fields. Later, a young man in Detroit found that an internal combustion engine which utilized the new fuel was practical.

This industrial progression needed—and still needs—capital to keep it running. Thus, the investment banking industry created a mechanism which is able to provide mature companies with additional capital as well as to manage the initial sale of the securities of new companies which have not yet developed a widespread public appeal. As new securities become seasoned, they may qualify for a listing on the Exchange which also improves their collateral value. That step generally makes the securities more attractive to more people and invariably enables the holders, when and if they wish, to liquidate their investments more easily and to put the proceeds into other enterprises.

Membership in the Exchange totals 1,366 individuals. A member may be a general partner or holder of voting stock in one of the brokerage concerns which, by virtue of his Exchange membership, is known as a member firm or member corporation. There are 649 such member organizations—484 partnerships and 165 corporations. About half of the members of this exclusive club are partners or officers in member organizations doing business with the public. These members execute customers' orders to buy and sell on the Exchange, and their firms receive the commissions on those transactions. Many firms have more than one member. About one fourth of the Exchange members are "specialists."

THE BALANCE WHEEL

The specialist deserves a detailed examination. In general, he provides a balance wheel for the whirling supermarket. During the wildest fluctuations the specialist is expected to buy securities in declining markets (when the public sells) and to sell stock in rising markets (when the public buys). He is the steely-nerved man in the middle who strives to make certain that prices move in an orderly way, usually within a narrow range.

How does the specialist function? Assume that the stock of a particular corporation has last been sold at $35 per share. The best

BUY				SELL	
50	1 *Loper* 2 *Haw* 1 *Green*			50	
1/8				1/8	
1/4	2 *Evans* ~~1 Brown C~~			1/4	
3/8				3/8	
1/2	~~1 Kind CDE~~ ~~1 Sail FGH~~			1/2	
5/8				5/8	1 *Ball* 1 *Lean*
3/4				3/4	1 *moon* 1 *Pike*
7/8				7/8	

(The orders to buy at 50½ have been executed and notations made indicating the selling Brokers. The order to buy 100 at 50¼ has been cancelled.)   **Excerpt from a specialist's notebook.**

public market is 34½ bid, 35½ offered; that is, 34½ is the highest any investor is willing to pay, and 35½ is the lowest price at which anyone wishes to sell. With one point separating the buyer and seller, the specialist would normally step in and narrow the quote by, for instance, agreeing to buy at a bid of 34¾ or to sell at the offer of 35¼ for his *own* account. The investor could then anticipate that the price of the next transaction would be either unchanged from the previous sale of $35 or very close to that price.

Stormy markets notwithstanding, the specialist must continually meet his other vital responsibility as a "broker's broker." Other brokers who are away from the current market leave orders with him. If, for example, the last sale of stock was $30 and an order is placed to buy 100 shares at $25, the specialist may hold the order until it can be executed at or below the designated price. For this the specialist receives part of the floor broker's commission.

To understand the controlled temperament and agility required of a specialist, consider what might happen when Outer Space, Inc. announces the development of a fantastic new product. Investors from coast to coast immediately act on the news. Orders to buy thousands of shares pour onto the Exchange trading floor simultaneously, and the sensitive balance between supply and demand is temporarily upset. The last sale before the flood of orders is $30. Because of the increased demand and the reluctance of public stockholders to sell, the price could jump several dollars unless the specialist helped to balance the scales by supplying stock out of his own account. As a result of the influx of buy orders, the price will no doubt rise, but it will remain orderly, since the specialist is helping establish the balance of supply and demand at a price reasonably related to the last sale. The reverse is true in a declining market, when the specialist buys stock to help offset a "dumping" of sell orders, which could cause prices to plummet.

How can the specialist continually buck public trends and still stay solvent? The answer lies in the nature of stock prices. While they are apt to fluctuate widely over a period of time, they almost never move in an absolutely straight line. On the way up they dip; on the way down they rise. During this zigzag the specialist is able to adjust his portfolio by buying or selling stocks while still playing his enormously important stabilizing role.

In a way, the specialist arranges financial "marriages" by offering a reasonable basis for fusion—the proper price. Moreover, he makes possible the split-second wedding between buyer and seller by subordinating his own personal interests. The specialist, for example, cannot buy stock for his own account in the Exchange market until he has executed all his public orders on that stock. The same principle applies to sales.

EXPENSIVE SEAT

Of course, all members of the Exchange—whatever their function—must own a "seat," a term that traces back to the early years when the brokers did remain seated while the president called out the list of securities.*

An Exchange "seat" is far from sedentary. On the contrary, during working hours an Exchange member is more active than the mother of year-old twins. From the balcony of the Exchange those on the floor appear to be engaged in a dizzy ballet. Their choreography, however, is specific and well-planned, but still the continual walking makes tough shoe leather an essential of the job and aching feet an occupational hazard.

In addition to members of the Exchange, there are some 3,000 partners in member firms. These partners are known as "allied members." Then there are about 1,950 holders of voting stock in member corporations who are also known as allied members. Allied members cannot do business on the trading floor, but are subject to the same rigorous rules and regulations as are members.

KEEPING HOUSE

The Exchange's housekeeping job is handled primarily by the Board of Governors. They keep the Exchange clean and orderly. The Governors, who are elected by the members, exercise broad policymaking and disciplinary powers. The group includes members and allied members representing all sections of the country. It also includes three representatives of the public with no direct connection with the securities business, who bring a broad outside viewpoint to the Board's deliberations. The Chairman, elected annually, must be a member of the Exchange. The President of the Exchange, who is selected by the Board of Governors, brings the Board's membership to thirty-three. He may *not* be a member of the Exchange nor a partner nor stockholder of a member organization.

Over the years the Exchange, largely through experience, has evolved a complex system of rules for self-management. But the underlying principles have remained the same:

---

* The price of memberships since 1950 has risen from $38,000 to more than $500,000. The initiation fee at present is $7,500, and dues are $1,500 annually.

1. Securities may be bought and sold on the Exchange only at prices openly and fairly arrived at.
2. Regulations for trading on the floor repeatedly stress the importance of the open market.
3. Bids and offers are made in multiples of the unit of trading (ordinarily 100 shares), and the highest bid and the lowest offer have precedence.
4. Bids and offers must be called out loud.
5. Transactions must be reported promptly over the Stock Exchange's nationwide ticker system. Therefore, practically every city in the United States is linked with the nation's marketplace. Although banks are not members of the Exchange, most have contacts with one or more member firms.

Some 500,000 miles of teletype and telephone wires connect the Exchange with 3,811 members' offices, many of which are in turn connected with 2,400 nonmember correspondents. Member firms have offices in 1,060 United States cities and 49 states, as well as in Puerto Rico, the Virgin Islands, and the District of Columbia. There are also member firm offices in 34 cities and in some of the Arabic countries, Argentina, Bahamas, Belgium, Brazil, Canada, England, France, Germany, Greece, Holland, Israel, Italy, Japan, Lebanon, Mexico, Monaco, Philippines, Spain, Switzerland, Uruguay, Venezuela, and Hong Kong.

JOINING THE CLUB

For a company to be listed on the NYSE requires a complete economic and financial examination. To qualify for original listing, a firm must be a going concern with substantial assets and demonstrated earning power. The Exchange places emphasis on such considerations as the degree of national interest in the company, the character of its product, the relative stability, and the position in its industry. The stock should have a sufficiently wide distribution so that an adequate auction market for its securities will exist.

A company's financial fitness depends on a variety of factors. It is considered in good shape if, under competitive conditions, it has annual earnings of over $2,000,000 before taxes and $1,200,000 clear profit. Moreover, it should have a minimum of 1,000,000 shares outstanding, with at least 700,000 shares publicly held among not fewer than 2,000 shareholders, including at least 1,700 round-lot (one hundred shares each) stockholders. The publicly-held common shares should have a minimum aggregate market value of $12,000,000.

Further, the Exchange keeps a motherly eye on its listees. If a company desires to list additional shares or a new issue, it must obtain Exchange authorization and in certain cases stockholder approval. All approved applications are promptly made public.

Another important Exchange activity concerns its vigilance over unusual situations in individual stocks. If a stock misbehaves, the Stock-Watcher takes over. Every day a computer runs over the price and volume movements of the 1,500-odd stocks listed on the Exchange. It spots any unusual variations in individual stocks and sets these aside for human investigation. When a stock "acts up" Big Daddy wants to know why. More often than not news events explain fluctuation. Sometimes a rumor will affect a stock. If false, the NYSE has it scotched; if true, it is aired. This may mean asking listed companies to clarify a situation via public statements. If stock manipulation is involved, the Exchange tracks down the facts to the limits of its authority and then turns the case over to the SEC* for official spanking.

The Exchange constantly checks the financial health of its corporate family. Factors involved in continued listing are not necessarily measured mathematically; the Board of Governors may act to suspend or delist a stock in any situation where the security in question is not suitable for retention. In considering a specific case, the Board will give weight to all factors affecting the security of the company.

For example, suspension of trading or delisting will normally be considered when the total number of shareowners is less than 800 and fewer than 700 shareowners own 100 shares or more;

---

* The SEC—Securities and Exchange Commission—is the Federal Agency that regulates and polices the securities industry.

when the number of publicly-held shares becomes less than 300,-000; or when for other reasons the Exchange believes that further dealings in the security are not advisable.

Delisting can be a grave matter for a company, since it is stripped of several prime benefits. A listing serves as a prestigious introduction to investors everywhere, institutions as well as individuals. It is an aid in raising fresh capital at a lower cost by sale of new "debt instruments" to the general public. A listed company generally has a ready hearing with banks, insurance companies, underwriters, and institutional investors. And finally, a listing offers an invaluable public relations advantage, since the company's name appears in the financial pages and stock tables of the nation's press.

ECONOMIC MUSCLE

Those stock tables evaluate the muscle power of the nation's economy. The more than 1,200 NYSE companies earn about two thirds of all the after-tax profits reported by *all* United States companies. They also pay their stockholders about 60 percent of all dividends disbursed.

Corporations listed on the Exchange provide jobs for over 15,-000,000 people. They produce practically all the automobiles and trucks made in this country, more than 90 percent of all steel, nearly 90 percent of all the electric power, over 95 percent of all the aluminum; they handle 95 percent of our railroad and air passenger travel. Last year they paid more than $14,000,000,000 in federal, state, and foreign income taxes.

Again, let me emphasize that this remarkable supermarket, with showcases extended around the world and countless products on display, neither buys, sells, nor sets prices. The Exchange merely provides the marketplace. When you buy or sell, you buy or sell to or from another investor. The Exchange is not organized to make a profit. It is a voluntary unincorporated association of brokers. Its revenues come mainly from members in dues and charges for services and facilities, and from fees paid by corporations whose securities are listed on the Exchange.

Incredibly enough, the main business of the Exchange is normally conducted without written contracts. It is done on the basis of verbal contracts.

THE AMERICAN STOCK EXCHANGE

The second largest supermarket, the American Exchange, traces its beginnings to a group of men who around the time of the 1849 California gold rush gathered daily in the financial district of New York City to deal in the securities of the burgeoning companies of the day. The exact birth date of the Amex is blurred by time and by the informality of its inception.

These outdoor brokers were men who at first traded among themselves and who later became agents for investors. They were on the street from early morning to sundown. As the number of regular brokers grew, they overflowed the curbstones into Wall and Hanover Streets. To find more room the curb brokers moved off a few blocks to William Street between Exchange Place and Beaver, where the market remained through the Civil War. Then during the 1890's they moved to Broad Street just below Wall Street. Outdoor trading reached its peak on Broad Street between 1900 and 1921. Powerful new industries—steel, munitions, marine, copper—grew during World War I and the years immediately following.

Visitors to New York in those earlier days could witness a scene not likely to be duplicated again in American history. Hundreds of tense, excited brokers milled in apparently aimless excitement, buying and selling stocks and bonds and waving and shouting to telephone order clerks stationed at windows in rooms above the street. In order to be recognized by their clerks, brokers wore yellow homburgs, green derbies, or loud striped jackets.

The volume of trading increased. And so did the number of stocks, new brokers, telephone clerks, and tourists, until finally there was so much noise that vocal communication became seriously hampered. Thus was born the handsignal, a one-handed version of the deaf sign language that still proves a most effective way of floor communication.

In 1908 a small group of leading outdoor brokers formed the New York Curb Agency, the first step toward formal organization. By 1911 the Agency had evolved into the New York Curb Association. Its Board of Representatives drew up and enforced trading rules. A five-hour trading day and a membership of five hundred were established. A listing department was organized to admit the stocks and bonds of qualified corporations to trading privileges and to keep records of their operations on file for public examination.

As the Curb Market continued to grow, the need for stock ticker services grew. On June 6, 1919, the Association decided to move indoors so that it could provide ticker service and improved trading, as well as stronger control over its members and list of securities. The first step was to purchase a building site on Trinity Place. To finance the venture, each member of the Association purchased stock in the New York Curb Realty Associates, Inc. On March 30, 1921, the Association's Board of Representatives approved a new constitution to become effective with the move indoors. To the regular memberships a new class of associate members was added. With the new constiution, the name was changed to the New York Curb Market. As word of the move indoors spread, the value of memberships jumped to $6,500 each, and fifty additional regular memberships were created.

The new Curb Market opened for business on June 27, 1921. The six-story building at 86 Trinity Place cost about $3,000,000. By 1929 the need for larger quarters had become imperative and in September, 1931, a fourteen-story addition to the original six-story building was opened. By 1929 the Curb Market changed its name to the New York Curb Exchange, and so it remained until January 5, 1953, when the present name, the American Stock Exchange, was adopted.

In general, the constitution, administrative organization, and broad administrative functions of the American Exchange are similar to those of the NYSE. Standards for listing represent the basic differences between the major markets. The minimum criteria for listing on the American Exchange are: (1) Tangible assets of at least $3,000,000; (2) pre-tax earnings of at least $500,000 and net earnings of it least $300,000 in the latest fiscal year (in addition, the applicant company is expected to demonstrate a reasonable prospect of sustaining its level of earnings); (3) public distribution of 300,000 shares (exclusive of holdings of officers, directors, con-

trolling stockholders, and other concentrated or family holdings);
(4) 900 stockholders, including not less than 600 holders of 100
shares or more; (5) a minimum selling price of $5 per share of the
company's stock for a reasonable period of time prior to filing the
listing application. In the case of recent public offerings, a higher
price is generally expected.

FAMOUS FIRSTS

The American Exchange is responsible for several notable pio-
neering efforts. It was the first to initiate an automated stock quotation system, the first to elect women members,* and the first to
formulate its own Market Index System covering the entire breadth
of the Exchange market.

THE OVER-THE-COUNTER MARKET

The Over-the-Counter, or OTC, is the largest and most demo-
cratic of the Big Three exchanges. While NYSE products are generally confined to the richest corporate plums and the Amex
displays are some ripe and some not-so-ripe, the OTC offers some
of the juiciest fruits in terms of United States Government Bonds,
municipal and corporate bonds, foreign bonds, and bank, insurance,
and investment trust shares, as well as bushels of red apples—it provides facilities for the initial distribution of securities of every
American company.

The over-the-counter securities market was thriving when Paul
Revere began his historic gallop. National debts incurred during the
Revolutionary War were floated through the OTC. During the early
years, private banking houses provided the facilities for OTC trading. The various transactions took place over counters similar to
those of the old-fashioned grocery store; hence the exchange's name.
As the economy expanded, this market's growth was explosive.

* The first two women members in American Exchange history were Mrs.
Julia Montgomery Walsh of Ferris & Co. and Mrs. Phyllis S. Peterson of Sade &
Co. In 1967 the New York Stock Exchange opened its doors—and dusted off a
seat—for its first female member, Miss Muriel Siebert.

About 3,000 stocks are available though the exchanges, compared to an estimated 50,000 on the unlisted market. Today the OTC is a network of some 3,700 securities houses and 5,000 branch offices, linked by telephone and telegraph.

The OTC is regulated and policed by the National Association of Securities Dealers, Inc., (NASD) under the Maloney Act, which provides for self-regulation through rules designed to promote "just and equitable principles of trade." Enforcement is implemented by limiting price concessions, discounts, and allowances to NASD members and withdrawl of such privileges for failure to abide by the rules.

One of the NASD services is the distribution of OTC securities quotations to newspapers. For national quotation a security must meet certain standards. The primary ones are: (1) There must be at least 1,500 stockholders throughout the country; (2) there must be at least 100,000 shares of the security in the hands of the public; (3) the security must have a market value of at least $5.00 per share. When the market value falls below $3.00 per share, the security may be listed on the appropriate local list.

Each local committee provides qualifying standards for quotation. The basic minimums are: (1) The market price of the security must be at least $1.00 bid (if the price falls below $.50 the security is deleted from the quotation list); (2) there must be sufficient inter-dealer interest in the issue to assure a realistic market. (For trade use there are sheets published by the National Quotation Bureau which give quoted prices at which dealers are willing to trade with each other. These sheets are know in the trade as the pink sheets.)

There are several fundamental differences between the listed exchanges and the OTC. The latter lacks a common meeting place and is scattered around the country. Its arteries are telephone and telegraph wires.

THE BIG DIFFERENCE

The prime distinction between the NYSE-Amex and the OTC is difference between an "auction market" and a "negotiated market." As noted previously, trading in the auction market is conducted with competition among buyers and sellers. The buyer making the highest bid and the seller with the lowest offer come together when the two agree on price. The OTC is primarily a negotiation or bargaining market. There is no set price at any one time. Seldom are there wide differences in price among dealers. Nevertheless, the professional bargainers usually perform in a prompt and efficient manner. More often than not it requires a few minutes to scout the best available sources for any one stock and a few seconds to negotiate the deal. There is also a thriving business done where the dealer acts solely as the agent for the customer. As a dealer, he sells the stock to you directly out of his own inventory, either at a profit or a loss, and adds a markup of not more than 5 percent above the prevailing price for his services.

Since the prices of many OTC securities are not published in newspapers, but only in the pink sheets, the average investor must rely on his broker's integrity in quoting the latest prices, as well as on his fairness in taking no more than a reasonable markup. Integrity between broker and investor—and between brokers—is the heart of the three major markets.

chapter three

Know Your Salesman

A woman's financial needs are affected by countless varied factors. Among them are annual income, age, health, training, temperament, ability to manage her own affairs, number of dependents, amount of time and attention that can be devoted to financial affairs, social and personal ambitions, and many others.

The aforementioned points deserve thoughtful attention before you go broker-hunting. It is difficult to generalize, but at least one factor should be available to every potential investor: time and attention to devote to financial affairs. A broker can help you more if you have the advantage of being able to help yourself.

Before choosing a broker, go over the following checklist:

1. Itemize your assets.
2. Total your income from all sources.
3. Estimate all expenses, including future needs:

   *Retirement
   *Money for college education
   *Money to support a parent
   *Income if you are disabled

4. Consider taxes to which you are subject.
5. Make certain you are in a position to check the prices of your securities at least once a month.
6. Study corporate earnings reports.
7. Carefully observe changes in management and management policy. Check new products and facilities that keep the individual company among the progressive in its field.
8. Check the external factor, such as vital legislation, development of new industries, trend of business and political activity—all the factors that influence investment values.

After you have done these things, then start the all-important business of choosing a broker.

Opening your account with him is as simple as sneezing in a dust storm. Among the information he will require is your name, address, occupation, social security number, citizenship, age (over twenty-one), and the name of your bank or other satisfactory financial reference. Choosing a broker is simple, but picking the *right* broker is difficult indeed. Actually the decision should be made as carefully as if you were picking a family doctor. Your financial health often depends on this basic choice.

WHOM DO YOU TRUST?

Unfortunately, too many investors choose brokers in a random, casual manner. Often they pick relatives, friends, friends of relatives, or relatives of friends, or some genial chap they met during a holiday cruise. Oddly enough, many persons who are careful, shrewd shoppers when it comes to purchasing a $19.95 item in a department store are impulsive buyers when investing thousands of dollars in stocks. I know a broker who was introduced to a widow at a party. Three days later he received her check for $50,000 and a note urging him to invest it for her. Such incidents are not uncommon. The problem, of course, is that some people are lured by the glowing illusion that purchasing stocks is the equivalent of making a deal with Santa Claus. More often than not, they wind up with Scrooge.

Proper investing technique demands patience as well as intelligence. Look before you plunge. Shop around and ask for assistance from reputable sources. Your banker, insurance agent, or Better Business Bureau knows responsible brokers. Or you can write to the New York Stock Exchange, 11 Wall Street, New York 10005, for a list of member firms with offices in your area. The biggest brokerages are members of the NYSE and Amex. The smallest are Over-the-Counter firms. Size, though, is not the sole criterion.

A broker's firm is one fact to consider. Fundamentally, in picking a broker you are choosing an individual. And it isn't enough to know his name—get to know him personally. This is all a matter of helping one who wants to help you. It pays to spend time before investing money. Further, be candid about the facts of your financial life, since your broker should know you as well as he does your money. In its way, the broker-client relationship is an extremely intimate one—especially if the client is a widow.

FOR WIDOWS ONLY

Almost immediately, and for many years afterward, the widow must make financial decisions. Unfortunately, not many are prepared for this stark confrontation. They generally turn their financial affairs over to others. But it is important that they become well acquainted with investment principles so as to understand the decisions made on their behalf.

Some primary problems of widows—or of their heirs—can be avoided by the proper creation of an estate. Estate planning is as intricate as it is delicate. It involves income and tax considerations, drafting of a proper will, selection of insurance executors and trustees, gift planning, and general investment policies. Some brokers make a specialty of these considerations.

The general investment requirements in estate planning are (1) tax relief on current income; (2) degrees of liquidity; (3) minimizing estate and inheritance taxes; (4) protection against inflation.

A trust involves the passing of property by deed or will from the owner who creates the trust to the trustee, who holds the property for the benefit of another. The relationship between trustee and beneficiaries involves the ultimate in mutual good faith.

There are diverse objectives for individual trusts, such as the support of dependents, education of children, support of charitable institutions, pension and profit-sharing plans and retirement. Anyone can set up a trust quite easily. All that is required is a simple agreement listing the names of the trustee or trustees, the manner in which the funds deposited with the trustee shall be invested, the distribution of income from the estate, and the disposition of any principal when the trust terminates. Again, it is wise to retain professional services—especially a broker's.

OTHER GUIDELINES

How do you know whether a broker is good? Eventually your profit and loss statements give the answer. Yet the practical response is more involved. Some brilliant brokers go sour. Occasionally they cannot pick a winner in a one-horse race. Still, the only fair and realistic test is the batting average over a prolonged period. It's not only how good you are—but how long you are good.

Compatibility is another test. Yours should be a comfortable marriage, able to survive stress. If he is unable to give your account sufficient time, or if he makes decisions you find uncomfortable, look for another account executive. Delay is costly. Basically the investment philosophies of the broker and investor should coincide. Such compatibility is essential on the basis of financial as well as psychological needs.

GOALS

Generally, there are a trio of investment objectives. One aims at safeguarding your principal, another at income from dividends, and a third at growth of capital. It *is* possible to buy one stock that will combine two of the three aims—safety and good dividends, or safety and growth potential, for example—but it is unlikely that you will ever find one stock that combines all three. Moreover, it is unrealistic to expect totally risk-proof stocks. Such securities are only traded in Paradise—and both you and your broker should know it.

Some investors have the emotional equipment which enables them to speculate; others get ulcers and heart attacks when they handle volatile securities. Some brokers specialize in speculative issues, while others concentrate on more stable stocks. Either may be right for you. But there are also brokers who focus on large accounts and give little attention to smaller ones. If a broker is uninterested in your account—no matter how small it is—then you should be indifferent to him. Ideally, a broker's attitude toward his accounts should be similar to a parent's attitude toward his children: he should devote himself to all of them on an equal basis.

The matter of compatibility is important to brokers too. Some function more effectively with certain types of people. I know one

Ivy League-honed broker who has been particularly successful with staid, well-heeled clients. On the other hand, one of the most successful brokers in Wall Street lacks a high school diploma, and many of his customers have a similar educational background. He understands them and speaks their language. Once again, the compatibility factor is all-important.

Although a friendly relationship between broker and client is significant, compatibility alone never brought Mother her mink. The ultimate test is the one previously mentioned: Does he make money for you? Be patient and exercise every benefit of doubt, but when you finally decide that during a reasonable period of time he has failed to fulfill his money-making function, then you should switch brokers. After all, you invest in the stock market to make money, not close friends.

The phrase "reasonable period of time" is crucial in a broker-switching decision. Often what is "reasonable" depends on attitude and temperament. Some consider six months a reasonable period of time; others might consider six years just as fair. But by and large, if you have confidence in your broker and if you are knowledgeable about his past record, patience can be rewarding. All brokers pick losers. The best of them merely choose more winners than losers, Again, check the averages.

A broker's buy-or-sell decision is frequently a simple procedure. Many large brokerages employ a large corps of analysts. Generally analysts specialize in different fields. Some center on the motor car industry, while others concentrate on food companies or chemical firms. Our industrial apparatus has become so complex that some analysts focus on a single service or product of a giant corporation. Their intensive research results in reports to brokers listing buy-sell-hold recommendations on different stocks offered by the same company.

X-RAY SPECIALIST

Superior analysts are called upon to unravel the tangled webs of variables. They study a company's annual report; evaluate its sales, earnings, and dividend record over the years; investigate other companies in the same industry, and judge the merits of the company's officers and its products. They must examine every strand. A company may be developing a remarkable new product, but it may also be manufacturing parts for an obsolete plane or have heavy investments in an overseas country threatened by revolution.

Myriad dynamics influence the market climate—corporate earnings, industrial trends, technological innovations, world-wide political and economic conditions, and public psychology. Hence choosing particular stocks may require the attributes of Sherlock Holmes, Solomon, and Freud. All in all, it is not surprising that analysts and brokers make mistakes. The remarkable fact is that they are not wrong more often.

Despite the intricate wheels-within-wheels machinery of stock selection, the fact is that some of the most successful brokers operate as good journalists. They create a network of informational sources within companies and among analysts and fellow brokers; they pick up fragments of information from various sources, check and evaluate them, and then put the pieces together into a significant story. Some of a broker's best sources of information are his clients. Now and again the client may provide the lead toward a bonanza by coming up with a fragment of information which solves the jigsaw.

Lately many brokers and analysts have taken to computers as a buying and selling aid. Nevertheless, the human factor cannot be discounted. Some brokers have "a feel for the market"—that is, a set of instinctive reactions which enables them to prosper. This nebulous asset comes from experience. In the same category is another factor I have never taken lightly. It involves that lovely charmer known as Lady Luck. In Wall Street her passionate embrace has made geniuses of some mediocrities.

INVESTOR BEWARE

Mediocrity is one of the failings among brokers, but there are more serious offenses. Like the medical and legal professions, brokerages are infested with quacks. Usually they are temporary nuisances, but they do exist. Of course the SEC enforces the law against illegal practitioners, but unfortunately there is no law against suckers; there's still one born every minute.

Commission-hungry brokers are a recurring problem. Some are merely greedy, while others are downright thieves. Naturally many a broker is interested in escalating commissions—that's the way he makes his living. Furthermore, his production enables the brokerage house to prosper. In recent years the struggling broker has become a rarity, thanks to record-breaking trading activity. Actually many collect lush incomes. But there is sometimes a small group of extremists who buy and sell at a furious pace merely to generate commissions. Along Wall Street this frowned-upon practice is called churning.

Examples of churning can be found in SEC records. One of the more flagrant illustrations involves a doctor with a $25,000 account. His broker turned over the account forty-six times in twelve months. Another concerns a farmer with a $15,560 account, which his broker turned over thirty-five times in six months. Both of them—the clients that is—lost money. So if you believe your broker engages in excessive trading, report your complaint to the SEC and get another broker. (Incidentally, the brokers involved in the churning of the aforementioned accounts lost their jobs following an SEC inquiry, and their brokerages were suspended from membership in the National Association of Securities Dealers for one month.)

The marks of a reputable broker are his refusal to accept accounts for speculation only, his reluctance to buy stocks on the basis of a tip you heard, and his basic caution. Some leading brokers discourage as many as 30 percent of those who wish to open accounts with them when they surmise these potential clients lack the emotional and financial stability to weather market storms. It's not enough to have the fortune-hunter's happy vision; you must have the stomach for accepting losses. Some women who are astute planners of family budgets become illogical when toying with stocks. The cash factor is also vital. Of course you must never, never buy stocks with money you require for mortgage payments, insurance fees, educational funds, or possible emergency needs. How much you hope to win may not be as meaningful as how much you can afford to lose.

An illusory Easy Street runs parallel to Wall and is frequently populated with outright crooks. The proportion of quacks in the financial community is small, just as they represent a fractional minority in the medical, legal, or any other profession. But they do—and will—exist. Their prime assets are the greed and gullibility of careless investors who pick brokers like new spring hats.

The Securities and Exchange Commission has warned again and again that Americans lose millions of dollars annually to broker frauds. Although all brokers are registered with the SEC, registration is not always a guarantee of integrity. As one SEC official has pointed out, "Just because a broker is registered with us doesn't mean he's honest. All it does mean is that he has not been convicted of a securities fraud in the last ten years. He could have been convicted of murder, robbery or rape. He could even run his operation from a penitentiary."

There are many ways to spot a phony. First, he may promise the moon as well as several other planets. Second, he is a fast talker and almost always operates over the phone. Third, he never puts his promises in writing.

His con job generally begins by the creamy-voiced phone caller promising to "let you in on a good thing. But send in your money today. The stock is going up and will cost you more tomorrow." More often than not this is a prepared pitch poured into a battery of different phones. This scattergun technique frequently manages to bag at least one pigeon.

The NYSE recently detailed a case history. A lady in New Jersey received a phone call from an alleged broker who offered to let her have 1,000 shares of uranium stock for $.25 each and promised to buy the stock back personally if it failed to double in price in the next few weeks. What could she lose—a mere $250? She sent off her check. The stock went up of course. If enough suckers buy, the upward movement is inevitable. When the broker called again and happily reported that the stock had doubled in price, she drew $2,000 out of the bank to get in on the further rise. Still urged on by the voice on the phone, she then sold a piece of farm land and some blue chip stocks that had paid her dividends for years. Evidently believing she had discovered a money-making machine, she wound up mortgaging her house and eventually lost every nickel.

Phony brokers are the slickest talkers. Often their sales pitches are models of warped genius. And they have bamboozled many successful and intelligent people. According to SEC records, their favorite targets are ministers, divinity students, schoolteachers, and doctors.

These con men sometimes operate out of tawdry offices in the Wall Street area. Anyone can open an office there. And some of the biggest thieves have the fanciest fronts, but wall-to-wall carpeting is hardly a measure of integrity.

Nevertheless, most of the crooked operators have some common characteristics. They are always in a hurry, for a good psychological reason. They don't want you to have second thoughts. They demand immediate decisions. No legitimate broker wants to rush you. He is aware that stocks gyrate. If you don't buy today, you can buy next week or next month. Sometimes you pay a little more, and sometimes you get a cheaper price.

The high-pressure operator rides the crest of the current fads. When uranium stocks are riding high, he sells uranium stocks. When computer companies are popular, he pitches computer companies. Almost always his stocks are in the low-price category. He promises thousands of shares for a few hundred dollars. Reputable brokers generally avoid the many penny stocks and even avoid issues as high as $5 a share. In an effort to discourage such speculation, some brokerages give their salesmen no commission for selling such stocks and even insist that the customer sign a letter stating that the order had been unsolicited.

HONESTY CHECK

The reputable broker will certainly recommend some prudently speculative stocks that seem to be a good investment. But he prefers to have you make the final decision, and he gives you time to think it over. Further, the legitimate broker never guarantees or promises a quick profit. He has no crystal ball, but he will give you the benefit of his own opinion. He makes no rash promises, and at your request, he willingly puts his recommendations in writing.

There is a confidential relationship between broker and client, and discretion is the basic element in his code of business ethics. Though you always buy from and sell to another investor, the actual transactions are executed in the names of the brokers representing the two parties, and neither broker knows the identity of the other's customer. The names of the brokers' customers never appear on the transaction ticket.

Next to outright fraud, hot tips and wild rumors are the prime pitfalls of the innocents. A Wall Street classic concerns the company official who made a casual remark in an elevator about his daughter's wedding. Another passenger recognized the official and immediately translated "marriage" into "merger." Within hours he told a friend who told other friends, and the rumor ricocheted around the financial community. As usually happens, the wildfire rumors were magnified and distorted. Soon the "inside story" was that the company would not only be involved in a merger, but would split its stock ten for one! Many such rumors are spread by honest people in good faith, simply because they want their friends to make a little money. All this would be a rather amusing illustration of mass psychology, except that it can result in heartbreaking financial disaster.

It is the better part of wisdom to go to a reputable physician rather than put yourself in the hands of a witch doctor who promises quick and easy cures. As in every field of endeavor, the brokerage profession's incompetents are at the bottom of the totem pole and the extraordinary are at the top. In between there are various shades of skill and ability. In the final analysis your own estimate of your broker's ability comes down to dollars and cents. If he makes money for you, he's good. If he doesn't, he isn't. The richer he makes you, the better he is. Period.

chapter four

The Information Gap—and How to Bridge It

In the twelfth book of his *Metamorphoses* the Roman poet Ovid wrote: "In the middle of the world there is a dwelling place, equally removed from the heavens, the earth and the waters. From that dwelling, everything can be heard and everything seen, no matter where it occurs. It is there that Fame resides, in a house built on the top of a mountain with a thousand entrances and thousands upon thousands of windows to receive the news about what happens everywhere. There are no locks on the doors, and all is wide open day and night. There are walls of bronze which recount in a piercing tone all they hear. In every part of that dwelling, the sound of talking can always be heard; rest and silence are unknown there. But neither are loud cries heard; the sound is as of a thousand voices whispering to each other. It is a sound just like that of the sea when heard from very far away."

Ovid could easily have been describing the office of one of today's brokers. He is deluged with information about the market all day long, and out of the multitude of whispers he must conclude which to listen to, and which to ignore. Practically the only "sure thing" on Wall Street is that information will always be needed, and hundreds of firms are only too happy to oblige—for a price. So when the investor wants information, he usually hasn't far to look.

At his beck and call are an army of researchers. Eleven thousand security analysts, over one hundred thousand brokers, thousands of statisticians and computer composers—all strive to be first with the most profits.

There are countless sources of information available to the average investor. For example, a quarterly report published jointly by the Federal Trade Commission and Securities Exchange Commission contains comprehensive data on the earnings and financial position of all manufacturing companies in the United States. In addition, the SEC is continually publishing reports about the financial realm in general and public corporations in particular.

The SEC requires that annual reports be sent to stockholders of registered corporations with more than $1,000,000 in assets and 500 or more stockholders. (But read company reports with a degree of skepticism: they naturally favor the company. It is not likely that a corporation will spend money on an effort to damage itself.) Interim reports are furnished by many large corporations. These may give comparative figures for periods of three, six, or nine months in the fiscal year.

The Federal government continually publishes pamphlets and surveys ranging from reports on specific issues to studies of general economic trends. For example, the Federal Reserve System, the Department of Commerce, and the Federal Trade Commission prepare and publish economic reports which provide business trends, industry earnings data, and other important information.

WALL STREET SCORECARD

Is one glass of water sufficient to determine the composition of an ocean? After all, one glass is a measure. Wall Street's most famous and influential market measure is the Dow Jones Industrials. The 30 DJ stocks, chosen out of some 1,300, are, by and large, top-grade securities. They account for roughly 27 percent of the market value of all listed stocks. Moreover, the DJ has a valuable historical background—it goes back to 1897—and for long years has been solidly implanted in the mind of the investment community as a measure of the market.

Over the years, various formulas, some very elaborate, have been devised to compensate for stock splits and stock dividends and thus have given continuity to the average. In the case of the DJ industrial average, the prices of the 30 stocks are totaled and then divided by a divisor, changed from time to time, which is intended to compensate for stock splits and dividends. As a result, point changes in the average have only the vaguest relationship to dollar price changes in stocks included in the average.

The DJ industrial and rail stock price averages have sprouted a theory—the Dow Theory—which says that the market is in a basic upward trend if one of these averages advances above a previous important high, accompanied or followed by a similar advance in the other. When the averages both dip below previous important lows, this is regarded as confirmation of a basic downward trend. The Theory does not attempt to predict how long either trend will continue, although it is widely misinterpreted as a method of forecasting future action. The importance of the Theory is simply that some people believe in it, or believe others do. In practice, the Theory has been right—sometimes. I'm inclined to put it on a par with tea leaves.

With all these reliable sources ready at hand, you'd think that investing would be a surer thing than it is, but such isn't the case. The big variable is that good old human element, emotion.

Wall Street is dominated by two pinnacles: A mountain of facts and figures, and the Mount Everest of psychology. After all, the last price of a stock is determined by what a buyer *thinks* it's worth. Some of the psychological factors involved are pride, survival, and greed. A stock going up can create magnificent delusions of grandeur; on the other hand, when it goes down, various types of anxieties and fears come to the surface. Frequently emotions run to extremes, and prices are exaggerated both upwards and down. Generally, the most poorly informed people are the first to panic and dump stocks when the market plunges and subsequently the first to personify remorse when the market recovers.

I will concede that it is easier to advise judicial calm than practice objectivity. After all, humans are, well, human, and subject to emotional flip-flops. Frequently even analysts are influenced by surrounding market psychology as expressed by the level and activity of the stock market. An analyst often finds himself taking his own standards from the public, like the famous politician who said, "I have to follow them, because I am their leader."

In general, however, markets react to what amateurs think the professionals will do and to what professionals think the amateurs will do. On balance, of course, pros outguess and outperform the novices, or should. However, how much you know is not as important as how much *good* information you have, and how well you understand "stock psychology."

A favorite Wall Street quip illustrates the crosscurrents of market thinking:

First Broker: "I'm optimistic about the market."

Second Broker: "Then why do you look worried?"

First Broker: "I'm not certain my optimism is justified."

Thus, being an amateur psychologist can actually pay off. There *are* "rules" that reflect the working of the human mind in business.

It is not necessary for you to be a professional analyst to join the diggers. You can do your own research, and the consequence might be educational and exciting as well as profitable. The fragment of information you may discover might be the missing piece in a jigsaw your broker is putting together. You never know.

THE PUBLIC EYE

How *does* a stock go up? Well, public companies perform publicly. When they show an impressive pattern of growth—or come up with a good idea or good product, which might result in unusual growth—they attract a following, and the following attracts a following. Result: The high demand causes an increase in price. As a matter of course, the initial followers are generally the more sophisticated analysts, the managers of funds, and the other bell cows of the Wall Street herd. But publicity attracts the novices too. Let a new company announce a new product, and its stock will usually jump.

But the average investor is often puzzled by the fact that when a company does announce good news—higher dividend, higher earnings, etc.—the price of the stock frequently goes *down*. It appears to go against the law of gravity, but the reason is simple. Insiders are presumed to have had knowledge of the good news well in advance of its actual publication. Consequently, it is also presumed that they purchased the stock when the price was low (i.e., before the good news had an effect). As the rumors are circulated within the market, the stock continues to rise in anticipation. Therefore, when the news is made public, the insiders sometimes sell since they believe the price has already hit its peak. This somewhat complicated sequence helps explain why good news can be bad. Furthermore, it explains why male analysts will equate market action with femininity: It is baffling as well as fascinating.

Nonetheless, companies like to create the "image" of having many new products constantly available, if only to bolster their stock prices. Accordingly, the proliferation of products has reached such proportions that it supports, among other things, a $50-per-year magazine. *The Products Digest,* published monthly, lists about five hundred new products per issue. Less than 10 percent of the new products on the market ever make it. Any research-oriented company always has up its sleeve something new which could become a major item in sales and profits. But if it can create a new *image* of growth for itself, then there is money to be made. Therefore, if you're relying on publicity releases to keep your portfolios plush, remember that your stock profits will be based on how good the news *seems,* not how good it really is. The next two examples illustrate the way fortunes are made and lost by publicity alone.

The impact of rosy prospects and thorny realities was illustrated by the Motorola experience in September, 1966. Similar patterns have applied to other stocks in the past and this classic case history will undoubtedly be repeated in the future. Early in 1966, Wall Street analysts and other projectionists had calculated that Motorola could and might earn as much as $9 per share. On the basis of the such buoyant prospects, the stock had wings. It soared to 232½. Obviously, visions of golden sugar plums danced in the heads of optimistic investors. But as the weeks passed, other analysts had second thoughts. By June, the projections were scaled down to $8 per share. By July, optimism had dwindled to $7 per share. The stock reacted accordingly and continued to decline from the high of 232½. By August, the stock dropped about 90 points. On September 27 the chairman of Motorola addressed the New York Security Analysts. He indicated that earnings for the year would probably be no more than $5.50 to $6 per share. In the year 1965 share earnings had totaled $5.23. Disappointed optimists and sudden pessimists dumped Motorola. Within ninety minutes the stock dived from 138¼ and closed at 119.

Another case history involved one of those hot new issues called Gamma Processing. It came to the market with a sophisticated concept: food preservation by irradiation. The possibilities of this form of food preservation were downright fantastic. Its beneficial effects in torrid climates was obvious. The stock came to Wall Street for sale at $5 per share. Within minutes it zoomed to $11. Several months later it had rocketed to $27 per share, even though the company had sustained losses during the first 23 months of its existence. (Later it showed small profits.) In May, 1968, the Food and Drug Administration suggested that this method of food preservation might cause cancer and still-born childbirths. The day the FDA announcement was made the stock hurtled downward to 15½ and recovered later in the day to close at 19. *The New York Times* quoted a Wall Streeter: "This shows you what can happen when people get carried away with an investment idea."

Individual stocks, of course, are usually affected only by news items concerning their particular company, but as a general rule, stocks are more like a team. In their progression or retrogression they are usually accompanied by companies in similar and allied fields. Steels, oils, chemicals, and computers do well or badly as a group.

On occasion there is a maverick among them. While reading financial news, you often come across the words "special situation." It is a term applied to the common stock of a company where the stock's potential is not related merely to the company's day-to-day business. A special situation may result from matters such as expected recovery under a new management, discovery of a valuable natural resource on the corporate properties, or the introduction of a popular new product. A special situation security will generally rise against a declining market and will outperform the averages in a rising market. And that, naturally, is what makes it so special.

However, the general rule is rather inflexible: You can get richer by buying a mediocre company in the right (fashionable) group than by buying the best stock in the wrong (unfashionable) segment. Example: In 1967-68 computer stocks were the favored group and steels were unpopular. In June, 1968, a small company in the computer group named Scandata sold for $130 per share in spite of the fact that it was losing money, while giant, blue-chip U. S. Steel sold for $39 per share. The irony of the group movements of stocks is that having picked the right group, you can be wrong and still make money. The hurricane force of the upward thrust of the group will carry your stock higher even if the company you've chosen is economically inferior.

NEWS OF THE DAY

Wall Street often has a knee-jerk reaction to Washington noises. A prime illustration was offered during 1967. Every time President Johnson called for a surtax the market spurted. But the market

went down whenever opposition to the surtax was voic
gressman Wilbur Mills, the House Ways and Means
chairman. As a matter of fact, almost everything a Pr
and does is promptly reflected by the stock ticker.

As a frame of reference for future effects of unpredictable news,
the following chart is useful:

	DJI % Loss*	Days of Decline	Losses Recovered
Battleship *Maine* sunk (1898)	16½	32	100% in 6 days
San Francisco Earthquake (1906)	11	14	82% in 26 days
Lusitania sunk (1915)	11	32	100% in 16 days
Austrian crisis (1938)	25	31	100% in 75 days
Munich crisis (1939)	14	53	100% in 11 days
Czechoslovakian crisis (1939)	22	24	100% in 130 days
Poland invaded (1939)	7	17	100% in 9 days
Fall of France (1940)	25	26	72% in 127 days
Pearl Harbor (1941)	9	14	77% in 9 days
Berlin crisis (1948)	9	72	82% in 18 days
Korean crisis (1950)	12½	13	100% in 43 days
President Eisenhower's illness (1955)	10	12	100% in 25 days
Cuban crisis (1962)	5½	6	100% in 6 days

* DJI % Loss: Percentage lost during days of decline.

In recent years a hypersensitive market has become increasingly
common. The trend will probably continue, simply because investors are recognizing public emotions as a valid index of financial success and are no longer afraid to use a little emotion
themselves, be it fear or enthusiasm.

The revolutionary change that has come over the stock market
was succinctly explained in the January-February, 1968, *Financial
Analysts' Journal*: "There's a new breed of fund managers. You
could characterize them as being open-minded, having a great respect for new ideas, and generally operating without committees.
One used to say that you had to be under forty to participate in the
new market, but it appears now that the age has been moved down
to thirty; there are a lot of people under thirty who did not witness

the 1962 break and who do not have the advantage or handicap of conventional wisdom and experience."

Naturally the long-term investor has always been searching for a pattern in temporary fluctuations. Theories have been advanced blaming everything from Gross National Product to sunspots. One may be worth mentioning: Over the last six years, four summers have produced definable rallies, based on advances by the common-stock index of the New York Stock Exchange. Rallies took place in 1963, 1964, 1965, and 1967. There was no rally in the hot summer months of 1966. In 1962 stock prices dropped sharply in the first half of the year and then more or less stabilized, leaving that year as a standoff.

Last year *The Exchange,* a publication of the Big Board, studied what it called the summer-rally "tradition." That study, utilizing the Dow Jones industrial average as "the market," went back to 1897. It found that stock prices during July advanced in forty-eight years and declined in twenty-two years. The conclusion was that, "The odds are better than two-to-one that the market will show a net gain during the summer."

Are Republicans or Democrats better for the stock market? Well, back in 1900 a man had two sons. One was a Republican and the other a Democrat. After one of their heated arguments as to which party would be better for the stock market, the father gave each a sum of $1,000 with the understanding that each son would invest his money in stock only in the years when his favorite party was in power. When the Democrats were in power, the Republican son would keep his money in cash. The other son did the opposite, investing only when the Democrats were elected.

During the sixty-eight-year period the Democrats were in power for thirty-six years and the Republicans for thirty-two years. In February of 1968 the old man asked them to figure out who had won, since he wanted to give a prize of $50,000 to the winner and get it over with. The Democrat son showed that he had made money in 7 of the 9 periods during which he had invested and that the cumulative value of his original $1,000 was now $5,557.90. The Republican son showed that he had made money in 7 of the 8 periods during which he had invested and that the cumulative value of his fund was only $2,478.90. But he argued that the results were not fair, since the value of the dollar had deteriorated so much during the years when the Democrats were in power.

So the father decided that they should adjust the results according to the change in the value of the dollar. After that was done the Democrat showed the value of his fund was $4,140.10, while the Republican showed that his fund was $4,609. Since they had not decided at the start whether the results were to be in constant or fluctuating dollar values, the father decided to divide the prize money equally.

The effect of politics on the stock market has been a long-running Wall Street debate. A study on the subject was made by Ralph Rotnam of Harris, Upham & Co. Conclusion: The party in power (whether Republican *or* Democrat) likes to see needed adjustments in the economy (which usually make the market decline) take place *early* in a four-year Presidential term. That way, the market has a chance to regain its healthy glow before the voters are again asked for their support at the polls.

To find out how this affects the stock market, Harris, Upham & Co. made a survey of the declines that had occurred each year from the high of the preceding year. The declines were indeed considerably *higher* in the first two years of Presidential terms than they were in the last two.

The record:

Declines from High of Preceding Year to Low in	Average for 1936-1967 Period	Average for 1948-1967 Period
First year after election	17.2%	13.6%
Second year after election	21.5	14.6
Third year after election	10.5	7.5
Fourth year after election	11.0	7.3
Average for 4 years	15.1	10.8
Average for first 2 years	19.35	14.1
Average for last 2 years	10.75	7.4

This means that with regard to the market the Chief Executive comes in as a bear and goes out as a bull. It also means that according to the law of averages, you'd do best to invest during the two summers preceding national elections.

Not all surveys on market psychology are so reliable. As a case in point, there is the following amusing illustration. Some years ago *Fortune* magazine drew a general portrait of women investors. The conclusions:

1. The richer the woman the less personal interest does she take in her investments.
2. They are more conservative investors than men.
3. They hate to touch capital.
4. They like preferred stock better than common.
5. They are likely to become emotionally attached to certain stocks.
6. They expect a great deal more from their investments than men do.
7. When they do speculate, they do it all-out.
8. They are highly susceptible to "hot tips."

After reading the conclusions, I instituted the "Jarvis Survey." I sent *Fortune*'s list of general observations to approximately thirty brokers and asked whether they agreed with it. Result: 18% agreed; 10% disagreed; 35% stated it was partially right; 37% reported it was partially wrong.

Since it's impossible to know *exactly* how the market's collective mind is going to react, I often feel the average female investor shouldn't bother to try. She should know, however, what the variables are, so that before a big change something in her mind will ring a bell, telling her to get off or jump on. Your intuition is just as good as a computer, but it also needs facts to keep it working smoothly. Keep looking for places where emotions can be traced to simple facts. Often small pebbles set off an avalanche.

Among the prime factors in stock success is managerial skill. This gift has transformed many lackluster companies into exciting, high-priced conglomerates, for instance. During the 1960's oils and phone companies were generally unpopular. But IT&T and Occidental Petroleum zoomed, thanks to the managerial wizardry of Harold Geneen and Armand Hammer. It is reassuring to note that despite the wonders of our technology superior brains remain the most dominant factor.

By and large, a company with 200,000 shares will move up more quickly than one saddled with 2,000,000 shares—if a demand for the stock exists. The company with the smaller stock capitalization will move down more quickly, too. The formula is elementary: Stock scarcity plus demand equals higher prices.

"Security psychosis" means the desire to "protect" one's capital. This is understandable, since most individuals toil hard over a prolonged period to accumulate it. But the harsh fact of economic life is that there is no absolute protection of the value of capital. Many blue chips are big enough to provide a certain stability, but they are too large to continue growing as fast as younger, more dynamic companies. The blue chippers in general are tied to the business cycle and generally cannot grow any faster than the industry they are in or than the economy as a whole. Furthermore, the industry giants tend to be the targets of organized labor, and they are often restricted in their growth by anti-trust legislation. Washington tends to be silent when labor asks for increases, but protests loudly and publicly when prices are increased.

Facts like those above have influence out of proportion to their *seeming* importance. You'll find reasonable reports helpful, but sometimes you'll be better off working the opposite side of the track. As a matter of fact, in my early days in Wall Street when I wrote market letters, I often would fly right in the face of a trend. Being right was very important. Frequently, when I was president of the New York Society of Security Analysts, I would ask for a vote of confidence in the market. Whatever the majority opinion was in those days, I'd find it profitable to go in the opposite direction. It always took a lot of nerve, and my courage was tested severely for a while. But the profits below the line backed me up.

To go where the weak fear to tread is difficult at any time, but I have done it many times and have enjoyed the caviar and champagne of solid profits.

One of my good friends in Wall Street had a $4,000 portfolio in 1939. In 1962, when the late President Kennedy disagreed on steel price increases, the stock market dropped a couple of hundred points in the industrial averages. Stock Exchange seats dropped from $225,000 to $150,000, and IBM dropped the equivalent of one hundred years' dividends in market value. My friend who had

had $4,000 in 1939 dropped $9,000,000—and brought his portfolio down to $18,000,000. A couple of years ago he was up to $62,000,000, and more recently he was up to over $100,000,000. All of this was done mostly by disagreeing with the majority and looking for special situations.

Of course there are many hazards in forecasting, and Mark Twain is reported to have named February as the most dangerous month for forecasting. He then added that March, April, May, and so on were also dangerous. However, he also said, "You must forecast frequently and always for the long term." Obviously anybody can prove you are wrong at some time or another, but forecasters like to remember the forecasts that have turned out right; it is sort of a disease.

The reasons so many forecasts don't turn out right is that none of the rules on which they are based are inflexible. And not all information is completely reliable, either. You have to be very careful with management and with public relations men, some of whom do not check their figures too accurately or who wish to create an up-beat impression.

Too often analysts say we should buy only the blue chips. I have always maintained that it is not necessary to buy leaders of an industry. On many occasions I have felt that the best profits are to be made in the so-called "doggie" stocks of an industry which seem likely to turn around. Frequently Wall Street analysts will find "stocks are good buys" only after they have gone up considerably.

I don't find it necessary to buy into only those companies with sales of over $100,000,000. You can frequently get a beautiful company with sales of only $500,000 or $1,000,000. Image, potentials, and glamour are often more important.

It is not always essential to insist on "capable" management. What is "capable" is debatable, but don't assume that the management is capable simply because the product is good. Manufacturers of products like Kleenex and Scotch Tape and Band-Aids cannot *help* but sell their product; these great products advertise themselves. However, competition may be lurking around the corner with truly capable management. Breadth of product line is not necessary either—this can be developed later. However, a well-staffed research division may be more important, because tomorrow's success can come from today's research.

Long-term forecasts are often misleading because they predict precise figures. A case in point is the laser industry. When the world's first laser beam was demonstrated in 1960, headlines greeted it as a modern miracle. Physicians saw it as a cure for cancer, generals as an awesome addition to their arsenals, and businessmen as a fantastic growth industry.

The word laser is an acronym for Light Amplification Stimulated Emission of Radiation. A laser is a source of coherent lights —the purest, sharpest, most intense light ever known. It can be focused into a very small spot to create temperatures several times hotter than the sun, reducing any known material to vapor. For communications scientists theorize that a single laser beam could carry all the telephone, television, and radio channels now in use on earth.

When the laser was unveiled in 1960 there were predictions of an industry of $1,000,000,000 by 1970. In 1967 the world-wide market for laser-related goods and services was $300,000,000. By 1970 it *may* reach $500,000,000, or about 50 percent of what it was expected to hit.

But the figures here are misleading. Lasers are still fantastically expensive—a single one costs in the tens of thousands of dollars— and therefore, only large industries may be able to use them. Until lasers become cheaper (like Xerox's machines or IBM's computers) they may not cause any permanent price leaps on the exchanges.

What devices or companies *will*? Well, successful investing is frequently the consequence of logical progression, a fact which enables non-experts to make sound economic forecasts. Let's take a well-known fact: Medicare is here and it is here to stay. Moreover, many of its benefits will be expanded in the future. Take another fact: More and more people are living longer. A third fact is hardly a secret: Medical group insurance has become an accepted fringe benefit in private industry and in government. Thus, it requires a minimum of analytical ability for you to conclude that there are exciting growth prospects for companies in the drug field.

There are some other facts you may be able to weave into a sound portfolio. Assets owned by United States life insurance companies have increased 77 percent to more than $149,000,000,000 at the end of 1964 compared with $85,000,000,000 at the end of 1954. And within the same 10 years insurance was up 140 percent to $800,000,000,000, and total premium income was up 96 percent to $22,700,000,000. Industry sources were predicting that insurance would reach $1,000,000,000,000 by 1970, but now this target has been advanced to 1968! Pension funds in 1950 were believed to own $200,000,000 worth of common stocks. In 1960, this had increased to $2,000,000,000. In 1968 the figure approximated $5,500,000,000, and by 1973 the total may reach $9,000,-000,000.

The growth rates projected for certain segments of the population appear especially favorable for the apparel industry. The fifteen-to-thirty age group, which buys the most apparel, is growing faster than any other age group. In 1968, it represented about 20 percent of the population and is expected to increase to 25 percent by 1970. These figures becomes more important when you realize that this age group buys nearly 40 percent of all the clothing sold in the country. They are fashion conscious, and their buying power is sizably increasing. Teen-age income now is said to be $13,000,000,000, and by 1973 it may reach $20,000,000,000. Since 1958 the percentage of teen-agers holding part-time jobs has increased to 40 percent among boys and 30 percent among girls. And 25 percent of all teen-agers have charge accounts in their own names.

The population of the United States as a whole is expected to rise to 350,000,000 by the turn of the century. By 1980 the population of the United States and Canada should increase from 211,-000,000 to 267,000,000. The population of the world is expected to double by the year 2,000 and exceed 6,000,000,000. This obviously means that the future of the housing industry is bright. Furthermore, every motorist and commuter realizes the dire need for improved mass transportation; it follows that industries involved in mass transportation have prosperous prospects.

The air pollution control industry at present is a fragmented one. Laws are needed to force industry to solve its problems. Up to now expenditures on pollution control have been very small. The market can grow only as fast as the industry is willing to spend money on it. Water pollution is another field where politics has been holding us back. But inevitably, *in time,* companies engaged in producing devices to control or eliminate air and water pollution will be part of an explosive industry.

Even a new slant on *how* you handle investment goals can pay off, especially if you're unorthodox for a reason. For example, one bank analyst observed in 1968, "We're doing something new at the bank. We're now putting electric utility stocks instead of bonds into our trust accounts. We ran some calculations that show that if you take a six percent bond and reinvest the interest semi-annually, in twenty-five years that thousand-dollar bond is worth four thousand four hundred dollars. On the other hand, if you buy a utility at fifteen times earnings and it's growing at five percent per year and paying out sixty percent of earnings, in twenty-five years your thousand-dollar investment grows to nine thousand four hundred dollars. We don't think utilities are *dynamic* growth stocks, but we're putting a lot of them into what we call our growing income accounts. We think they're a wonderful replacement for straight corporate bonds."

I like to think of myself as a practical dreamer. That is not a contradictory position. As a dreamer I can envision the potential of a good idea—and as a realist I am aware that some dreams remain dreams, that others eventually develop a partial reality, and that some take longer than others to materialize.

As we noted previously, if any tool or combination of instruments could predict the market with certitude, Wall Street would be compelled to go out of business. The fact to remember about all forms of technical analysis is that they are maps, not crystal balls. An investor has to dream in order to stay one jump ahead of the highly emotional, vastly well-informed, cautious, and whimsical public that constitutes the market.

Of course you have to know what you're dreaming about. And one of the best methods of becoming well-informed is by listening to the well-informed. The adult education curriculum in many community schools includes how-to-invest courses. Moreover, financial forums are being conducted in cities and towns all over the country by brokerage houses, banks, women's clubs, and firms associated with the New York Stock Exchange.

Beyond that, your single biggest advantage is your imagination. Use it to draw conclusions, to put yourself in the shoes of the other investor, and to fill in the gaps a financial report often leaves. That way the nest you feather has a larger chance of being your own.

chapter five

Reading a Financial Report

As a woman, you are a born shopper. But shopping means knowing what you're buying—whether it's a hat, a coat, a dress, or a peck of potatoes. By the same token, it is important to know what you're buying in Wall Street.

Let us assume that you have picked the proper broker. You are impressed with some of the stocks he has on his buy list. Yet the basic decision to buy is a subjective one; you must make up your own mind. Before you buy, you should examine the quality of the merchandise. How is this done? There are numerous buying guides on Wall Street. One of the most effective is the annual report, published by every public company you may be interested in.

At first glance, the annual report may seem to be an exercise in hieroglyphics. And the various figures and symbols can create the impression of being pure Sanskrit. But don't let that scare or discourage you; anyone of normal intelligence can decipher an annual report. If you require some assistance, ask your accountant, not only your husband, if necessary. Time and study will make you more expert than you—or your husband—ever imagined.

In simplest terms an annual report is the formal financial statement issued yearly by a corporation to its shareowners. The report shows assets, liabilities, earnings—how the company fared with regard to profits during the year and how it stood at the close. In addition, the annual report not only records the past, but also reflects the present and often looks to the future. Most annual reports include statements for both the current and previous years, and in many instances summaries for five- to ten-year periods are provided. Measuring the past record against the present sometimes helps you determine the pattern of future growth.

Although the standards of balance sheets (financial statements) vary according to the economic characteristics of particular industries, the following general pattern will apply to most of them.

Plus Signs

The plus signs in an annual report are:
1. Current assets
2. Cash
3. Receivables
4. Inventories
5. Fixed assets

"Current" assets are assets that can be turned into cash more quickly than "fixed" assets. "Cash" is exactly what the word denotes, generally in the form of bank deposits. "Inventories" include the raw materials, the work in process, the supplies used in operations, and the finished goods ready for sale. Sometimes these items are shown separately. Since the value of inventories changes with price fluctuations, it is important to know how the inventories are valued. Statements usually indicate the basis, which generally is cost or current market price, whichever is lower.

A steady decline in the "inventory turnover"—that is, the amount of goods left on the shelf as compared with the amount of goods sold—may be a warning. It could mean that the heavy load of unsold goods is dangerous, since it adds to the perils of falling prices. Or it could mean either that the company's sales program is faltering or that its buying could be inept or outdated as a consequence of shifts in public taste and style.

Fixed assets represents buildings, land, machinery, and equipment—less accumulated depreciation.

An increase in fixed assets, as well as increased sales, is the expected companion of expansion. Such an increase may also indicate that the company has made an additional investment in equipment, or built new plants, in order to cut costs.

If a large gain in fixed assets is not followed by a more or less corresponding gain in sales, management may have been the victim of pipe dreams, overestimating its ability to sell more goods. Or the industry may have reached overcapacity. In any case, if a company's fixed assets show little change for several years during a period of general business expansion, obviously the company could be in trouble. It may be losing its competitive position, or it may be that management has neglected to keep up with technological changes and innovations.

It would be a happy day if a company could produce and sell more merchandise, or mine more ore, without adding to its expenses, but this is practically impossible. If you make additions to your home and increase its value, you must also pay for the labor and products that go into the improvements. Sustained growth almost invariably requires an investment in additional facilities— either plant structures, machinery, and equipment, or in the case of oil and gas companies, additional acreage for exploration.

Good news for the investor comes in the form of additional efficient production as a result of capital expenditures. Failure to spend for increased efficiency in our competitive economy leads to higher costs and less business, just as when repair bills on a jalopy begin to equal the cost of a brand-new car.

Finally, there is one class of assets, known as intangible, that does not appear on a company's balance sheet, because it represents non-physical items. Intangibles include goodwill, trademarks, patents and copyrights, and other things. In computing the company's net worth or the book value of a stock, the value at which any intangible item is held is omitted in the balance sheet. It is the tangible net worth or tangible book value that is used for purposes of financial analysis.

Minus Signs

Liabilities and stockholders' equity
1. Current liabilities:
   (A) Accounts payable
   (B) Notes payable
2. Accrued liabilities
3. Reserves
4. Current maturity of long-term debt
5. Federal income and other taxes
6. Dividends payable

"Accounts and Notes payable" represents money owed to suppliers of raw materials, as well as other costs that have to be met in the course of business. Ordinarily, when sales are expanding, there will be some increase in this item. "Accrued liabilities" may represent such items as unpaid wages, salaries, and commissions.

Other items under the heading of liabilities and stockholders' equity include reserves, capital, long-term debt, and stockholders' equity.

"Reserves" earmark appropriations from surplus that are not to be used for dividend purposes. Such reserves may be set up against possible losses from declines in inventory value or for various other contingencies. Ultimately contingent reserves may be restored to surplus and become available for dividends.

"Capital" includes all sums used in business—funds invested by lenders and stockholders as well as the funds representing reinvested earnings. In the financial world the term "capital structure" is used frequently and simply means the total of all long-term debt, preferred stock, common-stock, and surplus. The company may have raised funds through the "sale" of long-term debt (mortgage bonds or debentures), preferred stock, and common stock; or it may have outstanding only bonds and common stock, or only preferred stock and common stock, or only common stock. In the last case it is said the capital structure is "simple," or that the company has a "one-stock capitalization."

The point to note whatever the combination may be, a company *must* have a common stock, though it may have other securities as well. Common stock represents ownership; the common stockholder takes the greatest risk but also stands to gain the most from a company's prosperity. A holder of a bond or debenture and preferred stockholders have certain legal priorities over the common shareholders. The investor should realize, however, that legal relationships do not determine values. Bonds and preferred stocks of one company may be inferior in quality to the common stocks of another.

"Long-term debt" is the face, or principal, sum due at maturity, less any amount that is payable in less than a year. Debt may consist of several different issues, representing money borrowed at various times and at different rates of interest. Usually long-term debt may be called or redeemed by the company prior to maturity at a premium of 3 to 5 percent over the principal amount.

Under "stockholders' equity" there is preferred stock. At one time the company may have raised funds through the sale of this stock. The rights of the preferred stockholder, like those of a holder of debt securities, are determined by contract. Usually a preferred stockholder is entitled to a fixed dividend before common stockholders may receive dividends and to priority in the event of dissolution or liquidation. Generally no dividend can be declared on the common stock if there are any dividends in arrears on the preferred. Most preferred stocks now have voting power in the event that four quarterly dividend payments have not been declared. Like bonds and debentures, preferred stocks usually are redeemable at the company's option at fixed prices. Common stock may be shown at "par value" or, if the stock has no par value, at "stated value." The thing to remember is that the par value or stated value is an arbitrary amount, having no relation to the market value of a common stock or to what would be received in liquidation. Market value is determined by buyers who take into account earnings, dividends, prospects, the caliber of management, and the general business outlook.

Incidentally, there is no "ideal" capital structure. Even so, the investor should be on guard against "too heavy" an amount of long-term debt and preferred stock in relation to common stock and surplus. Further, it is important to note that a one-stock capitalization may be attractive because there are no prior claims ahead of the common stock. But there may be an advantage in using senior securities (bonds and preferred stock) provided the funds borrowed can earn more than is needed to pay the interest on the debt or dividends on preferred stock. Obviously if the company can earn profits on the money it has borrowed, such a debt is an advantage as it provides excellent leverage for the common shares when the economies are favorable.

Additions

The Income Statement includes:
1. Sales
2. Cost of goods sold
3. Selling, general, and administrative expenses
4. Depreciation and depletion
5. Operating profit
6. Interest charges
7. Earnings before income taxes
8. Provision for federal and states taxes on income

9. Net income for the year
10. Dividends on preferred stock
11. Balance of new income
12. Earned surplus
13. Accountant's opinion

"Sales" tells you how much business the company did. It is always encouraging to see an increase, of course, provided it is accompanied by a boost in profits. Note, however, that whether or not a company has made a favorable showing depends on what other companies in the industry have done in the same period. If the *entire* industry has increased sales by 15 percent and the company you are interested in has boosted its sales only 7 percent, then the picture could be gloomy. It is always well to determine whether sales have expanded or whether the larger dollar volume is derived entirely or even partially from price increases.

The "cost of goods sold" represents the expense of doing business. It involves outlays for raw materials, wages and salaries, supplies, power and light, and other costs. The simple arithmetic of the story is this: If the company lowers the cost of goods sold, it automatically raises its gross profit. Keep an eye on that item.

Selling, general, and administrative expenses vary with the kind of business. For example, companies that ultimately sell to consumers usually spend larger sums for advertising than companies selling to other manufacturers or companies that obtain a large part of their orders from the government.

"Depreciation and depletion" are very important with regard to taxes. Every piece of machinery and equipment has a limited period of usefulness even when kept in good repair. Thus, the company makes a provision for "using up" the service life of each asset. The United States Treasury Department holds that depreciation for tax purposes can be related only to cost. It sets forth maximum depreciation allowances in computing a company's taxable income. If a company has not provided for the wear and tear on its production facilities, its profits and net worth would be overstated. Depletion is somewhat similar to depreciation, but in terms of natural resources. Timber, coal, copper, oil, and gas are examples of the type of assets that is subject to depletion.

The higher the amounts deducted for depreciation and depletion, the lower the net reported income. Conversely, large deductions make for a high "cash flow," which is the total net income plus deduction for depreciation and depletion. Cash flow is sometimes considered a better guide to future dividend policy than net income. However, working capital and projected capital expenditures should always be considered.

"Operating profit" is sometimes referred to as pre-tax profit. For a check on management efficiency, some analysts exclude depreciation and depletion in calculating pre-tax profit margin. By the way, small companies do not necessarily have the smallest pre-tax profit margins, nor big companies the widest.

"Interest charges" represent the sum required to meet interest payments on debt. Since interest is deductible as an expense before taxes, it is often less costly to borrow money than to have funds supplied by stockholders. Bondholders will sleep better when they see at least $3 of available earnings for $1 of interest that the company must pay.

"Earnings before income taxes" represent simply the operating profit minus interest charges.

"Provision for federal and state taxes on income" is Uncle Sam's bite, of course. Since the tax rate on corporate profits is 52 percent, the federal tax collector has more than a half-interest in the earnings of a company. The full implications of the 52 percent rate have been a matter of debate. Some economists and businessmen are sure that higher tax rates are passed on to the consumer, while others contend that prices are determined in other ways. Obviously, everyone wants lower taxes, if for no other reason than that the present tax rates unquestionably hinder small companies more than large ones. It is often more difficult for a small business to raise the needed capital.

"Net income for the year" is the acid test item. It is also known as earnings or profits. Earnings over the year sum up all the effort, achievement, progress, mistakes, and problems of the business. There are two standard tests of how good earnings are. The first is the relation of net income to sales. The second concerns the relation between net earnings and the amount of stockholders' investment. Grocery chains earn about 10 percent on the funds the shareholders have invested in business, but only 2 to 3 percent on sales. Again, average net income varies considerably among different industries.

"Dividends on preferred stock" is determined largely by the relation between the size of the net income and the annual dividend requirements. Careful investors should take note of the amount of interest required on a company's indebtedness, for interest comes before the preferred stockholders' dividends. The dividends requirement on the preferred stock is not an obligation in the same way as the interest due to a creditor. In a sense a preferred stockholder is a "limited partner."

"Balance of new income" represents the balance available for dividends on common stocks after deducting preferred-stock dividends. This is the item most commonly used to indicate earnings of the common stockholder when reduced to a per-share basis.

"Earned surplus" is also known as income retained in business. The amount retained from year to year depends on both net income and dividend payments.

The "accountant's opinion" expresses an opinion, not a guarantee, since the value of many items in financial statements are not subject to precise measurement. Nevertheless, the opinion of an independent expert, with experience and skill in auditing and accounting, serves three important purposes: It usually states (1) that the statements presented have been prepared in accordance with generally accepted principles of accounting; (2) that the financial statements are a fair picture of the end-of-the-year financial condition; and (3) that the accounting principles followed are consistent with those of the preceding year.

After completing your appraisal of the financial statement, try it on for size. Does it fit your bankroll as an investment? Is it in style with your needs? Does it match your hopes? Is the texture of the corporate merchandise as good as it appears? Your investment should be custom-tailored for you.

There are several ways of getting answers to these questions. Among the most effective are several ratios used by brokers and analysts. These focus attention on significant relationships in the income account and balance sheets. The ratios are fairly simple to understand and apply; they are merely exercises in simple arithmetic. Of course, there are not magic formulas for the appraisal of securities. They omit broad economic factors, public psychology, technological struggles, and the skill of management (although the balance sheet *is* one step in the final judgment of management).

The Big Seven Ratios

1. Ratio of profit, before interest and taxes, to sales
2. Ratio of current assets to liabilities
3. Ratio of cash equivalent to total current liabilities
4. Capitalization ratio
5. Ratio of sales to fixed assets
6. Ratio of sales to inventories
7. Ratio of new income to net worth

First is the ratio of profit, before interest and taxes, to sales. It is expressed as a percentage of sales and is found by dividing the operating profit by sales.

Second is the current working capital ratio (or "current" ratio), meaning the ratio of current assets to current liabilities. A 2-to-1 ratio is the standard for many industries, but it may vary. A gradual increase in the current ratio is usually a healthy sign of improved financial strength.

Third is the liquidity ratio, the ratio of cash and equivalent (that is, marketable securities) to total current liabilities. It is also expressed as a percentage figure, arrived at by dividing cash and equivalent by total current liabilities. This ratio is important as a supplement to the current ratio; if this ratio is low, the company's immediate ability to meet current obligations or pay larger dividends may be hampered despite a higher current ratio.

Fourth is the capitalization ratio, the ratio of each type of investment in the company to the total investment.

Fifth is the ratio of sales to fixed assets. This ratio is arrived at by dividing the annual sales by the value, before depreciation and amortization, of plant, equipment, and land at the end of the year. The ratio is important because it helps point out whether or not the funds used to enlarge productive facilities are being spent wisely.

Sixth is the ratio of sales to inventories, the so-called inventory turnover. This figure is important as a guide to whether or not the enterprise is investing too heavily in inventories. In this event a setback in sales or a drop in commodity prices could be particularly unfavorable.

The seventh ratio, that of net income to net worth, is one of the most significant. This figure is arrived at by dividing net income by the total of the preferred stock, common stock, and surplus accounts. This ratio answers the vital question of how much the company is earning on the stockholders' investment. Naturally, a large and increasing ratio is favorable. In a competitive society, however, a zooming ratio inevitably invites competition. Moreover, broad economic forces may change the general direction of this ratio. A higher rate may be due to general prosperity; a decline may be due to recession, to less favorable conditions, or to higher taxes.

There are many other quality guides, of course. You should be aware of two of them, the price-earnings multiple and the book value per share on common stock. Book value is found by adding the stated or par value of the common stock to the surplus accounts and then dividing the total by the number of shares.

MATHEMAGIC

But by far the most important indication of quality is the price-earnings multiple. This is a shorthand way of saying that a stock is selling in the market for x times earnings. If the common stock sells for $60 per share and earns $6 per share, it would be selling at 10 times earnings. What is the proper P-E multiple? That's a riddle within an enigma. No one knows what it should be, and this is one reason why they say Wall Street experts are distinguished by different degrees of ignorance. The fact is that P-E multiples vary constantly. And they vary not only with economic conditions but also with expectations for the future—that is, with the buyers' confidence that they will be able to sell their stock to other buyers at higher prices. Interest rates and the level of bond prices are other important factors.

For obvious reasons investors are willing to pay a higher price for the stocks of companies whose earnings may grow faster than the average or than for the stocks of companies in static industries. Once again, factors applying to individual companies—management, financial position, capitalization, dividend policy, and the market's appraisal of the stock of similar companies—must be considered in each case.

The rule of thumb used to be 10 times earnings. But that multiple is as stable as a candle in the wind. Actually a stock isn't necessarily high if it sells for 30 times earnings or even 50 or more, or low if it sells at 8 times earnings. As the saying goes, it all depends.

Rigid mathematical formulas cannot be applied to individual stocks or to the market in general. By and large, the arithmetic tells you what *has* happened, while Wall Street is primarily interested in what *will* happen. Reading the palms of our dynamic economy involves the imponderables of history as well as the intangibles of economic change. These forces cannot be measured by a slide rule, nor are they to be seen under a microscope. Often they defy imagination, but eventually they have an enormous effect on the arithmetic of Wall Street. Beneath the Sahara there may be a vast store of cosmic ray which will be to atomic energy what atomic energy is to the gas engine. Perhaps the aurora borealis can be harnessed; perhaps some subdivision of chlorophyll will cure all bodily ills. Over the years such fantastic forces have made Wall Street what it is, and what it isn't.

In brief, it is important to read a balance sheet, but you would get richer quicker if you could read a crystal ball clearly.

chapter six

Your Investment Channels

One broker tells of a nurse who buys stocks only in those companies she has discussed with businessmen who are patients at her hospital.

A New York woman who spends a lot of time in her garden once tried a new hand lotion. She liked it, reflected on its sales potential, asked her broker about the manufacturer, and bought the stock. She made a tidy profit.

Although stocks are often purchased on the basis of foibles, superstitions, and impulse, the hard fact remains that purchases should be motivated primarily by individual needs. You don't hear as much about the cautious investors, but their successes can be equally spectacular.

When Keith Funston was President of the NYSE, he told about a thirty-year-old New York executive secretary who once admitted that every penny she had was invested in her wardrobe. Then she started investing $50 per month through a monthly investment plan. This discipline not only enabled her to budget her money more efficiently, but it also allowed her enough excess capital to enlarge her selection of ball gowns.

In 1957 a Boston housewife invested $560. She studied the market carefully and kept in close touch with her broker. By 1966, her money had grown to $18,000.

And in Vermont, a sixty-two-year-old widow began her investment career after becoming a conscientious reader of financial publications. She used the profits to fulfill her dream of buying a small antique shop.

Prudent or not, all these ladies used a different route on their way to Easy Street. Some joined investment clubs affiliated with the National Association of Investment Clubs.

REAL AND COSTUME JEWELRY

The Wall Street shopping center offers a wide assortment of goods. On occasion the variety appears bewildering. Every category is included—luxury items as well as popular-priced products. There's something for everybody if you don't see it, as the saying goes, ask for it. There is quality, quantity, the quaint, and the quick. As always, what you choose or spurn is an individual choice. The decision depends on your pocketbook and your psyche.

If you're one of the upper tax bracketeers, you might be interested in pricing municipal bonds. These are issued by a state or a political subdivision, such as county, city, town, or village. The term also designates bonds issued by state agencies and authorities. In general, interest paid on municipal bonds is exempt from Federal income taxes. When you drive down a toll road or pay a bill for water, you are often contributing to the repayment of a municipal bond. For people in the 55 percent tax bracket the retained income from a taxable investment yielding 4½ percent is the same as the retained income from a taxable investment yielding 10 percent.

All bonds are graded on the basis of quality, liquidity, and short maturities. The ratings, which go all the way up to triple A, are given by two chief rating services, Moody's and Standard & Poor's. Any banker or broker will give you the ratings on various bonds. For example, United States Government Bonds have the highest rating. These are the savings bonds of the government, which, according to the provisions of their contract, cannot be sold to another prospective buyer. But they can be redeemed by the owner at predetermined prices at the United States Treasury, at post offices, and at most banks. Other obligations of the government *are* marketable, certain issues of which are listed on the New York Exchange. In addition, there are various types of high-grade bonds among corporate issues.

It should be noted that the value of any bond you buy will fluctuate, including government, corporate, and municipals. For instance, if you sell a municipal bond before maturity, the price can be higher or lower than its face value. In this case the capital gains may still be liable to tax and the capital losses may be deductible, even though the interest is exempt.

Roughly speaking, stocks rise two thirds to three quarters of the time and decline one third to one quarter of the time. In certain "depressed" periods, bonds are better holdings than stocks. The suggested proportion differs with each individual, from the affluent elderly widow with 30 percent of her funds mostly in municipals, to the young married couple who have about $500 to invest in dynamic and speculative securities.

Trust funds are in the luxury classification. The trust officer at your bank will have to determine if the amount you're prepared to invest fits into the bank's minimum. In some cases, this amount can be high—possibly $100,000. Many banks, however, will work with much less. In a typical situation a bank sets up a trust through your lawyer and arranges to have the assets in trust (your money) put into one of the bank's common trust funds. Many banks have several of these funds to meet your particular needs, such as safety, growth, or current income.

The tiara of luxury items is the investment counselor. Such counseling requires substantial investment sums—often $250,000 or more.

Blue and Gold

Naturally, "quality goods" is a synonym for blue chips. Let's take a look at the thirty companies that make up the Dow Jones Industrials:

1. Allied Chemical
2. American Can
3. American Smelting
4. American Telephone and Telegraph
5. American Tobacco
6. Bethlehem Steel
7. Chrysler
8. Corn Products
9. Dupont
10. Eastman Kodak
11. General Electric
12. General Foods
13. General Motors
14. Goodyear Tire
15. International Harvester
16. International Nickel
17. International Paper
18. Johns-Manville
19. National Distillers

20. National Steel
21. Procter & Gamble
22. Sears Roebuck
23. Standard Oil of California
24. Standard Oil of New Jersey
25. Texas Company
26. Union Carbide
27. United Aircraft
28. United States Steel
29. Westinghouse Electric
30. Woolworth

Many investors and brokers consider these stocks the bluest of the blue. Yet in recent years while many of these stocks have doubled or tripled in value, others are down 25 percent or more from the former highs.

Few people realize that many blue chips have left investors singing the blues. Like other stocks, blue chips fluctuate. If you bought them when they were high and had to sell them when they were low, their status does not prevent you from losing money.

For example, if you bought United States Steel in 1959, you could have paid about $108 a share; if you sold it in the spring of 1967, you might have gotten $46 a share. From a 1964 high of 75, American Telephone and Telegraph slipped more than 15 points in 1967; similarly, Dupont dropped from a 1964 high of 293 to less than 167. During the same period, Standard Oil of New Jersey fell from 92 to around 64, and General Motors lost about 30 points from its high of 113. GM, AT&T, U. S. Steel and Jersey Standard are among the Gibraltars of our economy, and rightfully so. Their quality, products, and dividend records are first-rate. Nevertheless, the Rocks of Gibraltar can sometimes look more like Jell-o.

The public image of blue chips is that they will turn bluer over the years, that they are guarantees against loss and will reap fancy dividends. Don't you believe it! Every stock and bond in Wall Street is subject to a definite maybe. Some blue chips are safer than others. Some will increase in value and continue paying ever-increasing dividends; others will remain constant in dividends payments, decline, or they could even cease paying dividends altogether.

In short, anyone who assures you that an investment is always safe from downside risks is talking through his fedora. Over the years those securities categorized as blue chips have *in general* been safer than others. By and large, they represent shares in companies that are well known for their high-quality, widely accepted products and for their ability to make money and pay dividends.

In many cases the slumps and rallies of the blue chips have little to do with the actual operations of the companies. They are caused by investors who bid the prices up and down and who in turn are motivated by anything from mass psychology to political and international cross currents. Blue chips, like other stocks, have their fads. Sometimes one becomes popular, and everybody rushes to buy. The binge causes prices to zoom, and then when people start trying to sell in order to collect profits, the stock drops, due to the ancient inexorable law of supply and demand. "Profit-taking" is the technical term for what makes a stock level out or dip. Often a stock that had a glamor lure a year before loses its attraction to investors, never regains its popularity, and is relegated to the Old Maid category even though the company is doing well but at a slower pace. Sometimes younger companies will make inroads, and a former leader will begin to slip. Nothing is as forlorn as a faded belle of the ball who is reduced to pleading for suitors.

You may be surprised to learn that several blue chips of twenty or even ten years ago have deteriorated badly. During the 1960's these standbys gave way just like the worst speculative stock:

1. Anaconda
2. Standard Oil of New Jersey
3. AT&T
4. Union Carbide
5. Allied Chemical
6. American Cyanamid
7. Dupont
8. U. S. Steel
9. Bethlehem Steel
10. Greater Atlantic & Pacific Stores
11. Alcoa
12. Parke-Davis
13. Goodrich
14. General Motors

15. International Harvester
16. International Paper
17. W. R. Grace
18. Safeway

Others are no longer even listed on the exchanges.

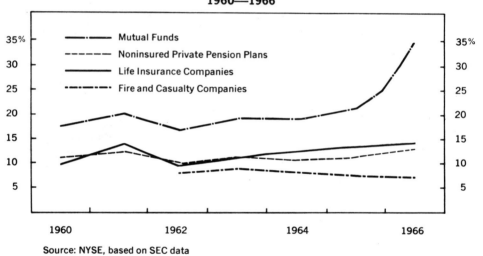

**TURNOVER RATES OF COMMON STOCK PORTFOLIOS
FOR SELECTED INSTITUTIONS
1960—1966**

Source: NYSE, based on SEC data

THE INSTITUTIONS

The leaders of the Plush Set are the institutions. These are some of the selected major types:

1. Noninsured private pension funds
2. State and local pension funds
3. Mutual funds
4. Closed-end investment companies
5. Personal trust funds

6. Fire and casualty companies
7. College and university endowments
8. Foundations

Their stocks or shares—when they bother to issue them—are particularly reliable.

A variety of factors determine the investment policies of the institutions. Each is custom-tailored, requiring certain specific methods and objectives. Goals are dictated by the needs of, and services sought by the people placing the money in each of the institutions. Another policy consideration is the legal restrictions imposed by different levels of government. Some types, such as foundations and college and university endowments, are virtually free to invest without legal restrictions. Others are tightly restricted in their investment activity. Life insurance companies are highly regulated by state laws on amount and types of securities held; but many have gradually increased their common stock limitations. Mutual Funds must maintain a stated diversification policy, unless changed by shareowners, and meet Internal Revenue Service diversification standards to obtain tax advantages.

Tax considerations are a prime factor with institutional investors. Certain types are tax exempt—foundations, for instance. Naturally their investment activity is tailored accordingly; tax exempt bonds, for instance, lose much of their appeal to institutions whose income is tax free.

Finally, there are liquidity requirements. Many institutions must keep liquid funds available to meet the needs of their clients, although short-term U. S. Treasury bonds are sometimes resorted to. The importance of this factor varies among institutional types, depending on the stability and predictability of the inflow and outflow of funds.

THE POWER OF INSTITUTIONS

Institutional investors have made giant strides during the past decade and a half; in fact, they have increased to the point where they threaten to overpower the market. The New York Stock Exchange reported that at the end of 1964 investment companies—

including insurance companies, noninsured pension funds, college endowments, and foundations—had combined assets of $347,-000,000 of which $109,000,000, or 31 percent, was held in equity securities. In addition, personal trust funds alone had assets of $105,000,000, of which $69,000,000 was in stock. Thus, corporate stock has a prominent position in institutional portfolios, in private noninsured pension funds, in investment companies, and personal trust funds. In each of these groups, not only are the dollar amounts in equities large, but over 50 percent of the total assets are in common stock. Institutional investors (not including bank-administered personal trust funds) now own over one fifth of the dollar value of the NYSE list, as opposed to one eighth in 1949.

The Exchange has projected that institutions are likely to own about 30 percent of the Exchange's list by 1970 and that they will account for 40 percent of total Exchange volume and 50 percent of the Exchange's public volume.

TYPES

Institutions come in assorted shapes and sizes. Some of the smaller ones are located in both large and small cities. However, the public they serve is for the most part drawn from locations relatively nearby. Local commercial banks, educational institutions, hospitals, religious organizations, and insurance companies provide the core of this market. Also important are local employers who may need brokerage services to implement their pension funds, profit sharing, or stock purchase plan activities.

Large institutions consist of the major financial institutions, usually located in large central cities. They include the largest commercial banks, insurance companies, and investment companies in the nation. Each invests the savings of thousands of Americans, and numerous Americans of average means are part of these luxury institutions.

The popular-priced institutions go under the general heading of management funds. They pool small and large investments by individuals and invest in securities with the assistance of professional investment counselors. Operating under the rules of the Se-

A COMPARISON OF OPEN-END AND
CLOSED-END INVESTMENT COMPANIES

	Open-end	*Closed-end*
1. Number of shares outstanding.	Constantly changing.	Fixed.
2. Public offering.	Continuous.	One time.
3. Redemption by issuer.	Yes.	No.
4. Redemption price.	Net asset value (sometimes less a per cent charge).	Not redeemable by issuer.
5. Where shares are bought or sold.	Although shares of some funds may be purchased from the issuing company or from the underwriter, most commonly shares are purchased from the dealer.	Over-the-counter or on an exchange.
6. From whom shares are purchased or to whom shares may be sold.	Purchased from underwriter through a dealer. Sold or redeemed similarly.	Purchased from another stockholder or from inventory of a dealer. Sold in same way as any common stock is sold.
7. Relation of purchase price to net asset value.	Purchase price is net asset value plus commission or sales charge. Net asset value is determined by the value of securities in portfolio.	None. Purchase price is determined by supply and demand. Thus price may exceed net asset value (trading at a *premium*) or be less than net asset value (trading at a *discount*).
8. Buying or selling costs or charges.	A sales charge is added to net asset value to determine the purchase price. Usually there is no redemption charge. The amount of the sales charge and the redemption charge, if any, must be clearly stated in the fund prospectus.	For both purchases and sales there is normally the equivalent of a stock exchange commission if the transaction is handled on an agency basis. For transactions on a principal basis there would be an appropriate mark-up or mark-down. .

curities and Exchange Commission, they have a tax exempt status with the Internal Revenue Service (the tax being paid by the individual investor on his own tax return).

A management fund is simply a service company; what it sells is not products, but investment wisdom. The performance of funds varies from good to bad to indifferent. In the end the quality of the fund depends on how well it does over a period of time. As always, the loss and profit statement tells the story.

THE MUTUALS

Most of the management funds are popularly known as mutual funds. They have become as popular with advertisers as deodorants and corn flakes. They are being merchandised via every medium of communication, and their proliferation during the past few years has been downright fantastic. With the inevitable population growth, it is obvious that these funds will continue to mushroom.

Before you invest in a mutual fund, figure the cost. Some mutual funds offer "contract purchase" plans. This is a long-term contract, usually for ten years, in which you agree to invest a fixed amount monthly over the life of the contract. Usually the sales charges for the life of the contract are taken out of the money you deposit over the first two years. For example, if you sign a contract for $5,000 for 10 years, you are required to pay $500 a year. If the fund charges 8 percent (which is quite common), the total charge will be $450. So if you deposit $1,000 with the fund during the first 2 years and the $450 is deducted for the mutual fund's overhead, actually only $550 is invested in the first 2 years of the contract. There is nothing unique about this form of payment in sales commissions; life insurance agents make their money in the same way.

The fact is that it isn't necessary to purchase mutual funds via long-term contracts. Many of them can be bought by paying only the sales load applicable to the amount invested at the time. It should be added, however, that long-term contracts may be worthwhile as a form of forced savings for those who toss their money around. As always in making an investment, the final decision must be determined by your needs, hopes, and ability to pay.

In the final analysis, what you pay for the management of your funds depends on your sense of values. If the mutual fund can do a better job for you than you can with or without your broker, then the expense is justified. On the other hand, if the performance of the mutual fund doesn't justify the cost, you can convert your mutual funds into cash.

BARGAIN FUND

The New York Stock Exchange has a discount quasi-competitor to mutual funds. It is called the Monthly Investment Plan. Like the mutual funds, it is designed primarily to provide the small investor with a means of sharing in equities, while at the same time offering protection.

The Monthly Investment Plan can begin with payments as small as $40 per Plan every 3 months, or as large as $1,000 per month. You pay as you go. There are no down payments, you don't owe any "balance," and you are never in debt. You are the owner of the stock you purchase. Your account is credited with both full and fractional shares. You get the amount your dollars will buy—less commission.

After you have made your first investment, you are entitled to your portion of any dividends on full or fractional shares held for your account. Your dividends will be automatically reinvested for you in the stock you are buying unless you elect to receive them in cash.

It should be stressed that the MIP is not designed for short-term selling and buying. Its advantages work best over the long haul. There is of course no guarantee against losses. However, if you continue periodic purchases when price levels are low, you'll do better (that is, get more shares for your money) than if you buy sporadically, and then only in bullish times.

You can instruct your broker at any time to sell all or any part of the shares you have accumulated. You will receive a check for the proceeds, less the commission SEC fee and transfer taxes. On MIP transactions the commission is a straight 6 percent when the amount invested is less than $100. For amounts of $100 or more the charge is progressively less than 6 percent. Of course, the more you invest at one time, the lower the rate of commission. There are no opening or starting fees, no dues, and no assessments or custody fees.

After the broker's commission is deducted from your payment, the exact number of shares your dollars will buy is figured to four decimal places. It's like buying $5 worth of gasoline. For example, $50 will buy 2.6206 shares of stock selling for $18 per share, and 0.2621 of a share of stock selling at $180 per share.

Incidentally, if you wish, you may have several MIP's and make payments on them either simultaneously or on alternating dates. Or perhaps you might want three quarterly Plans, with a payment due each month. The Plan is tailored to fit almost every pocketbook.

You can receive your full shares whenever you request them, or when you terminate your Monthly Investment Plan. There is no charge for delivery on termination of the Plan, or when you request 50 shares or more. If your request is for less than 50 shares and you are not terminating the Plan, there will be a C.O.D. handling charge of $1 plus mailing costs. When you take delivery of shares, your name will be registered on the company's books as a stockholder and your dividends on these shares will be mailed directly to you.

After each of your purchases you will be mailed a confirmation showing the amount of money received, number of shares bought, price, commission paid, and total shares held for your account at that time, together with a reminder of your next scheduled payment.

Regular periodic investing is the basis of the MIP. It is a healthy habit to cultivate and a lucrative one—if you choose the right stocks. By the way, in MIP you are not bound by contract to make purchases on a specific date. If you have some extra cash, you can always make a larger payment than usual, or you can send in payments of $40 per Plan or more at any time. Some people start their Plans with initial purchases of several hundred dollars and then continue with regular payments of a smaller amount. Should you have to skip one or two purchases, your Plan will remain in force. However, your broker reserves the right to terminate your account at any time and probably will do so if you show little or no interest in keeping up purchases.

Any time you decide to stop, your full shares will be registered in your name on the books of your company and mailed to you without charge. Any fractions will be sold, and a check for the proceeds, less charges, will be sent to you.

FUND MANAGERS

If you can envision Wall Street as one gigantic dish and the institutions as a single giant egg beater, then you can see that every whirl of the prongs makes continual changes in financial ingredients. The individuals who handle the egg beaters obviously exert considerable influence. They are known as fund managers.

How do these managers function? Some give considerable responsibility to brokers, who are repaid with reciprocal commission business. As always, the ultimate factor is determined by whether the brokers' choices are good (showing increased stock prices) or bad (showing decreased stock prices). The foregoing is illustrated by typical fund manager comments:

"Occasionally we talk to a broker who apparently hasn't done his homework as far as our portfolio is concerned. This definitely leaves a bad impression and may even be the deciding factor as to how much business that firm will receive from us."

"This firm has taken the trouble to familiarize themselves completely with our problems. They are always willing to talk to us in person about why a certain stock would be a good addition to our portfolio. Their knowledge of our situation has made it possible for us to get their views on many of our major investment decisions. We bend over backwards to give this firm business."

In recent years the "new breed" of fund managers has given Wall Street the "mod" look. Many of them are in their thirties or younger. They do not suffer from the overcautiousness that comes from experience. They have an archeologist's view of the 1929 market debacle, and the 1962 break is mere history to them. They are the go-go boys, intent on making as much money as possible as soon as possible, by-passing the traditional ways. They are extremely performance-conscious.

The traditionalist managers have as their objectives capital preservation rather than profitability. They seek an image of quality and conservatism. It follows that they seek to avoid risk. On the other hand, the new portfolio managers are profit-conscious and

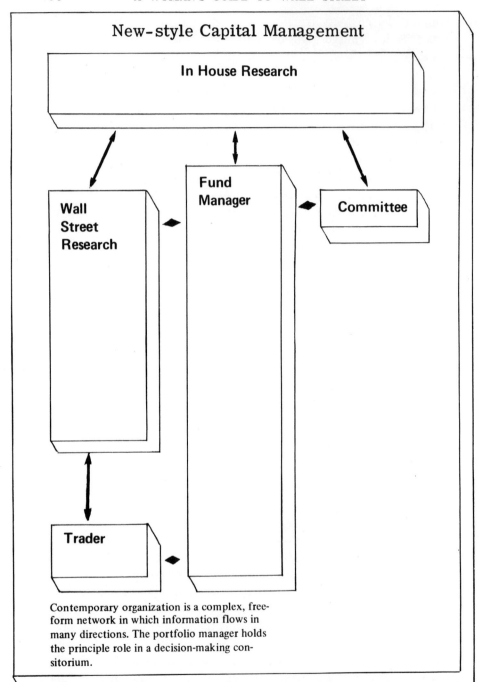

New-style Capital Management

In House Research

Fund Manager

Wall Street Research

Committee

Trader

Contemporary organization is a complex, free-form network in which information flows in many directions. The portfolio manager holds the principle role in a decision-making consitorium.

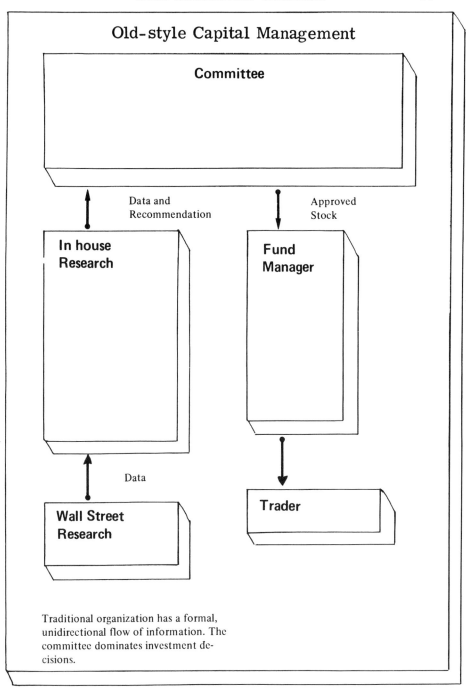

Old-style Capital Management

Committee

Data and
Recommendation

Approved
Stock

**In house
Research**

**Fund
Manager**

Data

Trader

**Wall Street
Research**

Traditional organization has a formal,
unidirectional flow of information. The
committee dominates investment decisions.

take risks. They envision the stock market as a competitive arena wherein investment managers buy and sell to each other.

The "new breed" sops up new ideas and is fascinated by the economic potential of the future. Moreover, they are aided by an enormous flow of information. They have at their command some 13,000 analysts who are digging, digging, digging. They are constantly on the prowl for new products, new companies, and even companies that have nothing more than an idea. All are eager to be the first to spot a basic trend, such as a given airline's changing from pistons to jets.

Incidentally, their mutual in-group buying and selling has occasioned some criticism. The hecklers insist they are "washing each other's hands" in their push for "performance" profits. In addition, their intramural trading keeps pushing share prices higher.

Many of the go-go fund managers have compiled enviable records. Some of their critics wonder whether their good fortune is just a temporary streak of luck. Only time will tell, but in the meantime they're giving old-line investors a decided jolt and they are very successful.

It is interesting to note that on May 19, 1968, *The New York Times* reported:

"Pressed by the need for more money, and prodded by the Ford Foundation, the trustees of American colleges and universities are beginning to be more adventuresome with the $12-billion they hold in endowment funds."

McGeorge Bundy, president of the Ford Foundation, spoke out on unexploited endowments. As he wrote in his first annual report: "It is far from clear that the trustees have reason to be proud of their performance in making money for their colleges. We recognize the risks of unconventional investing, but the true test of performance in the handling of money is the record of achievement, not the opinion of the respectable."

In other words, how you play the game is not as significant as how much you win.

Until now the basic rule in trusteeship has been, and in many cases still is, the "prudent man" rule, based on an 1830 Massachusetts court decision that the trustee who acts with prudence cannot be challenged on legal grounds. "Prudent" is commonly interpreted as "careful" or "conservative"—meaning blue-chip stocks and gilt-edge bonds, even though some of the best of these turn out to be inferior investments, as we've seen before. Is it better to be "respectable" and make less money than those who accept risks? Or is respectability a cloak for obsolete investment philosophy?

While the controversy rages, a Ford Foundation committee is trying to develop a yardstick so that institutions can compare their own performances against those of other institutions. One thing I'll wager—when and if the Ford Foundation comes up with that yardstick, it could still be a mighty flexible one.

In the meantime, I'd suggest you use the now-familiar yardstick of how much you can afford to lose. The more you can afford to lose, the better you're doing. As for blue chips, trust funds, mutuals, and MIP, you pays your money and you takes your choice.

PROSPECTUS

412,000 Shares

MANUFACTURING COMPANY, INC.

COMMON STOCK

(Par Value $.05 Per Share)

Up to 41,200 of the shares offered herein are being reserved for sale to employees or sales representatives of the Company, or distributors and franchisees of Robo-Wash, Inc. (see "Business, *Robo-Wash*") who are selected by the Company. The number of shares offered herein which are available to the public will be reduced to the extent such sales are made.

Of the 412,000 shares of Common Stock offered hereby, 100,000 shares are to be purchased by the Underwriters from the Company and 312,000 shares from certain stockholders of the Company (see "Principal and Selling Stockholders"). The Company will receive none of the proceeds from the sale of the 312,000 shares.

Prior to this offering there has been no public market for the Common Stock of the Company. The public offering price of these shares has been determined by negotiation between the Company, the Selling Stockholders and the Representatives of the Underwriters.

THESE SECURITIES HAVE NOT BEEN APPROVED OR DISAPPROVED BY THE SECURITIES AND EXCHANGE COMMISSION NOR HAS THE COMMISSION PASSED UPON THE ACCURACY OR ADEQUACY OF THIS PROSPECTUS. ANY REPRESENTATION TO THE CONTRARY IS A CRIMINAL OFFENSE.

	Price to Public	Underwriting Discounts and Commissions (1)	Proceeds to Company (2)	Proceeds to Selling Stockholders (2)
Per Share	$5.00	$.50	$4.50	$4.50
Total	$2,060,000	$206,000	$450,000	$1,404,000

(1) The Selling Stockholders have granted to Dempsey-Tegeler & Co., Inc. and Dabbs Sullivan, Trulock & Company, Inc. (the "Representatives"), for $.10 per share, options to purchase 15,000 shares each of the Common Stock of the Company at an initial exercise price of $5.00 per share (see "Underwriting-Options to Purchase Stock"). Any profit realized by the Representatives on the sale of the Common Stock received on the exercise of such options may be deemed additional underwriting compensation for purposes of the Securities Act of 1933. For information concerning the Representatives' right of first refusal in future financings and the right to designate two nominees for election to the Company's Board of Directors see "Underwriting."

(2) Before deducting estimated expenses of $11,400 payable by the Company and $35,600 payable by the Selling Stockholders.

The shares of Common Stock are offered subject to prior sale, when, as and if delivered and accepted by the Underwriters, and subject to approval of certain legal matters by counsel. The Underwriters reserve the right to withdraw, cancel or modify the offer and to reject orders in whole or in part. It is expected that delivery of the Common Stock will be made at the office of Dempsey-Tegeler & Co., Inc., 1000 Locust Street, St. Louis, Missouri, on or about May 29, 1968.

Dempsey-Tegeler & Co., Inc.

Dabbs Sullivan, Trulock & Company, Inc.

The date of this Prospectus is May 22, 1968

Page one prospectus of a hot new issue. Issued June, 1968 at $5-a-share. Within minutes after trading began, the price rose to $11.

chapter seven

Bringing Up Baby

HOT, HOTTER, HOTTEST

Janet is a successful New York designer. Over the years she has made regular investments in stocks by following the advice of her broker. The broker's choices have been generally good, and the value of her portfolio has had a 70 percent increase in value over a period of 5 years.

Janet has confidence in her broker. He is courteous and cooperative when she calls for information about specific stocks, and when he recommends a stock, he tells her exactly why he believes it would be a profitable addition to her portfolio. The relationship has been friendly as well as profitable. What Janet particularly likes about him is that his approach to her financial needs is thoughtful and individualistic. He never buys and sells just to roll up commissions; more often than not, he will discourage Janet from buying when she comes to him with a tip. Although by and large he is conservative, he will occasionally buy speculative stocks for her account. And he makes certain she understands that it is a speculation. "This is a speculation," he'll say, "but I believe it is a good speculation. You might lose some money, but I think you can well afford to risk the possibility of loss in a situation where you might reap extraordinary gains."

One day the broker called and said: "I suggest you buy twenty-five shares of India, Inc. It's a hot new issue and should come out at a premium."

A "hot issue" is a stock for which there is a great demand. Consequently, it will be bid up. When it is issued for public trading the stock will sell above its issue price. In this case, India, Inc. was issued at $10 per share.

Janet told some of her friends about the hot issue. They promptly called their brokers and asked to buy the stock at the $10 issue price. The brokers responded that they were unable to buy a single share for them.

There are two reasons for their inability to buy the new issues. First, the brokers they contacted might have been affiliated with firms that were not part of the selling group for the new issue. Secondly, new issues usually come in what are called small packages in Wall Street terms—often 100,000, 200,000, or 300,000 shares. Not many new issues have as many as 1,000,000 shares. Brokerages involved in the underwriting tend to distribute the hot issues to their prime customers. This is known as "reciprocal business." An individual or firm that takes hot issues is also expected to accept new issues that prove to be lukewarm or downright cold.

At any rate, Janet purchased 25 shares of India, Inc. at $10 a share. The day it was issued for public trading it was selling for $20 a share. If Janet had sold her stock 24 hours after she bought it, she would have made a profit of 100 percent on her investment.

The new-issue market erupts periodically. It exploded during 1960-61. After the 1962 market break many of the new issues stumbled, skidded, and crashed. Some new companies went into bankruptcy; others prospered and reached new highs. For about six years the new-issue market was tranquil. It exploded again in 1967-68.

At any rate, the remarkable dynamism of the new-issue market was revealed in the June 1, 1968, issue of *The New York Times*. It listed a batch of new issues and noted both the original price and the prices quoted for the stocks several weeks later.

	Original Price	*Latest Quote*
Wells Management	$ 7.75	$13
Block Engineering	$10.50	$21
Samuel Moore	$13.25	$17.75
Advanced Computer Techniques	$ 7.25	$25.25
Martin Brower	$19	$29.75
Clorox Co.	$27.50	$33.25
Citation Integrated Mfg.	$ 5	$12
Integrated Controls	$20	$54

	Original Price	Latest Quote
Nat'l Data	$15	$37
Aspen System	$10	$24
Unit Dollar Stores	$18	$28.50
Four Seasons	$11	$29
Boothe Computer	$18	$62.25
Petrie Stores	$30	$41.25
Standard Controls	$11.25	$15.25
Minnie Pearl's	$20	$43.50
Omni-Spec	$14.50	$22.50
Super Surgical	$11	$17.50
Downe Communications	$10	$69

As you can see, when the new issue market is hot, it sizzles. But when it cools down, it can really freeze. You must be able to jump fast in order to protect your profits if a deluge is in the offing. Nevertheless, if you are in a position to buy new issues when the market is boiling, by all means take advantage of the opportunity. There is no better way to get rich. I know a New York City police-man who got rich because a broker, who was a lifelong friend, was in a position to buy new issues for him. On the other hand, remember that there are always people who buy hot issues at the highest price, and they are the ones who get burned.

There are some brokers who come close to specializing in the markets for new issues and the stocks of other small companies. If some broker starts buying the stock of a company that has few shares outstanding to begin with, it would not take much to drive the stock up, simply because its supply is so limited. Furthermore, many of these small issues become smaller still when mutual funds decide to buy in. There's nothing like a scarcity to propel a stock price to new highs.

The birth certificate of a new issue is the prospectus, which pro-vides information about the company, generally under the follow-ing headings:

1. Capitalization
2. Application of proceeds
3. Consolidated statement of income
4. Description of business
   a. Description
   b. Personnel
   c. Offices
   d. Competition
5. Management
   a. Directors and officers
   b. Renumeration
6. Principal and selling shareholder
7. Description of common stock
   a. Non-cumulative or cumulative voting
   b. Dividends
8. Rights to purchase securities
   a. Stock options
   b. Warrants
9. Underwriting
10. Legal opinions
11. Experts
12. Miscellaneous information
13. Reports of certified independent accountants
14. Financial statements

The Securities Act of 1933 requires (1) registration with the SEC of securities before they may be offered for public sale, and (2) delivery of a prospectus prior to an order or any solicitation of an order for open-end investment company shares. It is very important to understand the significance of registration. The SEC does *not* approve securities registered with it and offered for sale. Nor does it guarantee the accuracy of the disclosures made in the prospectus or in the registration statement. Any representation to the contrary, however, is a criminal offense. What the SEC *does* do is to try to make sure that the prospectus contains a full disclosure of all material facts about the security so as to enable the prospective purchaser to make up his mind.

But to get back to the matter at hand—what makes a new issue hot? There are a number of factors:

Psychology rules the public passion for new issues. It should be noted that historically the new-issue sprees generally occur at the end of a bull market although not necessarily so. Some analysts consider such eruptions as a definite signal of an oncoming market collapse.

Stock fashions: In the late 1950's, uranium stocks were given a whirl. In the early 1960's new electronic companies were the leaders. During 1967-68 companies involved in new technologies as well as those engaged in franchise operations, computer leasing, and medical techniques sparked the new-issue boom.

A new product: In May, 1968, a new company called Applied Synthetics Corporation went public at $1.75 per share. It was a 260,000-share issue. By the end of the day, the lucky participants were holding stock worth $6.50 per share. The company had had a $12,000 loss in each of the two previous years, and there wasn't even a projection for a break-even point. But the company did have an interesting new product; it planned to make a fire-resistant industrial garment that would go into the ash can at the end of the day. When the company went public its production was zero; it had just a few samples to show around. (Incidentally, the company was organized in 1965.)

The underwriter: Some brokerage firms or investment bankers have a good reputation for underwriting hot issues. Consequently, any new issue that carries their names on the prospectus is automatically hot, it seems.

OLD BABIES

While the mortality rate is high among the baby companies, some grow up to be industrial giants. After all, every old company was once a toddler. Railroads were once high-risk penny stocks. Fortunes were made and lost on their rise and fall.

One of the bluest of chips is Dupont. Yet this corporate colossus also had its birth pangs. Irénée Dupont, the founder of the company, wrote to a friend on August 18, 1803: "I have spent my life here building up a very difficult industry, and the disappointments I have had to bear have given me an habitual dullness and melancholy. . . . I owe more than sixty thousand dollars, chiefly in notes at the banks, so that my debts amount to far more than my profits from the powder. The signatures that must be renewed every 60 days put me in exactly the situation of a prisoner on parole who must show himself to the police every month.

"It is cruel to ride 60 miles every five or six days to meet one's notes, and so to waste one's time and one's life. God grant that someday I may get to the end of it."

Women played a major role in Dupont's major step forward. On September 21, 1938, the newspapers reported that a patent had been granted to Dupont on a new textile fiber which was described with enthusiasm as "a new silk, made on a chemical base." It was in the first rank of American discoveries—the fruit of the chemical industry's first large-scale fundamental research program, costing $27,000,000 and 13 years of research. It struck another critical item from the list of materials which the United States had to import from foreign sources. It added many hundreds of millions to Dupont's sales and profits and joined peanuts, automobiles, cola drinks, photographic film, and hot dogs as an American institution: nylon.

In retrospect it is difficult to comprehend that General Motors too went through a stage of precarious infancy. The world's largest corporation had its origin in a small automobile company started by David Dunbar Buick, a plumbing supply man. Within a year his outfit was on the rocks. William C. Durant, one of Michigan's richest men, was asked to rescue the company from bankruptcy. He poured enough money into it to be able to buy personal control, and between 1904 and 1906 he raised Buick production from 16 cars to 2,295. In those days broken rear axles were a major problem for motor car companies. Durant lured Charles Stewart Mott's Weston-Mott Axle Company of Utica, New York, to move to Flint, Michigan where the Buick plant was. (Mott, incidentally, later became the largest individual stockholder in General Motors.) In addition, Durant made a deal with Albert Champion, the French racing driver, to manufacture his new AC porcelain spark plug for Buick. Meanwhile, Durant's stock salesmanship had increased the capitalization of Buick from $75,000 to $1,500,000. The citizens of Flint subscribed 500,000 shares in a single day. Those who invested $5,000 that day were destined to become millionaires within 25 years.

Ironically, Wall Street was originally blind to the potential of the automobile. When Durant went to Morgan & Co. and boasted that the time would come when a half million automobiles would be running on the roads of this country, one of the Morgan partners walked out of the room with the comment: "Utter nonsense. If that fellow has any sense, he'll keep those observations to himself." Unable to raise capital in Wall Street, Durant put together the GM combination through exchanges of stock.

Several years later Durant was the victim of the ultimate irony. His ambitious over-expansion resulted in several unprofitable divisions. Thus, in 1910, because of a Buick bank debt of $7,000,000, Durant lost control of GM to two investment banking companies, Lee, Higginson, and Co. of Boston and J. and W. Seligman of New York.

Eventually with the aid of Pierre Dupont's financial acumen and the organizing genius of Alfred P. Sloan, GM emerged as a corporate titan.

It is interesting to note that while GM, Ford, and Chrysler have prospered, literally hundreds of other automobile companies have appeared and perished. The automotive graveyard is sprinkled with the names of extinct buggies—Altham, Ajax, Crestmobile, Grant-Ferris, Lear, Mohawk, Niagara, Regas, Waterloo, Wolverine, Yale, Zentmobile, and many others. In other words, it's not enough to own shares of stock in the right industry—you must be a partner in the right company.

CARE AND FEEDING

Let's take a more recent illustration of baby-to-giant growth. Since 1960, when Xerox introduced one of history's most profitable single products, the Xerox 914 office copier, the company's sales have increased 18-fold. Its profits have grown 37 times, and its stock has increased in value 50 times. Xerox was founded as the Haloid Company, a maker of photographic papers. You could have purchased stock in Haloid at $.56 per share in 1906. In May, 1968, it was selling for close to $280 per share. Among the fortunate ones who purchased Haloid at $.56 cents and still held it at $280 is the University of Rochester.

Then there's the remarkable saga of a company Milady made successful. At the turn of the century David H. McConnell, then a young door-to-door book salesman from Oswego, New York, traveled New England on horseback selling copies of *The Pilgrim's Progress* and *The American Book of Home Nursing.* To get his foot in the door, he offered each housewife a small vial of perfume. The perfume made a bigger hit than the books, and McConnell decided to switch businesses.

A friend of his who had gone to California wrote back about the glory of West Coast flowers and also lent him $500 to start the California Perfume Company, a name that sounded more exotic than Brooklyn, where the business started. Along with the perfume, McConnell manufactured a line of household products called Avon Maid.

The first Avon lady was Mrs. P. F. E. Albee, a widow living in Manchester, New Hampshire, and a friend of the McConnell family who needed money to support her brood. Mrs. Albee traveled by train and horse-drawn vehicle to sell Avon products to the women of New England. To make a short story shorter, Avon is now the largest cosmetics concern in the world. Its sales, all made by women calling door-to-door, amounted to $474,814,000 in 1967.

In the late 1930's, you could have purchased one hundred shares of Avon for $25. In June, 1967, your $25 investment would have been worth about $15,000.

By now you have seen that Wall Street tots, when born with hope and dollar signs in their eyes, sometimes have a wildly profitable adulthood. Those who adopt them when they are babies, and have the faith and perseverance to survive their growing pangs, can get rich on a relatively small investment. This is the lure of new companes. Like mountain-climbing, the ascent is incredibly difficult and the descent awfully dangerous, but the attraction is almost irresistible.

DREAM STOCK

For every corporate pup that's a victim of distemper there are some that grow up to be prize-winning dogs. Take the experience of a Long Island housewife named Mary. One day she called her broker and cheerfully announced: "I have about three hundred dollars to invest. My husband and I would like to take a vacation next summer. We need about eight hundred dollars. Can you recommend a stock that will pay for our holiday?"

The broker replied: "I cannot guarantee that any stock will give you a profit. I would be a liar if I would tell you that a stock you buy could increase in value at a specified time period. Possibly by the time you are ready for your vacation, there'll be a market break and your stock could drop with the rest of them. Besides, hoping to quadruple an investment means speculating. If you can afford to speculate—that is, if you can afford to lose a major portion of your investment—then I suggest that you take a chance."

"I'm willing to take the risk."

"Well, then, I've been buying stock in a company called Mohawk Data Science. It's strictly a speculation. The company is engaged in the manufacture, development, and sale or rental of electronic data processing equipment. I've visited the company's plant and spent hours speaking with some of the executives. I'm impressed with management and the company's product potential. I also discussed the company with an analyst and an expert in electronic processing, and they're both impressed too. But I must warn you that the company is now losing money, and it will take at least a year or two before it goes into the black. The stock is now selling for two dollars and fifty cents per share."

Mary replied: "Buy me one hundred shares."

The time was 1965. Mary invested $250, plus commission and taxes. Several months later, the stock was selling for $9 per share. But Mary never used that stock for a vacation because her broker urged her to hold on to it. She sold the stock two years later for $190 per share. Mary used the profit—about $18,500—to make a down payment on a new home and buy new furniture, and she still had about $5,000 after taxes to reinvest in other stocks.

Of course, the Mohawk Data Sciences are few and far between. But that company is a fabulous illustration of the growth potential of companies engaged in the emerging technologies.

The company's initial product, which has accounted for about 70 percent of its revenues, is the 1101 Keyed Data-Recorder. The 1101 was designed to prepare computer information from source documents at greater speed and at lower cost than by existing methods.

Mohawk Data Sciences lost money in 1965 and 1966. The company has never paid cash dividends and management, it appears, does not intend to pay any in the near future. However, the company showed a profit in 1967, when it earned $.71 for every outstanding share. During that year it rocketed to its high of $198.50. In evaluating Mohawk Data Sciences, the traditional price-earnings ratio, and all other ratios, were tossed out the window by investors. Why? Because they were buying the possibility of fantastic growth potential, putting their money on a dream of the future. In the end, MDS may more than justify the projections, and in retrospect $198.50 may seem a bargain price. Moreover, through an exchange of stock the company absorbed two additional firms in 1967-68. Ability to merge is one of the great advantages that a high-priced stock brings to a company.

In general, the quick toddler-to-titan progression of a company generates its own excitement. It inspires the imagination and creates talk along Wall Street. The excitement—or glamor, if you will—makes a stock fashionable and results in the inevitable heavy popular demand that causes the price to boom.

In recent years almost every one of the major earnings increases has come about from a new product or a stream of new products. It follows that the roots of new products are unique ideas. In other words, what Wall Streeters are buying is brains. You should too. And finally, let us hope that your baby will grow up to support you in lavish style.

chapter eight

Wall Street Fashions

Jane is an editor for a book publisher. She has been in and out of the market for a decade. She knows enough about the market to realize that the computer field is probably the fastest growing in the world. At a dinner party she overheard someone discussing "a hot, up-and-coming computer company." She mentally jotted down the company's name. First thing the following morning she called her broker and told him to buy 100 shares of the stock. The broker tried to discourage the purchase, since he was unfamiliar with the company. He wanted time to check. But she was insistent. Jane bought the stock and in a few weeks realized a substantial profit, simply because enough other investors had heard the same story.

Sophisticated analysts also are subject to the power of fads, fashions, and fancies. The officer of one Boston-based mutual fund was quoted recently: "A stock often starts to move when an analyst builds up a good story about it. If you are being told a good story and you think you are near the top of the list of those being told, you buy because you know that the story will be told to others, and the stock will go up."

The stock-fashion researchers are constantly on the prowl for companies that will set popular styles. They are looking for the next Polaroid, Xerox, or IBM.

I'm not saying that fashionable stocks should comprise your whole portfolio, but that they do produce definite trends. As with all trends, the *only* way to beat 'em is to join 'em.

Fashion may, on occasion, be a fickle balloon, yet the lure of the vogue can be overwhelming. In the process fancy becomes fact. The saga of the miniskirt offers a trivial illustration: In terms of money, the mod fashion revolution has had an enormous impact on the economy, not to mention its influence on the social structure.

One problem of fashion is its quicksilver mobility. There is practically no handbook to guide you, and this is because the very essence of fashion is kaleidoscopic. It is a something-new narcotic that is more exciting than satisfying. Nevertheless, in Wall Street and elsewhere the power of fashion cannot be casually dismissed. Stock style enslavement may be almost as complete as the dress designer's worship of the Parisian fashion-gods. In the financial realm the mania for uranium shares in the 1940's was followed by the frenzy for utilities in the 1950's and the craze for airlines in the early 1960's. Subsequently, computer-leasing and computer software manufacturers were the rage, as well as electronics and office-equipment firms.

THE MIDDLEMEN

There is little chance for the housewife to go directly to the manufacturer for gowns, hats, or trinkets. She depends on a middleman to secure them, display them, and allow her to select. Likewise in Wall Street, the middleman is usually the broker and the products are confetti dotted across financial pages of newspapers as well as innumerable kindred publications. Thus, it's not unusual for a broker to attempt a little trend-setting all by himself.

In the Spring of 1968, a major brokerage chain (for professional reasons, I'd rather not mention names) created a splash with full page ads in various dailies and magazines. The ad brightly trumpeted the latest in stock fashions with almost breathless awe. In a way, the words in the ad were star-dusted and carried more than a hint of movie trailer sensation and sideshow barkerism, smartly coupled with hush-hush innuendoes as well as gossip-column confidences. For example:

"Oceanography: Which companies have the lead in building submersibles, the submarine-like vessels that can explore a mile or more down in the ocean and may eventually number in the thousands? . . . Which companies are doing work in fish protein concentrate—the tasteless, odor-free powder that many someday give populations of underdeveloped countries an inexpensive protein-equivalent of meat, milk and eggs? . . . Who is developing techniques for mining incredibly rich mineral deposits offshore?

"Learning Aids: Which company plans to introduce soon a black-and-white videotape recorder and camera for less than $1,000? . . . Which blue chip is pioneering computerized techniques for learning—and has already installed its system in 15

New York City public schools? . . . Who produces portable planetariums and will soon market a programmed learning system for $350?

"Medical Technology: Which company is already cashing in on the development of the heart-lung oxygenator and artificial-kidney machines? . . . What company now manufactures a robot that can perform as many as 120 hospital chemical tests an hour?

"Pollution Control: What company makes instruments, controls and equipment used by 80 percent of the water-treatment plants in the United States? . . . Which producer of water-cooling towers stands to gain from the growing use of nuclear power by the electric-utility industry?

"Nuclear Energy: What little-known company is currently operating at capacity in producing components for nuclear plants, already enjoys a 15 percent share of the market? . . . Which company played a major role in the first successful attempt to free natural gas from rock formations by controlled nuclear explosion, and has also been active in developing nuclear engines that could be used for deep space probes?"

The ad did not mention any names (you were supposed to go to a member of the firm, perhaps open an account, and then find out the contents of their little black book). The result, though, was that many investors started looking around for companies that might fit those rosy qualifications. And all stocks with oceanographic, pollution, or medical technology potential spurted accordingly.

By and large, those who were buying the fashionable science stocks were investing in a dream world—a world of pure air, pure and abundant water, ample food, model cities, and care for all the sick, with exploration of the ocean depths and outer space thrown in for an adventurous tang. The point is that if enough investors start dreaming, they start a fad which pays dividends on the spot.

In a way, therefore, you can make more money by reading Jules Verne than a double-domed library of economic studies. Aladdin's Lamp seems to be a more effective economic guide than any amount of statistics. But after all, what is an automobile but every man's seven league boots? What is the airplane but his magic carpet?

High fashion stocks are not confined to those engaged in or related to sophisticated technology. Some of the most popular stocks of 1968, with leaping price-earnings ratios, gilt-edge sales growth, and consequent upward zoom in stock profits, were restaurant and hotel chains. Their products consisted of hamburgers, hot dogs, ice cream, fried chicken, and motels where the ice machines functioned efficiently.

As you can see, sometimes a fashion originates in basic need. When women no longer had maids to fasten them up the back and care for the little hooks and snaps, the zipper was born. But frequently fashionable trends are created and accelerated by sheer propaganda. Thousands of companies spend millions of dollars per year on public relations programs. The function of a public relations operator is to present a favorable public image. Sometimes he tries to paint this picture with stardust and rainbows, and sometimes he succeeds. During the Wall Street electronic mania, one pencil company was thinking of changing its name Penciltronics to participate in the bonanza. Some stocks went straight up because of their "tronic" names.

John is Vice-President in Charge of Public Relations for a firm we'll call The Keeping Steel Company. At a private meeting with the corporation's Big Brass, he outlined his strategy:

"Nothing appreciates the value of a stock like popularity. It must be fashionable. What makes something fashionable these days? Ask your kids. It's the image of contemporary excitement. Today the big attraction is technology. Let's join the mainstream. Ship builders now say they are in marine systems. This steel company can describe itself as being in materials technology.

"Forget the balance sheet and the antique talk about assets, book value, and working capital per share. Let's talk about the nucleus theory of growth and the feeding of markets of higher technology. And don't forget to use the words 'emerging conglomerate.' In 1967 and 1968 those words will add at least ten points to the stock."

A little induced optimism is a good thing, but in extreme cases, fashionable trends descend to psychotic levels. Charles Mackay's classic *Extraordinary Popular Delusions and the Madness of Crowds* lists numerous historical examples of mass insanity. His outstanding illustration is the "Tulipmania" that swept across Holland in the 1600's. It almost left the entire nation bankrupt. Tulips became so popular that the desire to have them exceeded financial guidelines, to put it mildly. Demand quickly outdistanced supply. The craze for tulips and more tulips spiraled. One rare tulip sold for 4400 florins. (At that time one could buy a luxurious mansion for 4400 florins.) Thinking it was an onion, one sailor accidentally ate a tulip bulb, the price of which would have fed the crew of his ship for a complete year!

Tulip bulbs soon moved into the stock exchanges of Amsterdam, Rotterdam, and other cities. Mackay writes: "The stock jobbers, ever on the alert for a new speculation, dealt largely in tulips, making use of all the means they so well knew how to employ to cause fluctuations in prices. At first, as in all these gambling mania, confidence was at its height, and everybody gained."

Thousands of conservative Dutchmen sold their homes, their produce, everything, in order to get in on something that looked like easy money. New millionaires sprouted almost daily. People were no longer buying tulips for their beauty or rarity. Bidders were tumbling over each other to raise the price today because you might sell it for twice the price tomorrow. Then the inevitable happened. Prices became too high for even the most optimistic and the tulip market collapsed.

Is the foregoing incident an antiquated example of wild mass psychology? Well, early in 1961, while the market was flying high, *Newsweek* magazine quoted a broker: "Everyone has the idea that anything he buys will double overnight. The horrible thing is, it has happened."

Stock market analysts had their convention in Richmond, Virginia, in May of 1961. Remember, this was not Rotterdam in the early 1600's.

U. S. News & World Report covered the convention and quoted some of the analysts. One New York investment banker stated: "I think this market is crazy, just plain crazy. There are still good stocks around, companies selling at ten to twenty times earnings, and with good earnings prospects. But people seem to want to pay for stock selling at sixty to eighty times a company's earnings. I don't know why. This just isn't a thinking man's market."

Another was quoted: "It's an amazing market. How can stocks go up with profits no better than they are? People just don't seem to care about profits. All they want to know is: 'What's going up tomorrow?' "

One year later, on May 28, 1962, many of those who had been driven by the illusion that stock prices are perpendicular had their comeuppance. Castles in the air were transformed into financial dungeons for investors unable to sell.

Of course, the examples are the extremes, and stock fashions do not show themselves only through uncontrolled frenzies. There are different degrees in the popularity. Some of the glamor stocks may be more real than transitory—if you choose the right ones. I can remember when some of the traditional investment managers peered down their noses at one brokerage house after it had exhibited the Midas touch by buying Polaroid early. The traditionalists dismissed the Polaroid-buyers as "lucky traders," but time has proved them to be shrewd investors.

There is no question that fads are constantly changing, but, as always, it is important to buy the style that fits *you,* whether or not it is fashionable at the moment. For instance, the "proper" fashion for you may be companies with established histories of well-above-average sales and earnings increases, dominant industry positions, and adequate financial resources; these would be industries such as oil, steel, paper, chemical, and automotive.

Then again, you might wish to buy the smaller high-technology companies with dreams for the future.

If you do remain conservative, however, there will always be pioneers willing to accept risks and set the fashion. Over the years Wall Street has attracted the risk-buyers.

Naturally, uncontrolled speculation should be condemned and avoided. The idea that a lottery has more winners than tickets must invite catastrophe. And the fashionable craze that compels you to buy something simply because others have purchased it is downright irrational. It is equally ridiculous to declare that you can buy stocks without undertaking a measure of risk. In the end, the calculation of the risk is an individual decision.

As noted previously, the most fashionable stocks of the 1960's have been those with rapid growth in earnings per share, either in real or in anticipated earnings. These include:

1. Control Data	4. IBM
2. Jim Walters	5. Revlon
3. IT&T	6. Xerox

7. Eastman Kodak	13. Penn Central
8. Polaroid	14. Northwest Industries
9. Burroughs	15. Gulf & Western
10. Boeing	16. RCA
11. Johnson & Johnson	17. Texas Gulf Sulphur
12. Syntex	18. Howmet

To repeat, the majority of the rapid growers have been in the high technology fields, but there is no guarantee that such companies will be the great growth industries in the future.

Fundamentally, the mushrooming of per share earnings depends on various factors. A *new product* is a vital element. Prime recent examples are xerography, the jet plane, steroid derivatives, computer leasing, color television, and magnetic tape. Second factor to be considered is a dramatic internal change in the company, increasing its efficiency and profitability. A third factor would include any favorable specialized characteristics, such as low labor cost or a wide potential market.

SPOTTING TRENDS

Anticipating and playing fashion trends is important. To do this you can use insight about a special industry, knowledge about a specific product, an instinctive "feel" for the market, a network of sources among brokers and fund managers, and skill in evaluating the unpredictible, intangible, imponderable mass psychology. Once you overcome any—or all—of the foregoing hurdles, then you can start counting your profits, since fashionable stocks are self-generating. They *create* demand, and demand results in an upward thrust of prices.

As one of my analyst friends has noted: "Short term value, like beauty, is in the eye of the beholder. Often it defies statistical analysis. The only reason why they fought a war over Helen of Troy was that two men wanted her. In economic parlance, demand exceeded supply. There were enough women to go around, but there was a shortage of Helens. Too many economists and investment analysts overlook such vitally important decisions. No poet would be so stupid."

The poetry of stock buying requires a soaring imagination in addition to an appreciation of the power and beauty of motion. In Wall Street active stocks have a special fascination. When they move upward quickly, they attract cheering followers. Of course everybody loves a winner.

FURTHER GUIDELINES

Since fashions both reflect and influence the times, styles and historical forces are reciprocal. As a striking case in point, the emerging technologies dedicated to ridding the air and streams of pollution, providing sufficient food for all, reanimating cities, improving medical therapy, discovering cures for various diseases, enhancing and broadening the educational process give indications of being a new and burgeoning historical force.

Voluntarily and unconsciously, for reasons of profits or welfare, the new force has been harnessed by industry and government. Both have accepted the basic premise that there is "something rotten in the state of Denmark." For the most part, they have been activated as much by what they would *not* stand for as by what they stood for, and one of the things they would *not* stand for was anything but a realistic assault against the grimy citadels of poverty and ignorance.

Both politics and business have dismissed the American myth that this land of the free and home of the brave is loaded with happy, prosperous families, all of which enjoy an unparalleled standard of well-being that could only result from an omniscient God bestowing his gifts on the most deserving—a neat twist by which the Golden Calf became God's gift to the annointed. The people behind the new force do not quarrel with the Grand Myth, but with the dismal economic facts which belie it.

Solutions to the problem range from community remedial reading courses to vast plans for model cities. Of course, a magnificent beginning has been made, but it is only a beginning. Billions of dollars are being spent, and literally trillions of dollars are needed. But day by day we are making more fruitful use of our human resources with the aid of the emerging technologies. And this is a continuing progression.

By and large, the average investor, broker, or analyst lacks the time to think in broad philosophic and historical perspectives. Unconsciously, however, they are a *part* of the perspective, and they are influenced by it. They may think in terms of price-earning ratios or a quick profit when they buy stock in high-technology companies, but those factors are influenced by facts which are often deceptively simple.

Perhaps nothing illustrates the "secret sources" of economics so much as a touch of humor credited to the late President Kennedy during one of his private meetings with motor magnates.

The President said that a group of industrialists had gone holidaying in the Everglades. At sundown, they found an isolated tar-paper saloon far out in the swamp. They entered the dingy place to find it occupied by a sleazy barkeep and one highly inebriated gentleman who greeted them most happily as fellows-well-met.

The drunk asked them if they would like to hear the most important factor in their lives as of that moment. The industrialists answered with a polite negative. Nevertheless, he informed them that the very island on which they stood was a breeding place for alligators and that 50,000 eggs were laid there each year. The spokesman for the industrialists answered that he saw no importance in that. The alcoholic agreed; he added that the most important fact was that the flamingoes devoured 49,000 of the eggs.

The industrialists answered that they saw no importance in that either. With wide-eyed incredulity, the drunk declared: "You don't? Well, I can tell you that if it weren't for the popular consumption by the flamingoes, right now we'd all be standing in alligators up to our arses."

Strange as it may seem, fashions and fads begin when someone takes something like "popular consumption" into account *and* is able to convince somebody else that his theory had promise. In closing, the best advice I can give you is to look for areas troubled by the proverbial alligators—and then buy into a company that sells flamingoes.

A new product may make fashions but not profits. (The topless bathing suit, for instance, made a splash but didn't sell.) The best rule is: look for needs, not for tulip bulbs. You can always plant your garden later with the profits from a simple little hardware stock that got other investors excited and kept them that way.

† PRICE EARNINGS RATIOS

Published by
Standard & Poor's
Corporation

†Based on extremes of closing prices during period. The quarterly price-earnings are based on the total of earnings during the 12 months preceding the end of each quarter, applied to the high and low prices for the quarter.

		Industrials		Rails		Utilities	
		High	Low	High	Low	High	Low
ANNUAL	1931	30.28	12.96	38.48	11.16	24.84	11.30
	1932	23.78	11.55	17.53	5.81	18.20	8.49
	1933	27.23	11.28	21.09	8.55	22.43	12.05
	1934	23.60	17.08	18.47	11.60	19.34	10.09
	1935	19.50	11.98	13.56	8.56	17.03	7.93
	1936	18.50	13.76	13.14	9.03	17.86	14.06
	1937	16.69	8.97	18.00	7.95	17.57	9.38
	1938	24.30	14.93	12.80	11.23	14.08	9.00
	1939	16.19	12.27	9.63	6.23	13.38	10.71
	1940	12.24	8.58	7.56	5.10	13.56	9.89
	1941	9.57	7.64	4.49	3.41	13.12	7.56
	1942	12.18	9.25	2.53	1.95	9.13	6.85
	1943	15.62	12.40	4.06	2.89	11.92	8.26
	1944	16.23	14.07	6.23	4.56	12.84	11.22
	1945	20.07	15.25	8.65	6.26	18.27	12.07
	1946	17.46	12.86	12.00	7.32	13.03	9.39
	1947	9.32	7.89	7.41	5.38	12.05	9.66
	1948	7.22	5.79	5.64	4.37	11.27	9.73
	1949	6.88	5.51	6.18	4.80	11.95	9.54
	1950	7.04	5.58	5.27	3.62	12.50	10.69
	1951	9.58	8.21	7.60	6.11	14.12	12.74
	1952	10.92	9.45	7.25	5.75	14.99	13.27
	1953	10.37	8.72	6.70	5.28	14.10	12.41
	1954	12.90	8.60	10.38	6.87	15.70	13.24
	1955	13.12	9.43	8.77	7.00	15.73	14.13
	1956	15.09	12.95	9.39	7.61	15.28	14.03
	1957	15.21	11.99	9.75	6.25	15.24	12.87
	1958	19.99	14.64	11.90	7.46	18.26	13.64
	1959	18.50	16.17	12.50	10.52	19.10	17.60
	1960	19.17	16.32	14.25	11.09	19.24	16.26
	1961	22.76	18.06	16.42	13.79	24.36	18.43
	1962	19.44	14.16	11.89	9.24	21.28	16.41
	1963	18.69	15.44	12.80	10.34	21.11	19.03
	1964	18.90	16.51	14.01	11.39	21.42	19.37
	1965	17.89	15.69	12.95	10.32	20.15	18.56
	1966	17.08	13.22	12.83	8.64	18.12	14.19
QUARTERLY	1966—1	17.74	16.46	13.44	11.86	18.98	17.18
	2	17.11	15.43	12.06	10.11	17.40	16.42
	3	16.08	13.66	10.33	8.64	16.61	14.40
	4	15.02	13.22	9.78	8.64	16.70	14.79
	1967—1	16.96	14.81	11.29	9.87	16.84	16.38
	2	18.09	16.77	13.00	12.00	16.88	15.48

chapter nine

Shopping for Bargains

Some years ago, a magazine requested its female readers to list their ten favorite words. The overwhelming majority chose such words as "love," "children," "beauty," and "Christmas." A popular runner-up was "bargain," which is hardly a surprise to retail shops. As women, you are natural shoppers, gifted with intuitive price-appraising ability. Basically, the bargain-hunting instinct exerts an enormous psychological attraction. It introduces a feeling of excitement and accomplishment into what otherwise is often a socially and emotionally quiet existence. You who have witnessed, or been, a victorious bargain-hunter know the flushed excitement that was probably shared by Napoleon at the pinnacle of his military triumphs. And this triumph is never dimmed by your knowledge that even a bargain costs money.

Of course, the joy of getting a bargain is not confined to you alone. Let's face it—everybody likes to get more for less, which is the essence of a bargain. And Wall Street has more than its share of bargain-hungry customers. Generally, stock market bargains represent good timing. Since buying (and selling) stocks is simply a matter of the art of timing, every stock is a bargain, if you buy it at the lowest possible price. This applies to blue chips as well as to the cheaper issues.

Before grabbing a bargain, there are the usual precautionary checks. Determine your personal investment goal, set aside adequate cash reserves for emergencies, assume only those risks you can afford, get the facts about the potential bargain, and seek advice from an experienced broker. Naturally, you cannot discount the element of luck. As a case in point, I'll repeat another story told by Keith Funston when he was president of the New York Stock Exchange:

An elderly lady brought her portfolio to a broker for advice. Her selections, said the broker, were ideal. How had she picked her stocks? The secret of her success, the lady said, was that for years she had been buying only shares of companies that ran two-page, four-color advertisements in her favorite magazine.

The foregoing is a wry exception, of course. Slot machine methods are not recommended here. Nevertheless, I can't stress frequently enough that your every stock purchase involves an element of risk. Accordingly, bargain-type stocks are riskier than most.

As a logical step in bargain-hunting, you should familiarize yourself with the more-for-less techniques. Along Wall Street they have a term for such methods—leverage, which the dictionary defines as an "increased means of accomplishing some purpose." In the stock market that means getting more stock for your money.

Here are two ladies with their own definitions:

Mrs. A. is a part-owner of a Fifth Avenue dress shop. She hopes to build her capital by making one dollar do the work of two. It sounds dreamy, but it is a daily Wall Street reality. Mrs. A. had made less dollars do more work by acquiring both life insurance and mutual funds with a single payment. She pledged the shares and/or life insurance as collateral for loans with which to extend her buying power.

Mrs. Valery G. is a famous actress. She borrowed money against life insurance at 5 percent and put the borrowed money into securities that paid 7 percent, thus giving her a 2 percent gain over her 5 percent borrowing rate. See? Simple arithmetic for making money.

(*But:* Remember, both Mrs. G. and Mrs. A. are assuming a risk. It is certain that the market value of the securities they pledged as collateral for their loans will fluctuate. If the market value of their securities drops, they'll reach for the aspirin.)

There are numerous other leverage devices. One of the handiest is the "stock options." This device enables you to buy a mink for the price of rabbit, albeit you do risk the possibility of being stripped of your mink. The average investor can buy stock options in the forms of "Puts" and "Calls." First, let us examine the Call. When you buy it, you acquire the right to buy a specified number of shares (invariably in 100-share lots) of a specified stock at a specified price at any time during the life of the option. Ordinarily, options are effective for periods of thirty, sixty, or ninety days, or for six months and ten days, or for a year.

Naturally, this right has a price—a fee or a premium, which you pay in advance. The longer the option, the higher the premium. Options on high-priced stocks generally cost more than ones on the low-priced securities. Options on listed stocks usually cost less than

THE PUT AND CALL MARKET

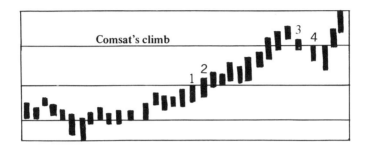

Comsat's climb

1 Option writer owns 100 shares of Comsat, which trades at $50 a share in the market. He sells to an option dealer a 90-day "call" on his stock at $50 a share. His selling price for the call is $500. He makes 10% on his $5,000 equity.

2 Dealer resells "call" to buyer for $550. His profit is the 10% spread, or $50.

3 Buyer exercises his "call" when Comsat reaches $60. He buys 100 shares from the option writer for $5,000 and sells 100 shares in the market for $6,000. His profit is $1,000 minus the cost of the "call," or $450 before commissions. That's an 81.8% return on the money he has risked—which is the option's price.

4 Option writer has made 10% in just under three months. If he does this three more times in a year, his profit adds up to a 40% return. But first he must reinvest his $5,000. He may decide to sell a "put"—the opposite of a "call"—to replenish his portfolio.

those on unlisted stocks. Options on popular, widely known stocks often cost less than those on lesser-known stocks. Options on stocks with market liquidity, on less volatile stocks, and on investment quality stocks generally also cost less.

As with anything else, the price is determined by the supply and demand for options. One of the chief motivations for buying a Call is to protect yourself against *undue* risk. For instance, you decide that Robsom Coppers is likely to go up from the present market in the thirties to a price in the eighties. You could either buy 100 shares, for instance, of the stock, putting at risk a large part of the cost of the shares, or you could buy a Call on 100 shares, giving you the right to buy the shares themselves later at the present price and risking only the premium paid for the Call.

If after you buy the stock there is a market break, there is the inevitable huge loss. However, if you bought a Call, you would lose only the amount of the premium, a small fraction of the actual stock price.

Now comes the worm in the bright red apple. Unless the stock *rises* sharply during the life of your Call, it would have been more prudent for you to buy the stock itself. Also, if Robsom Coppers leaps only *after* your Call has expired, your option is worthless. Obviously, buying a Call means you expect a stock to rise sharply during the period of your option. In other words, Calls are tickets to an optimists' convention.

There are other advantages in buying Calls on a stock rather than the stock itself. You can make use of them to further your overall investment program. Suppose you own 100 shares of Robsom Coppers, bought at 20 over 6 months ago. The stock is now at 30, and you believe it will go higher, but you are not certain. If you hold it for the expected rise and it goes down instead, you lose the capital gains tax advantage you would have had if you had sold. But if you sell the stock and it goes up, you lose the profit. So you decide to go ahead and sell, assuring your tax advantage, but at the same time you buy a Call on 100 shares, protecting your possible profit in case of a rise. This procedure has the additional advantage of freeing capital (proceeds of the stock sale, minus the price of the Call) for reinvestment in another security.

A Put is the exact opposite of a Call. Buying a Put gives you the right to sell a specified number of shares at a specified price at any time during the life of the option. Again, you pay in advance a fee or premium for this right. This is your price of admission into the bearish pessimist's club.

You use a Put when you have reason to believe that a stock will decline sharply. You should buy a Put only if you anticipate a relatively large *decline* in the price of the stock during the period of your option. You make money on a Put only when the stock goes down more than the amount of the premium you paid plus the commissions. Thus, Puts offer a way to be short * in a stock with a limited risk, the most you can lose is the premium. Since any market may have occasional unexpected breaks, you can pro-

---

* Being short is another way of saying selling short. Short sales are made by an investor who, thinking the price for a security is going to decline, borrows some stock and sells it at the present price. At a later date, he must buy the securities to replace those he borrowed—but if the stock has gone down, he pays less than he sold it for. Of course, if the security were to increase in price, he would lose money, having to buy back the securities at a higher price.

tect your long position with a portfolio of Puts. If the market goes down and the value of your position with it, profits from a Put could offset the losses on your long position, minus only the cost of the Put.

The buying of options, Puts and Calls, represents bargain goods —if you make money. Making a profit is the difference between a bargain and a blunder!

Now let's exemplify the happy arithmetic of successful option buying: Suppose you decide that Jekyll and Hyde Cosmetics stock is ready to move up from its present price of 25 to at least 35. You can buy 100 shares for $2,500, or you can buy 100 shares on margin,* or you can buy a Call on 100 shares for a premium of, say, $300.

If you buy the shares outright and the price, happily, moves up 10 points and then you sell, you make a profit of $1,000, less commissions to buy and sell of $68, plus $5 tax—a total of $73 —for a net profit of $927, or 37 percent profit. But if the stock *drops* 10 points and then you sell, you lose $1,000 plus commissions!

On the other hand, if instead you buy the Call on 100 shares and the price goes to 35, you can *then* exercise your option. You make a $1,000 profit, less $300 paid for the Call and $73 for commission and tax, for a net profit of $627 on your original $300, or 209 percent profit! Of course, if the stock drops, you simply let your option expire and you lose the $300 you paid for it. Better that than losing $1,000, wouldn't you say? (But remember, in terms of percentages, the $300 deficit would represent a 100 percent loss. As always, for every rosy bargain there are thorns.)

The leverage more-for-less factor works also on the market's downside. Assume you decide that Upp and Conning is ready to plummet from 25 to 15. To take advantage of this expected drop, you can sell the stock short (with all the risks involved in any short sale), or you can buy a Put on 100 shares for a premium of, say, $250.

---

* Margin means placing a certain amount of money with your broker as a deposit on securities whose value exceeds the money you deposited. In effect you borrow from your broker, using the securities he's purchased for you as collateral.

If you sell the stock short at 25, and it does drop to 15, you have a profit of $1,000, less commissions and tax, totaling $58.50, or a net of $941.50, a 38 percent profit. But if the short sale goes against you, there is the possibility of a substantial loss.

If, on the other hand, you buy a Put and your judgment is correct—repeat, *if* your judgment is correct—you make a profit of $1,000, less $250 for the Put and $58.50 commissions and tax, or $691.50 net on your $250 investment, for a 276 percent profit. If the Put trade goes against you, you lose $250. (Again, remember this is a 100 percent loss.)

PUT AND CALL DEPARTMENT

Puts and Calls can be very useful in periods of market uncertainty. Of course, uncertainty is an ever-present factor, which varies in degree, since the market is influenced by public confidence. And confidence is a variable that has been most accurately defined as suspicion asleep.

Options are particularly useful when the future appears more hazy than usual and consequently the market trend takes on the aspects of a shot in the dark. You can buy options instead of long and short positions and thus avoid the outlay of large sums of money during a dubious period. Naturally, your definitions of a large sum or small is as much your decision as your choice of lipstick.

However, suppose you consider Sterneast Airlines to be an attractive purchase at its current price of 50, but the overall market is listless and shows no direction. In such a case you might buy a 90-day Call on Sterneast at 50 for, say, $350. You thus take advantage of the current price while risking only your $350 premium. If the stock should rise sharply and you exercise your Call, you have purchased a bargain. If the stock goes down during the period of your Call, your loss is limited to $350.

The stock option apparatus is based on negotiation. Ordinarily, a Put-and-Call broker serves as a middleman between buyer and seller and earns his profit by doing so. When you want to buy an option, the broker tries to find someone who wants to sell one, in the stock you want, for the term you want, and at the price you want to pay. Sometimes this can be done easily; sometimes, as with lesser-known stocks, it may not be possible at all.

As in all market transactions, there are two sides to the story. One is told by the buyer, the other by the seller. Frequently, the endings are different. One can be sad, the other happy but both can be happy if each accomplished his objective. As I have indicated, Puts and Calls can serve as an umbrella to protect profits, insure against losses, and save on taxes. But if your judgment is wrong, you can lose the money you saved for the inevitable rainy day.

THE OTHER SIDE

Now we come to the Puts and Calls from the seller's point of view. Who sells stock options? Just who is it that, for relatively small payment, will guarantee to take over or deliver a specified quantity of stock at your specified price within your specified time limit? Clearly there must be benefits for the sellers of stock options as well as for the buyer. Well, in the case of stock options, the seller—or writer of the contract, as he is generally termed—is usually an individual or a corporation with large holdings in the security in question, who is willing to add to or subtract from that position—at a price.

Generally, the sellers of stock options are among the shrewdest of Wall Streeters. Girls are aware that a wolf can be a fox with patience, and in the financial market the wolf is a fox with money, experience, and sophistication. The buyer of stock options is bucking "smart" money, and the writers of option contracts keep well on top of the market. Options give them the opportunity to sell above the market or to invest at below-market prices. Basically, you see, the buyer's Put is the seller's Call, minus the fee.

The tempting fragrance of a bargain frequently emanates from something you can buy below the market price. The Wall Street shop window offers several perfumes in that category. One is called simply "rights."

BILL OF RIGHTS

Not long ago American Telephone and Telegraph Company raised close to $1,200,000,000 in new capital through a rights offering. That, of course, gives you an idea of AT&T's financial power and resources. And it helps explain why Mother Bell has a Tiffany rating. Many of the world's governments would have trouble raising that sum.

On Febuary 11, 1964, the 2,350,000 or so shareowners of AT&T were informed that they could buy one additional share for each 20 shares they owned. To buy one share, the shareowner would have to pay only $100. (At the time of the announcement, the stock was selling at about $146 per share.) Of course, this right to buy immediately acquired a value. After all, if you have the right to buy a security below the market price, this "right" has a value.

Telephone shareowners had several choices. They could exercise their right by paying the company $100 per share for each share they wanted and were entitled to. Or they could sell their rights. Or, if a shareowner owned, say, 15 shares, he could buy 5 additional shares, which (by giving him a total of 20) would allow him to buy one more bargain share.

In any case, Telephone stockholders were given a privileged position. The company had given them the opportunity to buy the additional stock *before* it was offered to the general public. In a way this is fair; selling additional shares dilutes the proportionate holdings of the original shareowners, unless they have the opportunity to maintain that proportion by buying into the additional shares.

A right, then, is in essence a privilege given by the issuing corporation to buy its stock—or bonds or debentures—at a price that is usually quite favorable in relation to the market price of the outstanding security. Offering rights is a common bargaining technique employed by many corporations. Surprisingly enough, the bargain rights are often overlooked by stockholders.

Securities subscribed to through rights can, under certain conditions, be placed in so-called "subscription accounts," which permit initial margin substantially below the usual margin requirements. This offers increased leverage. Incidentally, the rules relating to such subscription accounts are many, and "technical." For specific details, consult your broker.

Rights are often confused with warrants. The difference between the two is a Tweedledum-Tweedledee distinction. In the broadest terms, a right is a short-term privilege to buy a security at a favorable price; the privilege derives from the security you *own*. A warrant is the privilege to buy a security at a specific price, usually offered to facilitate the sale of a stock or bond which you do *not* own. You, the buyer, get the stock or bond plus the warrant.

FINANCIAL PERFUME

The seductive smell of money comes also in the form of a "tender." To you the stockholder, a tender is an offer to trade stock that you own for stock in another company. A tender is usually made by someone who wants to gain control of a company or to simplify his own corporate structure.

For example, some time ago, preferred and common stockholders of Eastern Gas & Fuel Associates received a letter: "Herewith is an offer by Eastern Gas & Fuel Associates which gives you the opportunity to exchange Eastern Preferred or Common Stock for shares of Common Stock of Norfolk & Western Railway Company."

In this case, Eastern Gas owned a large block of N&W shares as an investment. Eastern figured that disposal of the N&W stock would not only favorably modify their company's own capital structure, but also benefit Eastern common shareowners who accepted the tender (expectation of better dividends from N&W) and Eastern shareowners who did not accept the tender (possibility that income available for dividends would be distributed among fewer shares).

Another goal was to increase the percentage of shares held by Eastern's controlling stockholders. Thus, a tender may also be made by an individual or group seeking control of a company. The offer to buy will of course be above the market price, although, for obvious reasons, the market price quickly lines up with the tender price if there is no limit to the number of shares that will be accepted.

Rights and tender offers are not always a simple more-for-less deal; they can be very intricate. As always, consult your broker, banker, or investment advisor before making a decision. On occasion a tempting offer doesn't look so good on closer examination.

CONVERTIBLES

One of the more popular Wall Street bargains over the past few years has been the "convertible bond."

It is important to note that a bond is simply a contract to pay money. The contract binds the issuer of a bond to pay the principal sum and interest for the use of this money, the payments to be made as scheduled in the contract. A bond, then, evidences an obligation, or indebtedness, entered into by a company. This distinguishes it from a stock, the owner of which actually owns a part interest, however small, in a business.

When you look at a bond, you'll see the name of the issuer and the serial number. You also find the principal amount of the bond, the rate of interest, and the date on which the principal is to be repaid. An important provision is whether or not the bond is subject to "call." If it is, the issuer has the privilege of redeeming the bond at a stated price *before* the final date at which the principal sum comes due.

A note of caution: In order to avoid the possibility of loss, never buy a bond at a price substantially above its redemption value. A bond often shows little or nothing about the kind of activity in which the issuer engages, nor does it give evidence of the issuer's ability to pay as agreed. As always, when in doubt, consult your broker, banker, or investment advisor.

There are as many sizes and shapes of bonds as there are of gowns, shoes, and foods. The variety stems from the competitive nature of our economy. Not all businesses prosper; indeed, some go bankrupt. Therefore, the lure of higher yields shouldn't make you reach for lower quality bonds. A temptingly high interest rate is often an attempt by a weaker high-risk company to woo investors. Generally, the bonds of low quality companies are riskier than the quality of superior common stock. Gingham may come wrapped in silk, but it's still gingham.

The aforementioned convertible bond includes in its contract the privilege of converting the bond (at predetermined prices) into the common stock of the issuing company. This represents a significant change in the characteristics of a bond, for it permits the holder to participate in the growth of the company by exchanging the bond for common stock. By and large, convertibles are or could be, junior debt obligations, not measuring up to the credit standing of a company's other obligations. The convertible feature is a bargain tag, granted by the company in order to attract buyers who naturally believe in the company's potential without diluting earnings until they have increased.

The convertible offers the owner an opportunity to enjoy the sun when the company's business—or the nation's economy—is flourishing. It also presents a form of protection—a steady return on your money—when the rains come. The risk of a convertible is obvious, despite the cockeyed optimists who would have you believe convertibles are cartwheels from Heaven. Since the value of a convertible is to a large extent tied to the price of the common stock, it has a similar potential and risk.

Convertibles are influenced by interest rates and other primary factors, such as a company's growth of earnings and the quality of its securities. The advantage of convertibles is that their owners can change them at will or on certain terms into common shares of the company within the time limit in the indenture. If the common stock rises, the convertible prerogative can be tasty indeed. It is a way of eating your cake and having some left over to enjoy in the future. However, if the common stock should dive, that fund will fall along with it, possibly at a much slower pace or to a lesser degree.

Incidentally, some convertibles are issued with warrants. These warrants, usually detachable from the bonds, entitle the holders to purchase the common stock of the company at specified prices upon the payment of cash and the surrender of the warrants, rather than through the surrender of the bonds. If the price of the company's stock advances importantly, the bondholder can exercise his warrants at a profit, or he can sell them.

SIGNPOSTS

Another bargain guide in Wall Street is known as "capital turnover." You can appraise a company's performance by calculating how many dollars of sales are being generated by each dollar of invested capital—in other words, the capital turnover of a company. This can be done simply by dividing a company's annual net sales by the sum of what long-term investors have put into the company (represented by bonds, preferred stock, common stock, retained earnings, and other surplus accounts listed in its balance sheet).

The greater the turnover, the more productive the company. Obviously, a company showing a sales figure eight times as large as the amount of money put in by all long-term investors is using funds more efficiently than a company in the same industry whose turnover is, for instance, three.

The "Technical Position" is another item worth watching when shopping for bargains. This is a term applied to the various internal factors affecting the market (as opposed to external factors such as earnings, dividends, political considerations, and general market conditions). Some internal factors considered in appraising the market's technical position include the size of the short interest,* whether the market has had a sustained advance or decline without interruption, a sharp advance or decline on small volume and the amount of credit in use in the market. In a way, this is a method of checking the market's blood pressure and heartbeat—and of finding out whether the roses in its cheeks denote a high fever or good health.

HOT ITEMS

The desire by bargain-hunters for new issues has its periodic bursts of passion. During 1960-62 and 1967-68 buyers' passion for new issues was boundless. In general, though, their desire to embrace new issues during those periods was devoid of reason. Many buyers clutched them to their bosom simply because they were new issues; every other coldly logical consideration went out the window. Some new issues doubled and quadrupled in price within a day, and their buyers cleared quick profits. Other passionate purchasers hated themselves in the morning for holding on too long. Some new issues, in time, turned out to be busts.

As previously noted, among the problems of buying new issues is their scarcity. The limited supply plus the frenzied demand

---

* The total number of shares sold short, in each company.

gives new issues their rocket-like propensities. It should be added as a cautionary note that, in common with rockets, some new issues flare briefly and die later.

The new issue apparatus begins with the underwriter, who provides a major channel through which money flows to new as well as to established business enterprises. Let us assume you own Habeas Corporation. It is a moderate-sized business with a good earnings record and promising potential. The company needs money to build a plant, to develop an invention, and to expand its markets.

HOW IT'S DONE

The first step for you is to consult an underwriter. In Wall Street underwriters are known also as investment bankers. Whatever the title, the underwriter will discuss various methods of raising capital. Bank loans? Issues of various types of bonds or preferred stock? As the owner of Habeas Corporation, you decide that the best method is to seek equity capital. In other words, you decide to offer shares of common stock, shares which do not require interest payments or a fixed dividend. These shares, you and the underwriter agree, will offer the investor an ownership interest in your company, the possibility of dividends, and capital appreciation.

The solution requires much expertise. The underwriter probes every facet of your business—your history, your personal qualities, earnings, dividends (if any), capitalization, management, prospects, and products. The underwriter functions as an economist, psychologist, and crystal-ball gazer. Then there's the all-important question of price. What is a fair price at which to offer Habeas Corporation common, from the viewpoint of Habeas, the investor, and the market?

After the underwriter decides to accept the deal, the rest is simple for you as Habeas owner. You get a check from the investment banker for a previously specified amount, less expenses. Then it's up to the underwriter to successfully offer Habeas Corporation to the investor. The public offering, depending on its size, is made by the underwriter alone, *or* he may enlist the aid of other underwriters and form a selling group. The investor hears about the Habeas Corporation offering through the financial press, a prospectus, and his own broker. There are endless variations of this procedure, but basically, the underwriter functions as a middleman between the corporation seeking funds and the investor seeking the type of security he wants.

To repeat, when the love of new issues reaches feverish peaks, every new share may take on the aspect of being a rare jewel. But it has been my experience that for every Wall Street shopper who is fortunate enough to buy a valuable bauble at cut-rate prices, there are some who sadly discover that their prize is merely a five-and-dime trinket, hardly a promise of financial wedded bliss.

It should be noted here that there is a special tool to help you protect your profits, bargain or otherwise. It is known as the Stop Order.

STOP IN THE NAME OF CASH

Stop Orders were introduced on the Exchange more than half a century ago with the main purpose of trying to limit a loss or protect a profit. This is how they work: Suppose you bought 100 shares of Fyne and Dundee, Inc. stock at $10 per share and happily, within a year it leaped to $30 per share. Assume, too, that you are planning a vacation and you are concerned about the stock's action. You have no desire to lose all the "paper profit" during your holiday. So you tell your broker to sell your 100 shares of Fyne and Dundee at $20-stop, good until cancelled. If your order should be executed at that price, you'd be left with a profit of $10 per share. Remember, though, there is no guarantee that you will get that price, even though the market should decline low enough to put your Stop Order in effect. Eventually, while you're away, sales might take place dropping Fyne and Dundee to $20. When a sale takes place at $20, your Stop Order automatically becomes a Market Order and is handled just like any other Market Order. Usually the Market Order will be executed at a price close to the last price recorded on the tape. But within a few minutes a lot can happen to the price of a fast-moving, volatile stock. Your Market Order may have to compete with other orders when it gets to the trading floor. Your broker will do the best he can for you, but competition is a critical factor in the market place. The price you receive may not always be what you expect. In other words, if the broker cannot get $20, he may have to take a lower price (or he may even be able to get a price above $20); it depends entirely on the supply of and the demand for Fyne and Dundee at the particular moment. In brief, you may get all the *protection* you sought, but there's no guarantee as to the price. However, it is a form of market-profit insurance. Furthermore, the stock may even rally substantially and reach new highs later.

The New York Stock Exchange considers the Stop Order a vital protective instrument. Yet it is coupled with dangers. If there is a plethora of Stop Orders in a declining market, it can trigger an avalanche of sales. Recognizing the possibility that Stop Orders could accentuate price movements in a particular security, the NYSE Board of Governors decided that floor governors of the Exchange should be given authority to suspend Stop Orders in individual cases when, in their judgment, circumstances warranted. This would cancel Stop Orders already received by members and would prohibit acceptance of additional ones until further notice. Floor governors take into consideration such factors as the number of shares in the hands of the public, the reported short position, the current volume compared with past volume, and the price range. A ban on Stop Orders may go into effect only after the close of the market. Member firms of the Exchange which had entered Stop Orders on behalf of their customers would, of course, try to notify their customers promptly of such a suspension.

ADD BARGAINS

Reading the footnotes in annual reports is another bargain device. Not many investors give enough time to studying annual reports, and fewer examine the footnotes. They may provide a wealth of information for the alert investor. For example, investments may be stated at a specific amount, but the "Notes" may break this item up into categories such as Government bonds, long- and short-term obligations, and at times a repurchase of the company's own securities. The Notes may include explanations about litigation of a patent or about research on a new product. Such items can be invaluable buying and bargain guides.

WONDERS, INC.

Since the opening of the atomic age, some of the biggest bargains have been in small new companies involved in fields that come under the general heading of science.

Almost daily, newspapers headline mind-boggling scientific achievements, ranging from heart transplants to supersonic jets. The benefits of technology can be felt in almost every facet of life. The aura of the fantastic and incredible is the prime reason why companies involved in areas of sophisticated science have been wildly popular with stock buyers. For the time being at least, they defy such earthbound considerations as earnings, dividends, and price-earnings ratios. It follows that there is no realistic price limit to companies in the far-out category, since imagination is limitless. There probably could be a limit, however, to the advances of research. This was illustrated by a lady who went into a supermarket with four bubbling young boys and asked the manager if they had any breakfast food which would de-energize her rambunctious sons.

Nevertheless, you may have to put wings on your imagination to evaluate some stocks in the scientific field. The computer industry, for instance, despite its wondrous achievements, is still in its crawling stage. Only a decade ago the country had access to only about 1,500 computers; today there are more than 40,000. The numerical progression has been accompanied by giant strides in speed and capability. When computers reach adulthood, get together, and produce their remarkable technological babies, then the consequences—especially financial—will indeed be fantastic. More burgeoning industries will be explored in chapter thirteen.

Paying for earnings that you hope to get in the future is a game for the sophisticated and experienced, although there are occasional exceptions. A broker once told me about a woman who made substantial profits forecasting the rise and fall of stocks by the positions of the planets. Star-gazing as a form of market analysis is not recommended, but if you try it and find it really works, I'd be the last to tell you nay.

In 1935 John Maynard Keynes, the classical British economist, wrote: "The social object of skilled investment should be to defeat the dark forces of time and ignorance which envelop our future.

The actual, private object of the most skilled investment today is to 'beat the gun,' as the Americans so well express it, to outwit the crowd, to pass the bad or depreciating half-crown to another fellow.

"This battle of wits to anticipate the basis of conventional valuation a few months hence . . . does not even require gulls amongst the public to feed the maws of the professional; it can be played by the professionals amongst themselves. Nor is it necessary that anyone should keep his simple faith in the conventional basis of valuation having any genuine long-term validity. For it is, so to speak, a game of Snap, of Old Maid, of Musical Chairs—a pastime in which he is victor who says Snap neither too soon nor too late, who passes the Old Maid to his neighbor before the game is over, who secures a chair for himself when the music stops. The games can be played with zest and enjoyment, though all the players know that is the Old Maid which is circulating, or that when the music stops some of the players will find themselves unseated."

One way to avoid the Old Maid in the bargain-hunting game is by choosing an "undervalued growth stock." In general the ingredients of growth we look for are:

1. Able management
2. A growing market for products
3. Net earnings increasing at a rapid rate
4. Increasing profit margins
5. A low P-E ratio
6. Strong finances

The key qualities in management encompass the performance of useful services, the commitment to sound beliefs, and the ability to identify those individuals who generate ideas and innovations. In the market category, it is essential to be in a field of product proliferation. Today the computer industry is probably the fastest-growing field in the world. But there are many others. Within the science-technology field probably lies the next Polaroid, Xerox, or IBM.

The yardstick of rapid growth is a minimum of 50 percent annually in new earnings. As volume increases a company's profit margins should also rise as costs in many operations are fixed. In addition, the importance of a low price-earnings ratio is vital. Generally, the maximum P-E should be 15 times the latest 12-month earnings, but this is flexible. Of course, the basis for underlying growth is a good balance sheet. The company's fundamental financial condition often determines if there is a good basis to support growth.

On occasion, it seems to me that the race for supremacy in growth stocks can be compared to two men gazing at the same familiar optical illusion puzzle and each seeing it differently. The image in one man's mind is distinct, but so is the opposite image in the other's eye. "That's the bottom," says one. "No," says the other, "that's the top." Each sees his image clearly, but one will always see a different one from the one the other sees.

In appraising growth stocks, often the one who sees a special vision creates a form of mass hypnosis. Like a spellbinder working on an audience, his emotional chord deepens to meet the heightened tone of his enraptured listeners. They amplify each other. Thus, there is an important emotional factor in the success stocks —when they grow. All too often hopes fail to materialize, and the growth stock becomes Remorse, Inc.

During 1959 and 1960 zooming growth rates were forecast and documented by many Wall Street analysts, especially in space technology and electronics. As P-E ratios rocketed, the amplification process inevitably followed. Researchers produced a wide assortment of valuation methods, in an effort to justify the high prices of popularized stocks. For example, a growth stock purchased at $10 per share in 1960 with predictions that it would earn $2 per share in 2 years meant that you were buying a stock at the bargain rate of 5 times 1962 earnings. That represents quite a bargain, provided the company hits those earnings in the projected time. Projections for some stocks were made for 5 or 10 years, and the excited anticipation resulted in those issues selling for 40 to 100 times earnings.

BARGAIN BASEMENT

During 1959-60 the bargain stocks were not confined to space technology and electronics. They included dozens of consumer and business services, apparel manufacturers, savings and loan companies, and literally hundreds of others. They were all narrowly-based businesses which were hastily brought to the market by under-writers to satisfy investor demands for consistent growth during the period. I remember one superficial research report about a small photo company. The projection was that its per-share earnings would leap from $.50 to $5 in 3 years. Almost immediately the stock price arrowed into the air. It sold for $50 per share. The following year its earnings dropped to $.40 per share, and the stock dropped to $3 a share. The company's earnings picture later improved, and its stock price followed suit, but at this writing it isn't even close to the 1960 price of $50.

This phenomenon was repeated in the 1967 market. It became popular to ferret out companies that were not dependent on the overall economic environment and were "masters of their own destinies" because of unique products and superiority in technological development. Once again, investors were buying fragments of blue sky. Not only ordinary investors but sophisticated analysts joined the bargain throngs. As one top analyst confessed: "The game is being played by virtually everyone except for a few old-fashioned investors. I played it, made money, and had fun. But at the same time I hoped we would soon get back to some solid, sensible investment research and away from the shooting from the hip that has become so widespread. Frankly, I haven't bought a stock for over a year with any real conviction about its value— which is good, because if I had, I would not have made money."

The proponents of stocks involved in sophisticated technology —dynamic growth securities *—might be described as abstract idealists. They promulgate much theory, unclouded by many facts. Yet their theories represent the discovery of valid and fundamental patterns that contribute much to the philosophy of stock-buying. That is to say, the processes of the stock market have a new predictable pattern, and the old standards of growth are obsolete. Time will prove or disprove the validity of this assumption.

Since the Russians launched the first Sputnik, a Niagara of technological innovations has burst upon the world. Ultimately technological marvels will give the common man a standard of living

---

* During the middle 1950's, an article in *The Harvard Business Review* traced the contrasting investment results of growth companies and non-growth companies since 1937. This article was widely heralded as proving the merit of growth stock investment and helped provide the impetus for growth stock popularity.

beyond the imagination of the utopians of only a century before. After all, Eli Whitney, Robert Fulton, Alexander Graham Bell, Thomas Edison, and Henry Ford have had a much greater effect on American history than the Supreme Court. Laws are only recognitions that transformations of unusual importance have occurred. It is individuals and their research that supply those transformations.

OUR HEROES

In Wall Street there have been broker-pioneers who recognized these changes, acted upon them, and made themselves and their customers happily solvent. So it logically follows that the efficacy of bargain-hunting often depends on finding the successful bargain-hunting broker. There is no sure formula for finding him, albeit most people find it pays to shop around for the knowing one who, at the very least, can be expected to know what his fellow brokers are buying and selling.

Names of conquerors and their triumphs are well known in Wall Street. During the early 1960's, there was Sam Stedman, a creative, imaginative advocate of growth stocks. Polaroid was just one of his many successes. Unfortunately, Steadman's early death cut short his remarkable career. Over the years there have been many in his category. Some are heroes during certain periods and then fall by the wayside. Almost always, they are replaced by other prophets. During the latter part of the 1960's such portfolio managers as Gerry Tsai, John Hartwell, and Fred Alger have been the golden boys. In time they may be joined or supplanted by others.

If you find the golden broker, it is probably a good idea to have a "discretionary account," although many brokerage firms discourage the idea. The discretionary account arises when an investor, in effect, says to his broker: "I trust you, and I think your judgment is wonderful. I don't have the time or the acumen to worry constantly about my stocks. You buy and sell whenever you think best."

There are some formalities involved in such accounts, namely the New York Stock Exchange's Rule 408. To establish such an account, the investor must sign a statement, often a printed form, in which he absolves the brokerage firm of responsibility. That's to avoid having cry-baby investors who might blame their losses on the brokerage house itself. The New York Stock Exchange rule puts it this way: "No registered representative may engage in discretionary trading for any account without obtaining prior written authorization from the customer. It should be properly executed and on file with the member organization." In addition, every time a broker buys or sells a stock in a discretionary account, he must have the order "approved and initiated" by a vice-president or partner of the firm.

The golden boys capable of handling discretionary accounts are somewhat rare. The majority of brokers, it is fair to state, lack such capability. Again, the choice in a broker, like the choice of a stock, is a crucial one.

Another group of professionals, incidentally, concentrate on discretionary accounts. They are investment advisors. The average investor cannot afford them. Few of them will take accounts of less than $50,000. Some of the more prominent ones will not handle anything less than $250,000. The difference between an investment advisor and a broker is a simple one: The latter derives his income from commissions generated by the trading in his account, while the former usually charges a fee based on the asset value of the amount handled. In many instances the investment advisor charges a yearly fee of 1 percent of total assets. Thus the investment advisor is motivated not by commissions (or turnover) but by the objective of increasing the portfolio.

The offices of investment advisors, brokers, banks, and mutual funds are crammed with reports that strive to spot stocks of entire industries that appear to be breaking out of their usual earning pattern. As soon as a stock appears to be sprouting wings, the brokerage butterfly nets are in action. This phenomenon is not peculiar to science-oriented industries alone. For example, some years ago many investors were rather tired of looking at year-to-year fluctuation of earnings in basic industry, and research men quickly adapted to the mood of the market by "discovering" that a stock such as General Foods had shown higher earnings in 11 out of the preceding 13 years and yet was selling at a discount from market averages. Even utilities and banks, which had always been regarded as income vehicles, suddenly became regarded as growth stocks because of the consistent gains of their earnings.

Now we come to one of the most popular—and one of the most deplored—techniques of bargain-hunting. It is defined by a simple three-letter word: tip. Brokerage houses, the various Exchanges, analysts, books, magazines, and newspapers all have branded tips as a form of financial leprosy. The classic case of acting on tips from the shoeshine boy prompts warnings that have become so numerous and repetitive that they have taken on the tone of a symphonic dirge.

I agree that the quickest way to go broke is to put your money on hints you hear from a stranger at a cocktail party, who heard from someone who is supposed to know something. Obviously, this is the sheerest form of folly. There are stock-racketeers who boost the price of stocks by spreading rumors. And some gullibles will believe anything they hear as long as it's told in a whisper.

On the other hand, if someone at a cocktail party tells you to buy Gadfly, Ltd., and the price rises, and then later the same tipster urges you to go with Grasshopper Tech., and the value of its shares increases, then the *third* tip from the same source might deserve some degree of interest. Of course, you shouldn't hock the family jewels to comply with your tipster's choice, but it might be a calculated risk—*if* you can afford to speculate and lose. In a way, moderate speculating and losing can be a bargain in reverse, since it discourages you from walking into bigger booby traps in the future.

By and large, the best thing to do with tips is to check them with a broker. If your sanguine suspicions are confirmed, then go ahead and buy—maybe you have a bargain. Remember, though, it's better to miss four good tips than be hooked by one bad one.

I should add here that some of the most reputable and successful brokers rely on tips, although they call them "buying stories" or "information from reliable sources." They want investment ideas and they want them quickly and directly. They are dependent on a *few* good sources of information and follow them, sometimes without the detailed investigation usually associated with professional investment management. However, the professionals who act this quickly know from experience what sources are reliable.

Tips in their various forms have a striking similarity to "the wrong kind" of woman. Often they are publicly deplored and privately enjoyed. But there's one overwhelming reason why bargain-hunting in Wall Street requires enormous caution: You always buy a bargain from somebody who thinks it isn't one. And he's often in the best position to know.

chapter ten

The Wall Street Family

Some time ago, near Commerce, Oklahoma, twelve curious visitors descended into the main shaft of a flourishing zinc mine. They inspected every yard of tunnel and track. They asked about the efficiency of the equipment and the productivity of the labor force. After their return to the surface they reviewed assay reports and examined the company's books. The visitors were not professional metallurgists, geologists, or students from a school of mining. All in the inquisitive group were women, members of a small investment club in Kansas City. Their policy: Examine the facilities of a company firsthand before investing in it. This practice allowed them to prosper. Each member invested $10 per month for 6 years, and after the 6 years had passed, the ladies had earned enough on their investments to enable them to take a prolonged vacation.

The foregoing is a dramatic sample of the expanding interest women take in Wall Street. The statistics are as surprising as they are impressive. According to the New York Stock Exchange today approximately 10,000,000 adult women own over $100,000,000,-000 in shares of publicly held corporations. They *outnumber* male shareholders and dominate the stockholder's list of many of the nation's industrial giants.

At one time a woman's stockownership was generally limited either to what she inherited or what securities her husband had put in her name for tax purposes. But this is no longer the case. A 1965 New York Stock Exchange survey revealed that only 18 percent of the female stockholders received their first shares as gifts or through inheritance. Moreover, the same investment education courses for women that attracted only a handful of mildly interested housewives a few years ago now can pack hotel ballrooms.

The mounting female interest in finance reflects their progress within the economic community. Fifteen million married women earn a pay check today—more than twice as many as in the late forties. During 1967, for example, women have gone to work producing steel, building auto parts in Chicago, loading post office vans, delivering mail, welding and operating metal stamping machines in Fort Worth, driving cabs, and pumping gas. And when the old church bell rings out every evening in Ipswich, Massachusetts, the bell-ringer is a woman, for the first time in 333 years.

Some of the most dramatic female inroads have been made in the field of finance. As I have pointed out, this is a field that was until recently a male bastion. The single sex idea sufficed and, as Ben Franklin noted, money begat money, so there was no need for women in the process. But Eve is now entering the land of Adam in increasing numbers, and some have ascended to the loftiest levels. Julia Montgomery Walsh of Washington, D.C., is a good example. She has a husband and eleven children and is a senior partner in the investment firm of Ferris & Co. Her salary is said to be $200,000 a year. Mary Whelton handles from $2,000,000 to $10,000,000 worth of stocks every day as one of three traders at Boston's Massachusetts Trust, one of the nation's largest mutual funds. Of course, there is the aforementioned Muriel Siebert, who holds a seat on the New York Stock Exchange. Though the first woman to buy one, she has not taken advantage of her privilege to trade on the floor of the exchange. One reason perhaps is that the floor, with 1,366 men, has no powder room.*

HELP WANTED: FEMALE

Wall Street's recent explosive growth has made possible numerous employment opportunities for women. Parenthetically, it should be noted that the best Wall Street opportunities are not always in Wall Street. A brokerage house in your home town might be a more fertile field. The revolution in electronic communications, air travel, and branch office communications has fostered Wall Streets in all parts of the country.

At this writing, the majority of women in the securities industry hold office positions as secretaries, stenographers, typists, bookkeeping machine operators, and key-punch operators. Nevertheless,

---

* On occasion, she may go to the floor and execute a large order or a "cross," which is to buy and sell the same stock for different institutions.

women, with or without college degrees, hold supervisory and technical positions as well. Research departments now employ women security analysts, statisticians, and correspondents. Furthermore, with the introduction of larger computer centers, the data-processing departments now seek women college graduates trained as programmers.

LARGE OR SMALL FIRMS

It is important to decide whether you wish to apply for a job at a small or large firm. There are important differences.

Small firms tend to hire fewer inexperienced personnel, especially in clerical positions. A chief reason for this is their inability to conduct extensive formal training programs. But in a small firm you are likely to know everyone; the relations between management and employees are direct. And since the small firm maintains a smaller staff, your duties are likely to be varied. You may substitute in any of a dozen jobs in an emergency.

Working in a large firm, you are likely to perform only one function or a part of a function unless you show special ability to grow into more responsible positions. There are no hard and fast rules, of course, but the chances are that fringe benefits and specialized training opportunities will be superior in large firms. On the other hand, employment in a small firm probably will give you a broader experience in many aspects of the brokerage business, which could also pay off later in your career.

THE LADY BROKER

More and more women are becoming brokers. And there are no longer any raised eyebrows on learning that another woman has been made a partner in a securities firm.

Probably one third of all people employed by member firms of the New York Stock Exchange are brokers. In general, the initial requirement for a broker is adequate schooling, and many firms demand additional on-the-job training. Most large firms conduct their own training. Many small firms, unable to support a continuous program on a full scale, use outside facilities; some firms combine both methods. The length and scope of the training programs depend on the firm and the job. Programs to train brokers in member firms of the New York Stock Exchange range from six months to two years. Trainees are paid a salary while learning.

Some firms, both large and small, encourage employees to do independent study in the securities field by paying part or all of the cost of tuition in schools and colleges. The majority of such programs are on a strictly voluntary basis. It is up to the individual to take advantage of the opportunity.

Schools and colleges in many localities offer courses in finance and investing. For instance, broker trainee programs recommended by the New York Stock Exchange are given in colleges in eight large cities in the United States: Boston, Chicago, Los Angeles, Miami, New York, Philadelphia, St. Louis, and San Francisco. Private consulting and training firms have recently entered the field. Trade and management associations conduct conferences and workshops for the securities industry, as does the New York Institute of Finance.

Let us assume Mrs. A. is a broker in a member firm of the New York Stock Exchange. She grew up in Boston, attended public schools, and graduated from a liberal arts college. Though she majored in history in college, she became interested in a finance course which she took as an elective. After graduation she applied for employment with Smith & Smith, a member firm. Following a series of tests and interviews she was hired with the knowledge that she would have to be registered with the New York Stock Exchange before becoming a securities broker. This meant she had to be trained on the job for six months, attend courses in finance, and pass a test on security analysis, brokerage procedures, and the applicable regulations of the Exchange and of the government. The Exchange investigated her background as well before it approved her as a registered representative.

A DAY IN THE LIFE

Of course, there is no such thing as an average day for a broker. It is as varied, as simple, and as complex as the individual and as the world around her. Nevertheless, there are certain basic functions common to every broker. Since the market opens at ten o'clock, they begin by reading the news—especially the financial news— at breakfast. After arriving at the office, Mrs. A. surveys reports and checks her accounts. The phones begin their insistent ring. A few minutes before the market opens the Dow Jones news ticker announces a merger between Wilde and Woolsey Corporations.

Several of her clients hold blocks of Wilde stock. Mrs. A. calls the research department to get an opinion. The research specialist concludes that the merger would be beneficial to Wilde. Mrs. A. evaluates the opinion of the research specialist, jots down figures on a pad, mulls the possibilities, and then comes to a conclusion based on her long-term study of Wilde. She calls her clients and passes on the information as well as the analysis. One client decides to buy another 100 shares of Wilde.

In the meantime Mrs. A. continues watching the ticker, checking the news tape, and answering the phone. Another client calls later in the day and wants to sell Woolsey. She suggests that the merger and profits outlook, as well as the condition of the market in general, justifies holding the stock. However, the client tells her that he needs the money to pay an emergency medical expense; hence the stock is sold.

After the close of the market at three thirty P.M., Mrs. A. may receive buy and sell orders for the following day. She reviews her accounts and spends some time in studying various reports issued by her firm's research department. In addition, she may call friends in the Street, executives, public relations advisors, or anyone else who might provide valuable information.

Of course, not all days are crowded, exciting, gratifying, and profitable. Many of them can be dull, dreary, and frustrating, making you wish you had chosen some other profession. Brokers, male and female, are human, and all of them are subject to the constantly changing human conditions.

I believe that flexibility is a particular attribute of brokers. They must be able to detect a change of viewpoint whenever one occurs to revise their opinions in the light of changing conditions, which often change overnight. A sudden dramatic news event anywhere in the world can result in drastic economic changes. The classic illustration happened in the summer of 1929, when the stock market was booming. In Austria the Credit - Anstalt Bank failed. Incredibly enough, it started a chain of events which led to the market crash of that year. Moreover, a revision of the tax law on depreciation allowances, for example, may suddenly add new market appeal to a business that has been overlooked. A government anti-trust action may cast a gloomy new light on a whole industry.

Brokers' stock choices may not always be right, but they should be thorough. Their thoroughness is one of the best safeguards to a happy investment experience—meaning a profitable one.

THE SECURITY ANALYST

More and more women are becoming analysts. As previously noted, Mrs. A., as a broker, not only relies on her own sources and resources, but also on the research department of her firm or on an independent investment advisory service.

To put it simply, the security analyst's job is to study industries and companies and to form opinions about their future prospects as investments. In a way a company is a vessel in motion, and the stock market is a constantly changing shoreline. Between the two, imagine a fog of greater or lesser density. Also, it would be well to keep in mind that other vessels (competing companies) are in the area.

How can the analyst pierce the fog and determine the direction of the vessel? Among his various methods are communication with executives of the company and knowledge of the changing character of the company, its product and prospects, its planning and performance, and the actions of its competitors, as well as a knowledge of the general economic environment.

Our lady analyst had known that the Wilde and Woolsey merger was in the wind, and she had studied its probable effects. When the brokers in her firm called her, she had her opinion well documented with facts.

After the Wilde and Woolsey merger announcement she concentrated on an analysis of the Woolsey Company. She had gathered past annual and quarterly reports from her firm's library and had obtained further information by visiting the Woolsey plant the week before. A company officer had given her a tour of the plant and answered her many questions about earnings, research projects, expansion plans, management, and a host of other subjects.

A meeting of her firm's partners had been called for eleven thirty. At the meeting she gave a progress report on her study of Woolsey. Her preliminary findings indicated that the company would be an excellent prospect for investors in long-range growth stocks. That is, Woolsey would continue to be a growing company for years to come, and its stock should rise in value. Other analysts in the department also made reports on their research. It was decided that the results of her study would be included in the next monthly brochure of investment recommendations that the firm published.

Security analysis is a desirable career—a well-paid, prestigious position. It follows that competition is keen for positions in this field. A solid educational background in economics and finance is practically a prerequisite, and advanced degrees are becoming increasingly necessary.

A report by the New York Stock Exchange has noted that "in many respects, security analysis is a scholarly career. There seems to be a high correlation between success in this field and high grades in school. It takes a man or woman who is comfortable with figures and accounting, profit and loss statements and annual reports. It requires a self-disciplined person who knows the meaning of meeting a deadline. The ability to express oneself in good, concise English—written and oral—is important. An analyst should also maintain an interest in public affairs and government, as developments in these areas affect the stock market."

The foregoing neglects to include what I consider an analyst's prime asset, creative ability, the ability to see beyond the figures and to project in terms of imagination the possibilities of a particular company or a single product. Incidentally, as our industrial apparatus becomes more complex, more analysts tend to specialize in a single industry, or in a part of it.

Miss Muriel Siebert, the previously mentioned NYSE member, was once asked to explain her success as a broker-analyst.

"Actually," she replied, "I've had a lot of plain good luck. I started out as a research trainee at Bache in 1954, and there I covered five industries including aviation and investment companies.

What probably eventually made me was the institutions. I had got to know a lot of people at the analysts' meetings, including the portfolio managers, and they came to rely on me as an expert on certain stocks. After all, no institution with two hundred stocks can follow all of them the way I do. I actually follow three or four on the ticker every day, watch for current developments, and read all the literature on them that's available. I've never tried to cover the waterfront. That is, I've simply tried to have two or three winners of institutional acceptability going for me at any one time, and to add one or two new stocks a year."

How do you get a job? Your school's placement office or library can provide you with an appropriate directory. Once you have decided on several prospective employers, you can contact them or write a letter of application. You should know what you want in a job. Get to know a bit about the firm, its activities, and its organization. Most firms have brochures about themselves and their personnel policies.

The NYSE has compiled a list of jobs available to women:

1. *Accountant:*
   Training not provided in basic skills of the job.
   Training in accounting required.
   Duties: Determines bookkeeping policies and prepares financial statements.

2. *Bookkeeper:*
   Training not provided in basic skills of the job.
   Training in bookkeeping required.
   Duties: Records transactions in accordance with accountancy policies.

3. *Correspondent or portfolio analyst:*
   Training provided.
   College required, plus a basic knowledge of security analysis.
   Duties: Prepares letters to investors about their securities holdings, giving recommendations about specific stocks and bonds and

reasons for suggested changes in holdings. Correspondents work under supervision of security analysts.

4. *Programer:*
   Training not provided.
   College education required (mathematics background).
   Duties: Studies clerical operations being done by hand and figures out how they can be done by data-processing machines. This involves creating a flow-system of cards and forms which, when processed by machine, will achieve the same results as when done by hand.

5. *Key-punch operator:*
   Training not provided.
   High school education required.
   Duties: Operates a key-punch machine (similar to a typewriter) which transfers information onto cards by punching holes in the cards.

6. *Figuration clerk:*
   Training provided.
   High school education required.
   Duties: Calculates the total price of securities being bought or sold, the taxes, and the amount of commission to be charged.

7. *Receive and deliver clerk:*
   Training provided.
   High school education required.
   Duties: Checks stock and bond certificates which have been bought for clients to see that they are acceptable for transfer of ownership. Checks for accuracy number of shares and price paid and does the same for certificates which have been sold for clients and which are being delivered to the buyers.

8. *Secretary:*

No training provided.

High school education required, with secretarial skills. Business or secretarial school training is an asset.

Duties: Answers the telephone, takes dictation, types letters, files, and performs other secretarial-type duties.

9. *Statistician:*

Some training provided.

College education preferred, but not essential; knowledge of statistics required.

Duties: Prepares statistical analysis of company reports and other data for use by security analysts, brokers, and clients.

10. *Teletype operator:*

Training sometimes provided.

High school education required.

Duties: Receives and sends orders and messages between brokerage offices, using teletype machine. The job is sometimes combined with the job of order clerk in a small firm or a small branch office.

11. *Transfer clerk:*

Training provided.

High school education required.

Duties: Prepares the necessary documents to effect a change in ownership of stocks and bond certificates for the transfer agent of the corporation whose stock is involved.

As far as pay scales are concerned, the securities industry competes for the same people as do banks, insurance companies, manufacturing firms, department stores, and other businesses which hire large numbers of "white collar" workers. It is very difficult for an employer in any community to offer salaries, and fringe benefits, that are not competitive.

Of course, salaries will vary from firm to firm, city to city, and state to state. To get an idea of what you might expect to earn, check newspaper want ads. They are the best indicator of wage scales. The local Chamber of Commerce may also have local wage studies. Although the practice is not universal, many securities firms follow the practice of year-end profit sharing or bonuses. The initial salary is not important; it is what you do later to make yourself essential.

In addition, Wall Street offers some unique fringe benefits. By keeping her ears open, a secretary or typist can pick up investment information that might result in garnering more income than she can derive from typing and secretarying.

I once asked a blue-eyed temptress why she decided to work in Wall Street. Her reply was prompt, incisive, and feminine: "Wall Street is a great place for husband-hunting."

chapter eleven

Get Richer Quicker Hints

Brokers are frequently asked: "How much money should you have before you invest?"

The response cannot be general, but individual. It depends on age, income, emotions, and objectives. The answer to that question must be custom-tailored for you by your investment counselor.

Too many people rush into the market motivated by the question of "How much can I win?" To repeat it would be better if they moved into the market with another query in back of their minds: "How much can I afford to lose?"

What is the purpose of your investment? To fight inflation? To secure profits for spending? Spending for what? Luxuries? Necessities? Or do you go into the stock market to get richer and richer and richer and richer? Do you speculate because you enjoy the action? Or because you have some definite objectives? These questions—and many more—should be answered before setting up an investment program. Sketch your objectives and alternatives, even if they are nebulous. Then you can debate the pros and cons, the risks and the potentials, the dream and the reality.

In any case, it may be downright reckless to commit your entire reservoir of liquid financial resources to the stock market. You should always have sufficient cash in the bank for emergency purposes. Moreover, having cash on hand enables you to buy securities during the market's inevitable downswings. Liquidity is a major factor in a successful investment program. The size of this emergency fund should be determined by your age, number of your dependents, your standard of living, and your personal predilections. Though individual needs vary, a good rule of thumb is to have a reserve of from three to six months' income.

Since repetition has an educational impact, we would like to repeat the a-b-c of stock investment goals:

    a. Safety of principal
    b. Liberal income
    c. Growth

139

"Safety of principal" is for the investor whose primary concern is not to lose money. She might restrict her purchases to such issues as Federal bonds whose principal and interest are guaranteed by the United States Government. The emphasis is on conservation of money rather than income. Although market value and yield may fluctuate over time with such investments, their range is usually narrow. Municipals and highly rated industrials compensate for their slightly lower safety ratings by increased interest.

"Liberal income" is for the investor who wants stocks which have consistently paid good dividends and which probably will continue to do so. Here greater emphasis is placed on income than on the possibility of a substantial increase in the value of the security (capital gains). Stocks of public utility companies satisfy this requirement. When interest rates are generally high, some investors may consider bonds preferable.

"Growth" is for those primarily interested in securities that will "double their money" for them. Here relatively little emphasis is placed on income, since securities offering good growth possibilities often do not pay dividends. (Profits are retained and put back into the business to facilitate expansion.) The risk in purchasing such securities is greatest when the issues are new and untested, or when the history of earnings is negligible and the prospects for price appreciation rest squarely on the company's being a "glamor" industry. Of course, since growth-type companies are more responsive to economic and technological changes, they offer a risk of loss in conjunction with the possibilities of gain.

Therefore, you should buy stocks the way you buy shoes—they should fit your circumstances comfortably. If you're in your thirties and have above-average income, it might fit your needs to indulge in some speculation, (c) above. If you're in your sixties and your income consists solely of Social Security benefits, it might be wiser to measure yourself for (b), the securities that pay dividends, or the "good providers."

By good providers, of course, I refer to stocks that have paid quarterly dividends for thirty or forty years or more. Following are ten illustrations:

1. American Can	3. Coca-Cola
2. American Tobacco	4. Chase Manhattan Bank

5. Boston Edison
6. Texaco
7. Singer

8. Dow Chemical
9. Ingersoll-Rand
10. Corning Glass

There are two good reasons why capital appreciation is more attractive than ordinary income. The first is the tax structure which penalizes income and puts the emphasis on capital gains. The highest federal tax rate for long term capital gains is 25 percent plus surtax of 10 percent. But a married man with two children whose taxable income is between $12,000 and $14,000 pays 25 percent. Tax on ordinary income can go as high as 70 percent. A second reason is that the continuing inflationary spiral makes it more profitable to invest for capital appreciation than for traditional "income" sources.

One way or another, everybody can do something about inflation. For example, you can become a political activist. Contact your president, congressman, mayor, or councilman and voice your objections to unnecessary government expenditures and actual waste. Don't extend your vote to officials who believe all the answers are printed on dollar bills. (At this point I should debunk the popular fallacy about the stock market being enthusiastic about inflation. That just isn't true, simply because inflation tends to erode real profits and bring tight money and government controls. The market abhors the thought of controls on credit, wages, and prices.)

As a consumer, you can force adjustments in prices by prudent shopping—that is, by refusing to pay any price you consider sky-high. Prices are largely determined by supply and demand. If the demand drops, so must the prices.

Furthermore, don't be a pushover for easy-credit schemes. Borrow only when necessary and always shop and compare to be certain you are getting reasonable interest rates.

On a personal level, though, it is imperative that you own property as a hedge against inflation. This property, of course, can take many forms. The so-called perfect hedge is gold, but holding it at home or abroad is illegal. Partial hedges are commodities and commodity trading, but each is as risky as roulette. The purchase of precious metals or silver may be effective, as is the purchase of fine art. But there are drawbacks, such as no income, storage costs, and insurance. Real estate is, of course, a prime inflation edge, but it cannot always be sold quickly, and because of taxes may not produce much net income. Only common stocks give their owners the advantage of being able to sell them instantly if they need cash.

Quite simply, you can beat inflation by buying a stock that outperforms the economy and moves up faster than the dollar deflates. The complex part consists of choosing the right stock, particularly in an industry regarded as a hedge.

Bonds, on the other hand, except for convertibles, will not help you fight inflation for the simple reason that a bondholder is not a part owner of a business. He is a creditor. Even though bond yields normally average lower than the yields of common stocks, high-quality bonds are more stable in price. Hence if you desire maximum safety and stability, your investment portfolio should contain liberal representation in bonds.

The disadvantage of having all your capital in bonds is that at maturity a bond pays the owner only the amount specified in the contract. Thus, if the purchasing power of the dollar has declined by the time the bond matures, the money you receive will not buy as much as when the original investment was made.

In other words, the best hedge against inflation is to have your money make more money for you. To depend solely on bonds or savings banks is to expose your hard-earned money to the perils of inflation. We *are* going to have some inflation in this country over the next few years, and I don't see anything better to buy than growth equities which are available at 12 to 20 times earnings.

Whether you have a diversified investment program or put all your eggs in one carefully watched basket, make periodic reviews of your portfolio. Exercising your mind keeps you in good financial shape. The one constant in the market is its ceaseless change. Moreover, there may be significant changes in *your* life which dictate a change in investment strategy.

The Wall Street Road to Ruin is strewn with investors who were hell-bent for big money and neglected to notice the red lights along the way. There are some who believe that the longer you hold a stock, the richer you will become. But it isn't time that makes you richer—it's how you use the time.

In following the day to day movements of your stock, compare its price fluctuations with those of competitor companies. If competitors are moving ahead of your company in price, reappraise your investment. A widening difference can indicate a major problem. The company may be losing the battle for markets. In the end, even if your company doesn't lose the war, you will most certainly lose money.

When to sell is as vital as what to buy. There are myriad motives in stock-selling—you may need money for a new house, or for a son's college tuition, or for a new fur coat. But the rules remain the same.

Actually, stocks should be sold with the same careful guidance utilized in buying. Get your broker's opinion and check balance sheets and all other relevant information. If you purchased a stock because the company was in the process of developing an impressive new product and then either the new product never materializes or its competitors come out with a better product, the stock should of course be sold.

One of the massive problems in selling is ego. Both brokers and investors occasionally refuse to concede that their original opinions were wrong. And so they usually go down with the sinking ship. It's one thing to have confidence in a company's future despite temporary setbacks; it is quite another to refuse stubbornly to concede an error in judgment. There are some investors who sell only stocks that show a profit and who stick with their loss stocks. This type of attitude makes disaster inevitable. If you sell the good and keep the bad, in the end your portfolio is dominated by bad stocks.

Strangely enough, deciding to take a loss can be a profitable decision. If you cut your loss in a company headed downward, you still have the opportunity to retain the capital, which in turn enables you to invest in another company that will not only recoup your loss but earn additional profits. Nobody has enough capital to buy everything. So on occasion it may be a shrewd maneuver to collect profits on one stock in order to afford to buy another stock that is brimming with profit opportunities.

A warning with regard to selling: Don't be emotional. Give your heart to the man you love but keep your head about the stocks you buy. Some investors, especially women, cling to stocks with a Juliet-like passion, completely disregarding the fundamentals. I know one lady who purchased a stock on the basis of her admiration for the lipstick the company manufactured. Her adoration continued even while the company's sales and earning deteriorated. On the other hand, being fickle and panicky and selling stock on impulse can be equally disastrous.

One of the more effective selling guides is to watch for the first sign of a decline in profit margins. In some cases, the decline might be the consequence of extraordinary expenses, such as research and development, and thus the decline would be temporary. Nevertheless, when that profit margin dips, an intensive investigation should promptly begin in an effort to determine whether the company will continue to go downhill.

It is a rare stroke of luck to buy at the low and sell at the high. Nobody but nobody knows how high a stock will fly, or how low it will plunge. When a stock has gone as high as you anticipated, or higher, it is time to sell. Skim the cream, even if the investor who buys your stock eventually enjoys the milk.

Avoiding the obvious, however, is equally vital. A Wall Street maxim says: Don't sell on strike news. Harris, Upham & Co. compiled statistics for the Dow Jones industrial average during five steel strikes.

Year	Days of Strike	DJIA During Strike
1959-60	116	plus 4 percent
1956	34	plus 3 percent
1952	52	plus 6 percent
1949	42	plus 6 percent
1946	28	plus 4 percent

There are many stockholders who have profits and refuse to sell since they would then have to pay taxes on capital gain. More often than not, they remain locked in until a declining market wipes away their taxable profits. Remember, the *only* tax advantages you can get are by holding a profit-making stock over six months (to drive it into the long-term capital gains category) or by purchasing tax free bonds. Remember too that taxes will outlive you. If you hold profitable stocks until you die, then your executors and heirs will have to worry about inheritance taxes.

The proper tax counsel can result in substantial savings for stock-holders. For example, if you're self-employed—and this definition can fit any of a number of professions: doctor, lawyer, farmer—you should look into the special tax-sheltered retirement programs available under the Keogh Act. You get *100 percent tax deduction* for the money you contribute to your plan! And you don't have to pay taxes on the earnings of your investment until you withdraw the benefits after you retire (or become disabled). Bankers and brokers have brochures on various tax problems. But it would be wiser and safer for you to consult competent professionals, meaning accountants and tax attorneys.

In this connection it should be noted that during the past few years there has been a deluge of books and magazine articles describing do-it-yourself methods of estate planning. All knowledge is helpful of course. But in the long run it would be wiser and cheaper to enlist the assistance of the aforementioned competent accountants and attorneys.

The average female investor should also be aware of the laws created to protect her against illegal activities. In 1911 Kansas adopted the first "Omnibus Securities" law to outlaw shady stocks. Over the next few years about half of the states adopted similar laws, but variations resulted in many problems for underwriters when issues were to be marketed on a nationwide basis. In 1929 the Uniform State Securities Act was approved. This is the so-called "Old Act," which has served as a basis for many states' securities laws. A new Uniform State Securities Act was approved in 1956 by the Conference of Commissioners on Uniform State Laws and the American Bar Association. At the present time all states except Delaware have securities acts. If you believe that you have been cheated or that your stockholder rights have been violated, contact the SEC and state regulatory agencies—and get a lawyer.

Patience can be rewarding. Women know some things cannot be hurried. It takes nine months to produce a baby. Sometimes it takes longer for a stock to come to life. Avoid following the rampaging mob. You may believe a stock is worth buying, but after consulting your broker, you decide to wait and see. While you wait the stock may increase in price, but there is no reason for regrets. Generally, on mental bets you pick as many losers as winners, although you tend to remember only the winners. The stock-I-shoulda-bought is a classic Wall Street lament. But actually there are literally thousands of rising stocks, and if you miss one, another will soon come along. In the end, the preservation of capital is all-important, and the only time you have really lost is when you lose your capital.

Be skeptical. Actually, genuine inside information is on a par with military secrets or milady's age; that is, it is difficult to secure. The SEC has rigid regulations about privileged information. However, there are times when reliable information *is* leaked. If you are in the fortunate position of getting inside information without infringing on SEC regulations, then of course take advantage of your opportunity.

While you're being hard-nosed, remember there is no guarantee that a mutual fund will be profitable. In 1962 the SEC reported: "With respect to the performance of mutual funds, it was found that, on the average, it did not differ appreciably from what would have been achieved by an unmanaged portfolio consisting of the same proportions of common stocks, corporate bonds, government securities, and other assets as the composite fund portfolios."

That is not to say that some funds do not perform more spectacularly than others. Dreyfus, one of the major funds, enjoyed fabulous growth as a result of buying Polaroid during an early stage in the company's development. Perhaps you could have done the same by having bought the stock for yourself.

A more personal form of mutual funds, the investment clubs, are now becoming more popular among sewing circles and ladies' auxiliaries. They are usually composed of friends, neighbors, or relatives. There are now over 50,000 such clubs with a membership estimated at more than 700,000. Information on starting a club is available in the form of a kit costing $3 from the National Association of Investment Clubs, Washington Boulevard Building, Detroit, Michigan 48226.

Sometimes being a successful investor consists of keeping your eyes open and recognizing the obvious. For example, during the early 1960's anyone who walked or drove through our urban centers could see blocks and blocks of substandard housing. This fact, coupled with the fact of our population increase, brought many people to the conclusion that stocks involved in housing or related to that industry would eventually rise in value. Thus, between 1967 and 1968 numerous companies involved in real estate or building supplies had an enormous boom. Some of them doubled, tripled, and quadrupled in price during that period.

One way to discover a specific growth company is to spot relative earnings increases. Look for shortage areas, low labor cost companies, or companies benefiting from surges in segments of the economy, such as consumer spending, capital goods, or changing money rates.

Lastly, keep your securities in a safe deposit box or a locked metallic box. A duplicate list of the securities should be prepared (one to remain in the box) showing the number of each security, the amount, the name, the maturity date, and the rate and dates of income payments. Many brokerages will hold the stock certificates for you. Oh, yes—keep the buy and sell slips as well as the monthly statements from your brokerage in a safe place. They are essential for tax purposes.

COMPANIES THAT HAVE NEVER SHOWN A LOSS

	Date Incorporated		Date Incorporated
Abbott Laboratories	1900	Campbell Soup	1922
American Can	1901	Chesebrough-Pond's	1880
American Electric Power	1906	C. I. T. Financial	1924
American Home Products	1926	Coca-Cola Co.	1919
American Natural Gas	1901	Colgate-Palmolive	1923
American Tel. & Tel.	1880	Commonwealth Edison	1913
American Tobacco	1904	Continental Can	1913
Beatrice Foods	1924	Corn Products	1906
Bell & Howell	1907	Corning Glass Works	1875
Beneficial Finance	1929	Detroit Edison	1903
Boise Cascade	1931	Diamond International	1881
Borden Inc.	1899	Duke Power	1917
Bristol-Myers	1933	Dupont	1903
Burroughs Corp.	1905	Eastman Kodak	1901

El Paso Natural Gas	1928	National Dairy Products	1923
Family Finance	1927	National Lead	1891
Federated Dept. Stores	1929	National Steel	1929
General Acceptance	1933	New England Tel. & Tel.	1883
General Am.		Outboard Marine	1936
Transportation	1916	Pacific Gas & Electric	1905
General Electric	1892	Pacific Lighting	1907
General Foods	1922	Parke Davis	1875
General Mills	1928	Pet Inc.	1925
General Tel. & Electronics	1935	Pfizer (Chas.) & Co.	1900
Gillette Co.	1917	Philip Morris	1919
Hercules Inc.	1912	Procter & Gamble	1890
Hershey Foods	1927	Public Serv. Elec. &	
Household Finance	1925	Gas	1903
Idaho Power	1915	Reynolds Tobacco	1899
Int'l Business Machines	1911	Safeway Stores	1926
Johns-Manville	1912	Southern Calif. Edison	1909
Kresge (S. S.)	1912	Standard Brands	1929
Lily-Tulip Cup	1929	Standard Oil of Calif.	1911
Lorillard (P.)	1911	Standard Oil Co. (N.J.)	1882
Macy (R.H.)	1919	Sterling Drug	1901
May Dept. Stores	1910	Union Carbide	1917
Merck & Co.	1934	Union Oil of California	1890
National Biscuit	1898	U.S. Gypsum	1901

chapter twelve

Just Between Us Analysts

I write periodic confidential reports for high-level executives at Hayden-Stone. Here's one I wrote during July, 1968. Naturally, it's sort of a stream-of-consciousness form of writing, but it's also the best way to provide facts for the informed investor.

This year the gross national product will probably be up 7½ percent to 8 percent. The Federal Reserve Bank indicators should be up 4½ percent including an increase of 4 percent in prices. Consumers have finally decided to spend more money; hence summer has arrived. Research and defense expenditures are likely to rise more and will probably level out later. A tax increase is likely, which is psychological, and we have to look to Wilbur Mills, who is either a Joan of Arkansas or a tough poker player. The balance of payments is in bad repair, and the trade balance has been getting worse, although I think it will improve: the rate of growth this year may be smaller, and the rate of imports is expected to be less. Exports are likely to increase. But it may be a long, long road to Tipperary, to Rangoon, or wherever it is going to be for the peace conference.

Inflation continues at a rate of about a 4 percent, but I do not believe we are going to have a 1966 money crunch this year if the Federal Reserve Bank doesn't want it. They, like many others, learn not to repeat old mistakes, but are always subject to making new ones. I think there is a fairly good chance that the money picture may be easier later this year, but that is just a guess. Corporate pre-tax income this year could very well be up by 10 percent, but it is difficult to say what it will be after taxes. It will be a mixed industry pattern of earnings this year, and we may have to be more flexible on the market now than ever before. The market is like a dog on a leash—it depends on its length for profits and for its pull on money supply, and it depends on its strength for purchasing power and current rate of savings. The public attitudes can carry the market a long way.

An eventual tax increase and a cut in federal expenditures may not be bullish for the economy, but it would be bullish on the dollar in the long run and bullish on our way of life. We could then be more optimistic for a greater recovery. Can we afford to wait? Prudent investors are cautious now, but the more courageous ones usually do not end up with holes in their shoes and shiny pants. Over the years high-grade common stocks have been interesting, challenging stocks that have proven themselves to be profitable investments, and I like these under any foreseeable economic environment. I don't know of a better way to protect myself against the likelihood of further erosion of the buying power of the dollar. Emotionalism can very well prevail for a long time, prompting the panic buying which is a typical American investor phenomenon. I feel that the money managers who play the waiting game will come late to the feast if they don't choose to begin looking and making some major commitments now. Anybody can appreciate the feeling of ebullience that seized investors on the last night of March and for weeks thereafter when President Johnson got the Vietnamese to talk about talking. When the time comes to discuss actual issues, if not before, we will begin to realize that the country is or may be on its way to experiencing the first major failure in global politics. For months to come a great deal may rest on psychological reactions. It's another change in the national posture: the Administration has responded to the popular wish for peace. We will see if we want it on Hanoi's terms. The bird of Wall Street is obviously the dove and not the hawk. As Bernard Baruch once said, "A successful speculator or investor looks into the future and acts before it occurs."

After LBJ's startling announcement on March 31, we have had the most exciting and explosive days in the history of the stock market, and I think we will have more of the same. The name of the game is still the same: Vietnam, high interest rates, a likely increase in taxes, an exciting Presidential race looming up, and talk-talk-talk-talk peace negotiations. Some day peace will come, and peace is bullish on business and life. We are now a war-oriented economy with housing, automobiles, leisure time, and easier money.*

But for some time we may very well experience "the worst

* lower interest rates

of war and the worst of peace" at the same time. Interestingly enough, however, only about 9 percent of our total output is going into the war effort as against 41 percent at the peak of World War II and 13 percent at the height of the Korean War. So peace may not be a problem. And when and if peace comes, the sums to be spent on housing, education, cities, poverty programs, and other non-defense purposes, plus the Cold War, will be at record levels.

When I come back from abroad, I am confident that I will feel more optimistic about the U. S. A. Europe and other areas have political problems too, perhaps more serious than ours (with regard to race, gold, and the Hammer and Sickle). I think the American challenge is to invest only in American stocks. I think that compared to European companies we have absolute superiority in management, research, and market analysis. Germany seems to be coming up fast, but France is depressed. Ours is the only market for real trading and for substantial investments. The favorite stocks are the high technological ones, and never mind the P-E ratios. Many don't look at the old companies and yields any more; they may later. We have no choice. We have to "live" with the bomb, debt, money, and English pound, the franc, Vietnam, the Viet Cong, Red China and the Middle East.

There was an old saying, "When Wall Street sneezes, London catches a cold." No longer does this seem to be true. In 1967, when the DJ fell below 900 and Wall Street had the worst drop in 2½ years, London had the highest closing in 17 months, and this during a period of austerity.

Each year has its problem. We have lived with such problems as:

        1948—Berlin crisis
        1949—Nationalists overthrown in China
        1950—Korea
        1951—Iran oil crisis; China seizes Tibet
        1952—Iran oil crisis; Egyptian revolution
        1953—French-Indo-China crisis
        1954—Dien Bien Phu
        1955—Quemoy and Matsu crisis
        1956—Suez, Cyprus, Algeria
        1957—War in Middle East
        1958—Lebanon crisis—atomic threats

1959—Cuban revolution
1960—U-2 incident; Civil War in Congo
1961—Berlin Wall
1962—Cuban Missile crisis
1963—JFK killed
1964—Tonkin Bay
1965—Vietnam escalation
1966—Bank squeeze
1967—Arab-Israeli War

The United States economy grows each year; it has learned to live with danger. And this is not a 1962, 1932, or 1909, to say nothing of a 1929. But remember this—this is a year of political expediency.

Pollution control promises to make headway. In Michigan, for example, the state grants tax exemptions to firms installing equipment for controls. New equipment is exempt from property, sales, and use taxes. Over 250 Michigan firms have received tax exemptions for installing equipment to reduce air pollution. Most firms are in the southern half of the state, which is the most heavily industrialized. Water pollution control starts this year with similar tax exemptions. It is estimated that over 100 firms have applied for exemptions for control equipment. It is generally conceded that the Great Lakes Area, with Michigan in a central position, is a major hazard area, and that it will take years to clean up the lakes.

It is always a trick to find stocks that will outperform the market, because their companies must outperform economy. One of the most difficult things in this business is to try to convince institutions and individuals to buy stocks in a declining market. This is probably one of the times when you should find a situation to recommend, because institutions and individuals want to keep a certain percentage of their assets in cash—at certain times, that is. You might even say that no matter how many times the name of the game changes, the game itself remains the same. When I pick a stock, I hope it will be one that is going to be good in time, if not right away.

It is difficult to make projections on the short term, but certainly it is much easier to predict the long term. The 21st century is only 32 years away. Meanwhile, we are involved with a question of survival. We have a good life, we are still rich, and we are technologically advanced. Life is easy, but death is easy too. We should be a happy people, but we are not happy or complacent. We have problems with labor, traffic, balance of payments, money rates, taxes, Vietnam, the pound, the dollar, the franc, and public opinion, in various countries. The computers are coming into the picture more and more; they may even have the right to deny us or to approve us. Many of us are IBMized on everything. There is a great deal of cruelty, violence, and crime, as well as a decline in religion and sentiment.

We are all charged with taking care of portfolios over which we have varying degrees of responsibility. If we are no good in handling our own, what place do we have in assuming responsibility for others? When it comes to those others, we usually get the shakes (the goldfish bowl psychology) and end up by *not* doing unto others what we would do for ourselves. This ambivalence in the handling of investments means we have to run two types of portfolios in our minds, do two types of thinking and, so to speak, keep two mental sets of books and investment policies. I think it's a mistake to recommend any equity for another which you would not buy for yourself, with due allowance for tax considerations, size, objectives, and the time factor. For example, I might be interested personally in a three- to five-year time equation, whereas for clients this limit might properly—and necessarily—be stretched anywhere from ten years to life, especially if they were insurance companies, institutions, or the proverbially well-provided-for grandchildren.

In these days of the scientist, the economist, and the statistician, the tendency in investments is to overcomplicate the subject and to accumulate an excessive amount of information—facts piled on facts and details piled on details—to take the place of thought, experience, courage, and judgment. As an investor, you are deluged by brokers and investment services and all sorts of information centers which can only offer *daily* facts and figures and rumors and alarms. Obviously, they cannot decide for the owner as they do not know his frame of reference, and what is one man's meat may be another's poison. Hence a great deal of unmilled ore is shipped around, instead of refined metal. If the investor or the investment manager wants to get snowed under with reading all this stuff—including the various letters from Washington, the pseudo-confidential international news bulletins, and the technical magazines of government and trade compilation—then the job becomes quite hopeless. A certain amount of reading and inspection is necessary on various fronts, but this should be rigorously controlled, as there is no substitute for thought, no serum for courage, and no IBM for judgment.

Perhaps my approach today is somewhat sobering when we remember Chesterton's warning. He wrote that when wise men stand up and talk about coming events, humanity sits in the audience, nodding assent and saying, "Isn't it remarkable what these people know and how clever they are." Then humanity buries its wise men and does just the opposite of what the prophets predict.

"When the cock in the barnyard crows, the weather will change, or stay steady as she goes."

When the radio announcer declares on Saturday that Sunday's weather will be fine, not everyone is delighted. Most are pleased at the prospect of a sunny weekend, of course, but there are those gloomy souls who think that the weather man is about as reliable a prophet as a barn fowl.

Foreseeing the unforeseeable, what if some of the things that could happen actually did happen? What kind of world would we have if the "low probability" future actually came to pass?

At 5:13 a.m. on April 18, 1868, a cow was standing somewhere between the main farm and the milking shed on the old Schaffer Ranch in California, minding her own business. Suddenly the earth shook, the skies trembled, and when it was all over, there was nothing showing of the cow above ground but a bit of her tail sticking up! Huge outside forces—constructive and destructive—enter and change configurations. Be alert to upheavals! There are going to be a lot of new things coming around in the next few years, and no one knows what new technologies will be discovered. No doubt we will have more reliable weather forecasts, and perhaps regional weather control. Maybe we will be able to translate languages by computers. Maybe we will have a blanket immunization against infectious diseases. Maybe we will be able to produce primitive artificial life or economically produce synthetic protein foods.

There is an old saying or an old cliché about someone being the right man at the right place at the right time. I am sure that has been used to describe other people in other circumstances. In most cases it has been misused, but being asked to capsulize the market and special situations in a few minutes is very intriguing. I feel that I am somewhat of a student of price movements but certainly not a technician.

Who makes money in stocks? With rare exceptions the people who have become wealthy through stock ownership bought well-managed young companies operating in growth areas and refused to sell as long as the outlook remained favorable. This is investing! It is not involved with the random fluctuations of the market. Consider what $10,000 invested in the following companies ten years ago would be worth today:

> Dr. Pepper—$102,000
> Baxter Laboratories—$212,000
> Delta Airlines—$196,000
> Avon Products—$190,000
> Xerox—$744,000

Even in the last five years an investment in Avnet, Occidental, or Polaroid, would have paid off many times.

chapter thirteen

Growth Stocks of the Future

The Rand Corporation, one of the nation's prominent think tanks, has probed the future and pinpointed probable dates for a wide range of social and technological breakthroughs. Accordingly, the pinpoints sketch the stock market of the future.

SCIENTIFIC BREAKTHROUGHS

(Predicted Median Dates)

Economically useful desalination of sea water............ 1970
Effective fertility control by oral contraceptive or other simple and inexpensive means...................... 1970
Development of new synthetic materials for ultralight construction.. 1971
Automated language translators................................. 1972
New organs through transplanting or prothesis........... 1973
Reliable weather forecasts... 1975
Operation of a central data storage with access for general or specialized information retrieval........... 1978
Reformation of physical theory and simplifying particle theory.. 1980
Implanted artificial organs made of plastic and electronic components... 1982
Widespread and socially widely accepted use of nonnarcotic drugs (other than alcohol) to produce specific changes in personality characteristics........ 1983
Stimulated emission ("lasers") in X and Gamma ray spectrum region... 1985
Controlled thermo-nuclear power............................... 1986
Creation of a primitive form of artificial life (at least in the form of self-replicating molecules)....... 1988
Economically useful exploitation of the ocean bottom through mining, other than off-shore oil... 1989
Feasibility of limited weather control, in the sense of affecting regional weather at acceptable cost.... 1990
Economic feasibility of commercial generation of synthetic protein for food...................................... 1990
Increase in the relative number of psychotic cases amenable to physical or chemical therapy............. 1991
Biochemical general immunization against bacterial and viral diseases.. 1993
Feasibility (not necessarily acceptance) of chemical control over some hereditary defects by modification of genes through molecular engineering...... 1999
Economically useful exploitation of the ocean through farming, with the effect of producing at least 20% of the world's food............................ 2000
Biochemicals to stimulate new organ growth.............. 2008
Feasibility of using drugs to raise the level of intelligence (other than as dietary supplements)...... 2012
Chemical control of the aging process, permitting extension of life span by 50 years.............. 2050 or never
Breeding of intelligent animals (apes, etc.) for lowgrade labor... 2050 or never
Economic feasibility of commercial manufacture of many chemical elements from subatomic building blocks............................... after 2050 or never

Control of gravity through some form of modification of the gravitational field............. after 2050 or never
Feasibility of education by direct information recording on the brain......................... after 2050 or never
Use of telepathy and ESP in communications
.... after 2050 or never

AUTOMATION

Increase by a factor of 10 in capital investment in computers used for automated process control.. 1973
Air traffic control—positive and predictive track on all aircraft.. 1974
Direct link from stores to banks to check credit and to record transactions... 1974
Widespread use of simple teaching machines............... 1974
Automation of office work and services leading to displacement of 25% of current work force _........ 1975
Education becoming a respectable leisure pastime...... 1975
Widespread use of sophisticated teaching machines.... 1975
Automatic libraries, finding, reproducing copy........... 1976
Automated looking up of legal information................ 1978
Automatic language translator—correct grammar 1978
Automated rapid transit... 1978
Widespread use of automatic decision making at mgt. level for industry and nat'l. planning............. 1978
Electronic prothesis (radar for the blind, servomechanical limbs, etc.).. 1985
Automated interpretation of medical symptoms........ 1985
Construction on a production line of computers with motivation by "education"............................ 1986
Widespread use of robot services, for refuse pickup house slaves, sewer inspectors, etc...................... 1987
Widespread use of computers in tax collection, with access to all business records—automatic single tax deductions.. 1988
Availability of a machine which comprehends standard IQ tests and scores above 150 (where "comprehends" is to be interpreted behavioristically as the ability to respond to questions printed in "English" and possibly with diagrams...................................... 1990
Evolution of a universal language from automated communication.. 2000
Automated voting, in the sense of legislating through automated plebiscite................................. 2000
Automated highways and adaptive autopilots............. 2003
Remote facsimile newspapers and magazines, printed in home... 2005
Man-machine symbiosis, enabling man to extend his intelligence by direct electromechanical interaction between brain and a computing machine.... 2010

International agreements which guarantee certain economic minims to world population through high production from automation............ 2050 or never

Centralized (possibly random) wire tapping................ never

WEAPON SYSTEMS

Extensive use of devices which persuade without killing (water cannons, tear gas, etc.)...................... 1967

Miniature improved sensors and transmitters for snooping, reconnaissance, arms control................. 1967

Rapid mobility of men and light weapons to any point on earth for police action............................ 1968

Incapacitating chemical agents................................. 1969

Use of lasers for radar-type range sensors illuminators, communications................................. 1969

Incapacitating biological agents................................ 1969

Cheap, light-weight rocket-type personnel armament (silent, plastic, match-lit projectiles, capable of single or gang-firing)............................. 1969

Lethal biological agents................................. 1969

Perishable counter-insurgent arms........................... 1970

Orbiting space reconnaissance station...................... 1972

Advanced techniques of propaganda, thought control, opinion manipulation.............................. 1972

Accurate intelligence correlation with computer......... 1972

Effective anti-submarine capability, at least against contemporary submarines...................................... 1974

Longer endurance aircraft, perhaps nuclear-powered, for logistic supply or bombardment....... 1974

Biological agents destroying the will to resist.............. 1975

Penetrating nuclear weapons for deep cratering.......... 1975

Automated tactical capability (battlefield computers, robot sentries, TV surveillance.................. 1975

Effective terminal defense by ground-launched anti-missiles... 1975

ICBM's with other than nuclear warheads (such as snipers)... 1976

Rapidly mobile public works and logistics units for war recovery and refugee support........................ 1980

Directed energy weapons (electro-magnetic radiation, particle beams, lasers)................................. 1979

Massive civilian defense and post-war recovery plan... 1979

Weather manipulation (for military purposes)............ 1990

Effective terminal defense by air-launched anti-missiles... 1989

Large orbiting satellite weapons for blackmail............ 1994

Domesticated porpoises or dolphins for anti-submarine reconnaissance... never

Mass hypnotic recruitment of forces from enemy population... never

Mindreading.. never

SPACE PROGRESS

Increased use of near-earth satellites for weather prediction and control... 1967

Unmanned inspection and capability for destruction of satellites.. 1967

U.S. manned lunar fly-by... 1970

Manned lunar landing and return................................ 1970

Rescue of astronauts stranded in orbit...................... 1970

Operational readiness of laser for space communications.. 1970

Manned scientific orbital station—10 men.................. 1970

Development of reusable booster launch vehicle.......... 1974

Solid core—nuclear reactor propulsion........................ 1974

Ionic propulsion (nuclear-generator powered)............ 1974

Temporary lunar base (two men, one month)............ 1974

Manned Mars and Venus fly-by.................................... 1978

Permanent base established on moon (10 men, indefinite stay)... 1982

Deep space laboratories and observatories for high vacuum, zero-g and space research......................... 1984

Manned landing on Mars and return.......................... 1985

Establishment of permanent research stations on near planets.. 1990

Commercial global ballistic transport (including boost-glide techniques)....................................... 1999

Establishment of a permanent Mars base (say, 10 men for an indefinite period)................................. 2006

Manned landing on Jupiter's moons........................... 2050

Pluto fly-by.. 2050

Inter-galactic communication.................................... 2050

Long-duration coma to permit a form of time travel... 2050 or never

Manned multi-generation mission to other solar systems... 2050 or never

Regularly scheduled commercial traffic to lunar colony... 2050 or never

Communication with extra-terrestrials.......... 2050 or never

Non-rocket space drive—anti-gravity............ 2050 or never

Manned Venus landing............................ 2050 or never

Military force on moon........................... 2050 or never

Radiation immunization (through pills or other means)... 2050 or never

What of the future? As each minute drops into the past, it becomes clearer that the wide-ranging communications and automation revolution, plus the population growth, will continue to have an enormous impact on our economy. All segments of our economic structure, every type of company—science-oriented and otherwise —will be affected.

As noted in preceding pages, the group mobility of stocks is a basic market phenomenon. Accordingly, it is as critical to choose the right group, as it is to pick the right stock. In general, the growth group comes under the headings of new materials, new methods, and new products, encompassing such diverse fields as health, education, communications, electronics, agriculture, oceanography, automation, transportation, power, and many others.

Growth industries, by and large, are powered by extensive research and development, a comparative freedom from competition, lower labor costs, and government controls.

Following are some selected illustrations:

Electronics   The wonders of space research and the resulting breakthrough developments are adding more remarkable earthbound products, ranging from electro-optics to microelectronic items involved in color television, tape recorders, and lasers.

Drugs   Wondrous weapons in the war against disease are in a state of continual proliferation. Antibiotics, steroids, antihypertensives, diuretics, cortisones, vaccines, veterinary drugs, food, and cosmetic chemicals are only a few of the products enabling people to live longer and look younger.

Chemicals   Among the unbelievables this industry has produced are synthetic fibers, fertilizers, fuel cells, various types of plastics, and liquid nitrogen for food freezing. Incredibly, most of these products were unheard of two decades ago.

Office Machines   Computers, duplicators, and copying machines are becoming more sophisticated and efficient. Few companies can exist or expand without them.

Labor Saving Machinery   In the hurry-up world of business, any instrument that can do something faster inevitably increases efficiency and enhances profitability. Today there are a hundred different tools for every one that exist ten years ago.

Petroleum Industry   Any motorist who has observed our highways or has been trapped in traffic-clogged cities is aware of the growth of this industry. Moreover, many oil companies are expanding to include the coal and nuclear fields as well as the production of fertilizers.

Electric Utilities   More people mean more homes, more heat, more light, and more appliances. In addition, many utilities are starting to use nuclear power. According to the Federal Power Commission, electric power consumption in the United States will more than double during the next decade.

Life Insurance   Marriages and increasing population, improved health, and automation add up to a growth industry.

Recreation   The arithmetic is simple: Automation means more money plus more leisure time.

Education and Publishing   It is hardly news that we are in the midst of an education explosion. The simpler answer to the problem of additional schools and students is additional textbooks and readers.

The following 23 stocks were culled (in January, 1969) from Standard & Poor's * compilation of more than 10,000 companies. Arranged in alphabetical order, they are my candidates for unusual growth during the next 5 to 10 years.

---

* A prominent investment advisory and research service.

AMERICAN SMELTING & REFINING

INCOME STATISTICS (Million $) AND PER SHARE ($) DATA

Year Ended Dec.31	Sales & Serv. Revs.	Oper. Inc.	% Op. Inc. of Sales	Depr. Depl. & Obsol.	[1]Net Bef. Taxes	[1][2]Net Inc.	Earns.	Divs. Paid	Price Range	Price-Earns. Ratios HI LO
1968–	– – –	– – –	– – –	– – –	– – –	– – –	– – –	0.75	78-7/8–64-3/4	– – –
1967–	511.2	41.94	8.2	10.59	72.62	56.27	5.16	3.00	74-7/8–58	15–11
1966–	653.8	68.21	10.4	11.02	99.23	69.23	6.34	3.30	82-3/8–50-3/4	13– 8
1965–	614.5	81.88	13.3	11.53	83.52	52.46	4.80	2.80	76-1/4–48	16–10
1964–	608.0	73.63	12.1	13.54	68.80	41.92	3.77	2.10	56-1/2–41-5/8	15–11
1963–	544.5	51.44	9.4	13.34	47.66	29.29	2.41	1.35	44-7/8–28	19–12
1962–	488.5	48.79	10.0	13.69	45.22	27.72	2.22	1.15	32-1/2–24-3/8	15–11
1961–	470.8	34.27	7.3	12.17	32.80	21.42	1.64	1.00	36-1/8–27-3/8	22–17
1960–	475.6	42.62	9.0	11.41	38.88	23.74	1.86	0.87½	29-1/2–21	16–11
1959–	390.4	22.57	5.8	10.68	18.54	12.98	0.87	0.50	28-3/8–20-5/8	23–24
1958–	417.1	24.52	5.9	10.27	22.29	17.28	1.27	0.75	31-7/8–17-5/8	25–14

PERTINENT BALANCE SHEET STATISTICS (Million $)

Dec.31	Gross Prop.	[3]Capital Expend.	Cash Items	Inven-tories	Receiv-ables	Current Assets	Current Liabs.	Net Workg. Cap.	Cur. Ratio Assets to Liabs.	Long Term Debt	[4]($) Book Val. Com. Sh.
1967–	336.52	46.74	85.2	122.4	38.8	263.3	71.6	186.7	3.7–1	35.20	38.73
1966–	293.21	36.21	126.4	102.9	60.9	305.3	91.8	213.5	3.3–1	36.42	35.91
1965–	262.72	10.95	119.3	84.4	60.5	278.5	86.8	191.7	3.2–1	40.00	32.82
1964–	315.78	11.42	94.6	93.7	57.3	264.4	78.3	186.2	3.4–1	40.93	30.97
1963–	309.28	7.27	40.1	120.9	51.1	230.3	65.2	165.1	3.5–1	40.93	29.02
1962–	312.44	7.92	62.9	139.4	39.9	242.7	62.5	180.2	3.9–1	Nil	31.44
1961–	309.00	14.78	34.1	137.6	39.4	211.7	57.7	153.9	3.7–1	Nil	30.39
1960–	301.02	22.57	13.1	158.2	29.1	200.8	66.0	134.8	3.0–1	Nil	29.75
1959–	281.18	6.89	18.5	156.1	27.9	203.0	68.6	134.4	3.0–1	Nil	28.30
1958–	286.80	15.21	14.6	134.7	30.5	180.6	70.4	110.2	2.6–1	Nil	26.48

[1]Aft. depl. [2]Excl. equity in earns. of non-consol. subs.; also excl. spec. credits of $1.45 a sh. in 1959, $0.48 in 1960, $0.27 in 1964, $0.34 in 1965, $0.09 in 1966 & $0.69 in 1967. [3]Excl. $60 million in 1955–60 invested in Southern Peru Copper. [4]Adj. for 100% stk. divd. in 1964.

A leader in the non-ferrous metals industry, Asarco's wholly owned operations include substantial copper mines, smaller silver, zinc, and lead properties, and extensive refining operations in the United States. Other interests include 51½ percent ownership of the huge Southern Peru Copper Corporation, a 54 percent holding in Mount Isa Mines in Australia, minority interests in 2 leading United States fabricating companies, and 49 percent ownership of zinc-lead-silver operations in Mexico.

Profits are influenced by the demand for and prices of copper, zinc, silver and lead here and abroad. The earnings potential is enlarged by several new projects, by expansion of older mines, and by growth of affiliates.

BAUSCH & LOMB

[1]INCOME STATISTICS (Million $) AND PER SHARE ($) DATA

Year Ended Dec. 31	Net Sales	% Oper. Inc. of Sales	Oper. Inc.	Deprec.	Net Bef. Taxes	Net Income	-[2]Common-			Price-Earns. Ratios HI LO
							[3]Earns.	Divs. Paid	Price Range [2]Common	
1968-	-----	-----	11.99	---	-----	-----	-----	0.40	72 - 42-3/4	-----
1967-	115.29	10.4	11.99	3.74	6.78	3.82	[4]1.58	0.80	81-3/4 - 54-7/8	52-35
1966-	111.90	12.9	14.49	3.50	10.56	5.91	[4]2.70	0.75	61-1/2 - 31-5/8	23-12
1965-	88.34	11.9	10.53	2.99	7.35	4.07	2.04	0.60	35 - 20-1/2	17-10
1964-	80.73	11.0	8.89	2.88	5.53	3.05	1.53	0.60	23-3/8 - 16-5/8	15-11
1963-	73.18	9.7	7.11	2.75	3.69	1.94	0.93	0.60	18-7/8 - 13	20-14
1962-	70.48	8.9	6.26	2.44	3.20	1.61	0.76	0.60	18-1/2 · 11	24-14
1961-	68.20	9.0	6.15	2.42	3.41	1.68	0.80	0.60	24-1/4 - 17-5/8	30-22
1960-	66.09	10.2	6.74	2.09	4.34	2.31	1.18	0.57½	29-3/8 - 17-1/4	26-15
1959-	63.15	11.2	7.07	1.75	5.17	2.49	1.35	0.50	21-7/8 - 13-1/2	16-10
1958-	53.34	9.6	5.10	1.57	3.43	1.70	0.93	0.48	18 - 9-3/8	19-10

[1]PERTINENT BALANCE SHEET STATISTICS (Million $)

Dec. 31	Gross Prop.	Capital Expend.	Cash Items	Inven-tories	Receiv-ables	--Current-- Assets	Liabs.	Net Workg. Cap.	Cur. Ratio Assets to Liabs.	Long Term Debt	[2]($) Book Val. Com. Sh.
1967-	59.61	7.77	1.82	45.48	20.50	68.46	22.82	45.64	3.0-1	20.05	23.03
1966-	53.18	6.37	2.02	39.33	19.27	61.29	27.87	33.42	2.2-1	9.30	22.28
1965-	44.05	3.88	1.53	29.48	17.17	48.44	15.72	32.72	3.1-1	13.89	19.75
1964-	42.04	3.41	1.67	27.65	15.11	44.75	14.06	30.69	3.2-1	16.49	18.43
1963-	40.42	3.28	1.01	26.80	15.80	43.91	14.34	29.57	3.1-1	17.10	17.52
1962-	38.92	3.76	1.55	28.33	13.72	43.91	14.48	29.43	3.0-1	17.70	17.36
1961-	36.50	5.43	2.00	28.13	12.79	43.36	11.29	32.07	3.8-1	18.34	17.68
1960-	32.24	4.91	3.31	25.37	10.95	39.85	7.89	31.96	5.1-1	19.03	17.50
1959-	28.39	2.29	3.58	23.36	11.74	38.92	8.07	30.85	4.8-1	14.39	16.96
1958-	27.47	3.11	2.75	21.66	9.09	33.72	11.71	22.01	2.9-1	6.50	16.33

[1]Consol.; incl. foreign subs. (except South American) & Houston Instrument aft. 1965. [2]Adj. for 20% stk. div. in Jan., 1958 & 2-for-1 split in Apr., 1966. [3]Based on average shares. [4]Pro-forma earns. assuming conv. of debs. & exer. of options would be $1.45 in 1967 & $2.28 in 1966.

The company's line of conventional optical products is expected to show steady growth. Under a sub-licensing agreement with National Patent Development Corporation, the company is test-marketing a hydrophilic contact lens. Unlike regular contact lenses, this product absorbs rather than sheds water and thus will presumably aid comfort. Cost of the lens is estimated to be far below that of lenses presently on the market.

BRISTOL-MYERS

[1] INCOME STATISTICS (Million $) AND PER SHARE ($) DATA

Year Ended Dec. 31	Net Sales	% Oper. Inc. of Sales	Depr.	Net. Bef. Taxes	Net Inc.	[2] Common Share ($) Data			Price Range	Price-Earns. Ratios HI LO
						Earns.	*Cash Generated	Divs. Paid		
1968--	---	---	---	---	---	---	-----	0.25	74 −59-1/4	----
1967--	730.1	14.4	8.37	100.27	52.02	1.86	2.15	0.95	83 −52-5/8	45−28
1966--	645.8	14.3	7.09	91.47	44.24	1.59	1.75	0.75	58-3/4−41-5/8	37−26
1965--	391.4	16.3	3.98	64.96	33.36	1.32	1.48	0.65	49-7/8−33-5/8	38−25
1964--	324.1	17.6	3.68	58.17	28.09	1.12	1.26	0.52½	35-1/2−29-3/8	32−26
1963--	230.5	17.2	2.53	41.60	19.13	0.91	1.05	0.45	31-3/8−21-1/2	35−24
1962--	198.8	16.7	2.47	34.33	16.09	0.77	0.89	0.37½	24-7/8−15-1/8	33−20
1961--	164.4	15.9	2.27	27.77	12.96	0.62	0.73	0.30	25-7/8−16	42−26
1960-··	146.7	14.6	2.18	23.07	10.77	0.52	0.62	0.26¼	16-5/8− 9-5/8	32−19
1959--	131.5	13.4	2.18	18.59	8.89	0.43	0.54	0.21¼	12 − 5-5/8	28→l3
1958--	113.9	9.3	1.87	13.69	7.24	0.37	0.47	0.18¼	6-1/2− 4-3/8	18−12

[1] PERTINENT BALANCE SHEET STATISTICS (Million $)

Dec. 31	Gross Prop.	Capital Expend.	Cash Items	Inventories	Receivables	--Current--		Net Working Capital	Cur. Ratio Assets to Liabilities	Long Term Debt	[2]($) Book Val. Com. Sh.
						Assets	Liabs.				
1967--	184.70	36.13	48.1	98.37	107.82	262.01	101.65	160.36	2.6 − 1	78.7	5.89
1966--	151.02	30.89	39.5	88.58	80.67	215.51	102.30	113.21	2.1 − 1	27.1	4.89
1965--	76.38	8.06	28.8	37.28	33.01	102.04	45.80	56.24	2.2 − 1	Nil	4.68
1964--	69.71	9.13	37.6	30.03	24.44	94.67	36.20	58.47	2.6-- 1	4.6	3.99
1963--	50.73	4.81	39.9	18.61	17.52	78.09	32.62	45.46	2.4 − 1	5.2	3.38
1962--	46.44	3.33	40.4	15.30	12.99	70.38	30.96	39.42	2.3 − 1	6.8	2.95
1961--	43.82	2.48	34.0	13.71	10.94	58.68	27.94	30.74	2.1 − 1	7.9	2.62
1960--	42.18	2.16	17.5	11.66	9.99	39.14	12.13	27.01	3.2 − 1	8.7	2.37
1959--	40.68	3.76	14.4	11.40	10.56	36.35	11.22	25.13	3.2 − 1	10.1	2.19
1958--	39.00	8.62	13.4	9.70	11.72	34.84	8.46	26.38	4.1 − 1	10.7	2.25

[1] Incl. all wholly-owned North American (U. S. & Canadian) subs; incl. Drackett Co. from 1964 & Mead Johnson from 1966.
[2] Adj. for splits of 2-for-1 in 1966 & 3-for-1 in 1959 & for 100% stk. div. in 1963. *As computed by standard & Poor's.

This leading domestic producer of toiletries and proprietary * drugs also holds important positions in the ethical ** drug and household product fields. Further diversification was achieved through the acquisition of Mead, Johnson & Company, maker of nutritional products and drugs, and Javax Company, Ltd., Canadian manufacturer of household cleaning products.

Continued good growth is expected in its Clairol Division as well as the division devoted to such dietary products as Metrecal. Superior marketing ability should facilitate broader penetration of the Canadian market through its Canadian subsidiary. Strong research and acquisition programs and growing foreign operations enhance growth prospects.

* Proprietary drugs are sold over the counter and are usually trade-marked brands.
** Ethical drugs are high-quality drugs generally purchased by prescription only.

CASTLE & COOKE

[3]INCOME STATISTICS (Million $) AND PER SHARE ($) DATA

[1]Year Ended Apr. 30	Gross Rev.	% Total Inc. of Rev.	Total Inc.	Depr.	Net bef. Taxes	[5]Net Inc.	[5]Earns.	Divs. Paid	[2]Price Range	Price-Earns. Ratios HI LO
1968—	-----	-----	-----	-----	-----	-----	-----	----	45-1/2 - 31-1/2	-----
1967—	-----	-----	-----	-----	-----	-----	-----	[6]1.00	39 - 26-1/4	-----
1966—	336.38	9.1	30.50	8.14	18.80	10.08	2.34	1.00	34-7/8 - 24	15-10
1965—	318.50	10.5	33.56	7.89	24.18	10.34	2.54	0.95	33 - 21-3/4	13-19
1964—	237.36	10.8	25.65	6.43	18.25	8.16	2.13	0.91	24-1/2 - 19-3/4	11- 9
1963—	185.50	13.0	24.10	4.97	19.13	7.80	2.04	0.91	22-3/4 - 16	11- 8
1962—	166.49	7.1	11.88	5.01	6.87	2.81	0.74	0.73	29-1/2 - 14-3/8	40-20
1961—	155.33	8.9	13.82	4.59	9.23	4.59	1.19	0.95	32-1/2 - 19-1/4	27-16
1960—	30.56	-----	-----	0.89	3.94	2.99	1.13	0.59	21-3/8 - 18	19-16
1959—	28.14	-----	-----	0.84	4.28	3.03	1.17	0.58	22-3/8 - 18-1/4	19-16

[3]PERTINENT BALANCE SHEET STATISTICS (Million $)

[1]Apr. 30	Gross Prop.	Capital Expend.	Cash Items	Inven-tories	Receiv-ables	Current Assets	Current Liab.	Net Workg. Cap	Cur. Ratio Assets to Liab.	Long Term Debt	[4]($) Book Val. Com. Sh.
1966—	229.73	20.49	13.82	73.36	36.33	128.00	65.04	62.96	2.0-1	52.81	31.97
1965—	211.09	21.16	13.88	63.09	32.55	113.57	60.40	53.17	1.9	28.85	32.19
1964—	193.79	6.36	17.34	53.70	31.46	105.92	42.56	63.36	2.5-1	22.66	31.66
1963—	130.03	9.91	5.68	42.23	20.35	75.84	25.71	50.13	1.9-1	10.22	28.00
1962—	123.82	5.92	5.66	40.94	22.22	76.50	25.04	51.46	3.1-1	9.35	27.47
1961—	120.38	5.94	12.33	39.35	20.68	79.95	22.14	57.80	3.6-1	10.23	26.94
1960—	22.87	1.39	4.25	2.98	2.98	11.58	7.75	3.83	1.5-1	3.57	13.31
1959—	22.14	2.13	3.77	2.90	2.12	9.98	6.11	3.86	1.6-1	3.80	13.04

[1]Of foll. cal. yr.; cal. yr. pr. to 1961. [2]Cal. yr. [3]Incl. Dole Corp. & Bumble Bee Seafoods, Inc. aft. 1960. Standard Fruit & Steamship from Oct 4, 1964, Dole Philippines, Inc. aft. 1963, & Ames Mercantile aft. 1964. [4]Adj. for stk. divs. of 2% ea. in 1959 & 1960 & 10% in 1965 & 3-for-2 split in 1966. [5]Excl. $2.41 a sh. capital gain in 1964. [6]Plus 5% stk.

One of the largest of the Hawaiian-based companies, its principal product in Hawaii is Dole pineapple products, and its best-known mainland brand is Bumble Bee seafood. It has other interests in Hawaii, on the mainland, and abroad, including extensive real estate holdings and investments in services in financial and other areas.

Plans call for gradually converting the sizable acreage held in Hawaii into a real estate development and transferring pineapple growing activities to Philippines and to Central America.

COLT INDUSTRIES

[4]INCOME STATISTICS (Million $) AND PER SHARE ($) DATA

[1]Year Ended Dec. 31	Gross Rev.	% Op. Inc. of Sales	Depr. & Depl.	Net Bef. Taxes	Inc. Taxes	[3]Net Income	—[2] Common— [3]Earns.	Divs. Pd.	————Price Range———— $1.60 Pfd.	[2]Common
1968—	- - - -	- - - -	- - - -	- - - -	- - - -	- - - - -	- - - - -	0.40	41-1/2-35	75-3/4-48-5/8
1967—	306.75	9.5	4.45	21.46	9.44	12.02	[6]3.05	[5]- - -	38-1/8-23-3/4	65-3/4-19
1966—	251.78	8.8	4.24	14.95	7.02	7.93	[6]2.15	Nil	29-1/2-21-1/2	29-1/2-13-5/8
1965—	199.02	7.4	3.90	8.50	2.61	5.89	1.73	Nil	32-3/8-25-1/8	25-3/8-12
1964—	171.70	5.8	3.60	4.19	0.56	3.63	0.94	Nil	26 -21-1/4	21 -10-3/4
1963—	148.48	2.5	3.43	d0.97	Nil	d0.97	d0.55	Nil	21 -15	18-3/8-12-3/4
1962—	150.80	0.0	3.81	d4.85	Nil	d4.85	d2.19	Nil	23-1/2-15	26-3/8-12
1961—	141.29	3.2	3.70	d0.18	cr 0.10	d0.08	d0.27	Nil	28-1/2-21	44-5/8-22-1/2
1960—	145.37	3.6	3.76	0.20	0.06	0.73	0.06	Nil	28-7/8-20-5/8	36-3/4-16-7/8
1959—	149.45	6.8	3.25	6.50	3.30	3.20	1.05	Nil	28-7/8-21-3/8	30-3/4-21
1958—	70.46	1.4	1.93	d2.42	cr 0.57	d1.84	d1.23	Nil	23-3/4-13-5/8	26-1/4-10-1/2

[4]PERTINENT BALANCE SHEET STATISTICS (Million $)

Dec. 31	Gross Prop.	Capital Expend.	Cash Items	Inventories	Receivables	—Current— Assets	Liabs.	Net Workg. Cap.	Cur. Ratio Assets to Liabs.	Long Term Debt	[2]($) Book Val. Com. Sh.
1967—	106.03	7.95	12.92	72.11	57.19	143.88	57.28	86.60	2.5-1	44.97	16.13
1966—	98.64	5.56	10.01	73.14	44.79	130.18	58.44	71.74	2.2-1	40.15	13.37
1965—	94.25	4.40	7.66	58.32	35.78	102.57	43.09	59.48	2.4-1	39.24	11.47
1964—	92.41	3.44	5.49	53.72	35.53	96.25	41.52	54.73	2.3-1	38.56	9.83
1963—	89.71	3.67	8.73	47.23	24.04	81.22	29.32	51.89	2.8-1	38.30	10.32
1962—	89.57	2.19	9.26	42.00	25.63	77.82	33.67	44.15	2.3-1	29.48	10.90
1961—	91.28	4.44	9.77	55.87	28.93	95.16	30.06	65.10	3.2-1	32.47	21.97
1960—	91.30	3.02	12.22	52.34	28.05	93.94	26.72	67.22	3.5-1	31.79	22.25
1959—	91.15	4.07	15.58	56.91	24.83	98.40	23.70	74.69	4.2-1	39.12	22.19
1958-	86.75	1.79	14.78	57.56	20.66	93.97	30.87	63.10	3.0-1	25.95	25.80

[1]4½% stk. [2]Adj. for 1-for-3 reverse split in 1964. [3]Bef. net spec. charges of $8.22 a sh. in 1962 & $0.39 in 1958; aft. spec. cr. of $0.24 in 1960. [4]Incl. Quincy Compressor Co. & H. H. Wilson Inc. aft. 1963 & Elox Corp. aft. 1965. [5]5% in stk. [6]Pro forma earns. assuming issuance of all shares reserved for conversions and options would be $2.74 in 1967 & $1.93 in 1966. cr Credit. d Deficit.

In view of the continuing perilous world crisis, shipments of firearms and aircraft components should continue at a high level. Early in 1968 Colt acquired Holley Carburetor Company, which manufactures automotive and aviation fuel systems. Since the company is a prime producer of industrial equipment, it is expected to benefit from the improvement in the level of industrial activity as well as from projected increases in capital spending.

CONSOLIDATED ELECTRONICS

[3] INCOME STATISTICS (Million $) AND PER SHARE ($) DATA

Year Ended Dec. 31	Net Sales	% Oper Inc. of Sales	Oper. Inc.	Deprec.	Net bef. Taxes	Inc. Taxes	[4] Net Inc.	[4] Earns.	Div. Paid	Price Range	Price-Earns. Ratios HI LO
1968--	---	---	---	---	---	---	---	---	0.50	44 −34-3/8	---
1967--	316.41	11.3	35.75	6.25	27.87	12.23	12.46	[5] 2.81	1.00	57-3/4−35-1/2	21−13
1966--	317.18	11.3	39.62	6.04	32.18	15.20	13.87	[5] 3.15	1.00	45-3/4−31	15−10
1965--	259.29	10.8	28.08	5.34	21.58	9.52	10.16	2.31	1.00	38-1/4−28	17−12
1964--	223.91	9.3	20.84	4.92	15.21	6.53	8.16	1.86	1.00	50-7/8−30-1/8	27−16
1963--	177.84	9.5	16.82	3.45	12.81	6.56	5.56	1.75	1.00	39-5/8−27-1/2	23−16
1962--	165.86	8.9	14.75	3.35	10.64	4.92	4.98	1.57	1.00	49-1/2−25	32−16
1961--	144.44	9.2	13.25	2.99	10.07	4.50	5.00	1.58	1.00	51-7/8−36-1/8	33−23
1960--	92.94	10.2	9.45	1.94	7.88	3.96	3.57	1.26	1.00	60-3/4−42-1/4	48−34
1959--	86.90	13.2	11.43	1.79	10.30	4.52	5.03	1.80	Nil	47 −26-3/4	26−15
1958--	77.31	[2] 8.3	[2] 6.41	---	6.81	2.72	3.42	1.23	Nil	35-3/4−15-5/8	29−13

[3] PERTINENT BALANCE SHEET STATISTICS (Million $)

Dec. 31	Gross Prop.	[1] Capital Expend.	Cash Items	Inven-tories	Receiv-ables	Current Assets	Current Liabs.	Net Working Cap.	Cur. Ratio Assets to Liabs.	Long Term Debt	($) Book Val. Com. Sh.
1967--	105.41	11.53	30.65	66.23	51.46	149.59	45.31	104.27	3.3−1	45.34	24.76
1966--	97.06	10.71	21.90	61.59	53.31	138.08	56.63	81.46	2.4−1	24.75	23.08
1965--	89.24	6.86	15.89	48.71	47.17	112.82	45.60	67.22	2.5−1	15.22	21.37
1964--	82.70	7.10	14.44	44.88	37.30	97.74	37.99	59.75	2.6−1	13.40	20.07
1963--	45.84	6.13	16.86	33.53	31.49	82.98	34.22	48.76	2.4−1	4.47	20.42
1962--	40.29	5.28	15.57	26.63	26.94	70.05	30.09	39.96	2.3−1	4.10	19.62
1961--	35.01	1.21	13.76	25.32	24.83	65.05	24.50	40.55	2.7−1	4.83	19.15
1960--	38.02	7.37	16.30	13.85	16.24	47.16	16.71	30.45	2.8−1	1.73	17.37
1959--	33.00	3.21	20.35	13.49	15.64	49.94	16.10	33.84	3.1−1	2.63	17.01

[1] As reported to SEC. [2] Aft. depr. [3] Inc. Anchor Brush Bo. aft. 1965. [4] Bef. spec. cr. of $0.03 a sh. in 1967 & chge. of $0.01 in 1966. [5] Pro forma earns. assuming conv. of debs. would be $2.59 in 1967 & $2.80 in 1966.

Through its own operations and those of majority-owned subsidiaries, this company has representation in such diverse areas as electrical-electronic products, chemicals, pharmaceuticals, and public utilities.

Its growth future is enhanced by improved chemical and pharmaceutical operations as well as by the expanding market for its customer industries: Color television, automobiles, and home appliances. The company's indirect ties with Phillips Lamp, a major European electronics and drug manufacturer, and an active acquisition program enhance long-range prospects.

DOVER CORPORATION

[1] INCOME STATISTICS (Million $) AND PER SHARE ($) DATA

Year Ended Dec. 31	Net Sales	% Oper. Inc. of Sales	Oper. Inc.	Depr.	Net Bef. Taxes	Net Inc.	---[2]Common Share ($) Data---			Price-Earns. Ratios
							Earns.	Divs. Paid	Price Range	HI LO
1968–	---	---	---	---	---	---	---	0.60	60-3/4–47-3/4	----
1967–	123.35	14.1	17.35	2.08	14.47	7.63	[3]3.46	1.12½	61-1/2–30	18– 9
1966–	112.85	15.9	17.97	1.92	15.15	7.97	[3]3.60	1.02½	36 –22-5/8	10– 6
1965–	98.07	16.0	15.70	1.92	13.31	7.00	3.21	0.85	34-1/4–24-7/8	11– 8
1964–	83.92	16.6	13.92	1.66	12.16	6.07	2.78	0.75	31-5/8–20-1/4	11– 7
1963–	67.68	15.9	10.79	1.53	8.56	4.26	1.98	0.58	22-5/8–14-3/8	11– 7
1962–	54.89	15.7	8.60	1.24	6.96	3.32	1.54	0.50	15-1/8–10-1/4	10– 7
1961–	47.21	15.5	7.32	1.16	5.74	2.69	1.31	0.50	15-1/4– 8-7/8	12– 7
1960–	43.42	12.8	5.54	1.11	3.99	1.91	0.93	0.75	15-1/2– 8-5/8	16– 9
1959–	45.34	18.2	8.26	1.06	6.62	3.28	1.67	0.69	16-7/8–12-1/8	10– 7
1958–	27.72	17.8	4.93	0.84	3.88	1.92	1.25	0.64	12-7/8– 7-1/2	10– 6

[1] PERTINENT BALANCE SHEET STATISTICS (Million $)

Dec. 31	Gross. Prop.	Capital Expend.	Cash Items	Inventories	Receivables	---Current---		Net Workg. Cap.	Cur. Ratio Assets to Liabs.	Long Term Debt	[2]($) Book Val. Com. Sh.
						Assets	Liabs.				
1967–	32.89	2.44	1.58	29.41	21.77	53.55	15.01	38.54	3.6–1	16.02	17.61
1966–	30.00	2.65	1.78	26.43	20.75	49.75	13.01	36.73	3.8–1	16.87	15.80
1965–	25.23	1.88	1.41	20.22	14.11	36.33	13.39	22.94	2.7–1	6.65	12.94
1964–	23.91	1.63	1.16	18.61	13.50	33.83	15.01	18.82	2.3–1	7.36	10.42
1963–	20.04	2.01	1.18	15.32	10.39	27.41	10.48	16.92	2.6–1	8.11	9.47
1962–	18.71	1.19	2.33	13.23	8.32	24.43	8.28	16.15	3.0–1	9.50	8.30
1961–	14.21	0.67	4.00	11.31	6.71	22.44	5.88	16.56	3.8–1	6.79	8.41
1960–	13.64	1.19	2.78	11.34	5.53	20.00	5.06	14.94	4.0–1	7.05	7.61
1959–	12.70	0.90	3.60	11.95	5.04	20.86	5.64	15.22	3.7–1	7.17	7.90
1958–	9.79	1.26	2.34	8.30	4.13	15.04	3.41	11.63	4.4–1	6.80	7.13

[1] Incl. OPW Corp. aft. 1958 & Walter O'Bannon Co. aft. 1961. [2] Adj. for 3-for-2 split in 1965 & stk. divs. of 2% ea. in 1965, 1964 & 1963. [3] As reported by Co. assuming full conv. of pfd. stk.

Dover is the third largest elevator company in terms of units installed and component parts manufactured. Sales and service of electric and hydraulic elevators account for some 37 percent of the company's revenues, with the balance derived from sales of gas heaters, air conditioning parts, and oil field products, nozzles, and valves for petroleum marketers.

EDO CORPORATION

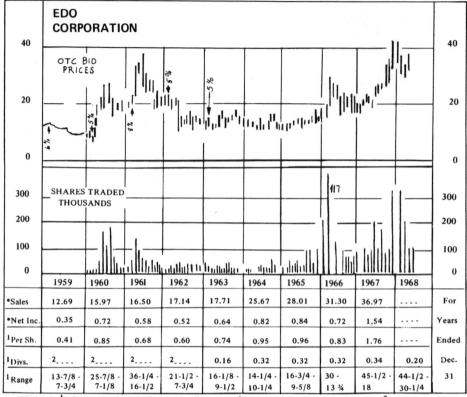

	1959	1960	1961	1962	1963	1964	1965	1966	1967	1968	
*Sales	12.69	15.97	16.50	17.14	17.71	25.67	28.01	31.30	36.97	....	For
*Net Inc.	0.35	0.72	0.58	0.52	0.64	0.82	0.84	0.72	1.54	....	Years
[1]Per Sh.	0.41	0.85	0.68	0.60	0.74	0.95	0.96	0.83	1.76	....	Ended
[1]Divs.	[2]....	[2]....	[2]....	[2]....	0.16	0.32	0.32	0.32	0.34	0.20	Dec.
[1]Range	13-7/8 - 7-3/4	25-7/8 - 7-1/8	36-1/4 - 16-1/2	21-1/2 - 7-3/4	16-1/8 - 9-1/2	14-1/4 - 10-1/4	16-3/4 - 9-5/8	30 - 13 ¾	45-1/2 - 18	44-1/2 - 30-1/4	31

*Million $. [1]Adj. for stk. divs. of 5% in 1963, 5% in 1962, 8% in 1961, 5% in 1960 & 6% in 1959. [2]Paid in stk. See note 1. [3]Indicated rate.

This leader in the sonar field derives nearly 77 percent of sales from military contracts, although commercial operations contribute a substantial amount to earnings.

While sonar equipment continues to be the most important product line, sales of commercial products are enjoying steady growth. Edo Western Corporation is a manufacturer of sonic transducers and related equipment for off-shore drilling and other commercial oceanographic applications.

GENERAL FOODS

[1] PERTINENT BALANCE SHEET STATISTICS (Million $)

[2] Mar. 31	Gross Prop.	Capital Expend.	Cash Items	Inven- tories	Receiv- ables	Current Assets	Current Liabs.	Net Workg. Cap.	Cur. Ratio Assets to Liabs.	Long Term Debt	[4] ($) Book Val. Com. Sh.
1966–	569.24	59.32	109.3	260.6	180.0	563.9	237.9	325.9	2.4-1	61.00	23.61
1965–	516.94	64.69	91.2	261.3	158.9	526.9	218.7	308.2	2.4-1	54.38	22.26
1964–	477.44	53.58	53.6	214.3	159.9	443.9	173.2	270.7	2.6-1	37.42	20.31
1963–	436.36	69.90	28.6	256.4	140.8	435.7	201.5	234.2	2.2-1	23.11	18.89
1962–	375.12	56.90	72.8	204.7	125.9	410.9	162.0	249.0	2.5-1	34.12	17.52
1961–	328.15	41.55	90.9	183.5	107.5	386.8	141.4	245.4	2.7-1	35.43	16.16
1960–	289.28	39.90	69.5	189.1	92.4	360.4	123.0	237.4	2.9-1	37.39	15.08
1959–	247.31	34.61	107.5	157.4	86.0	356.5	126.2	230.4	2.8-1	39.74	13.89
1958–	220.80	23.55	92.6	148.6	82.2	329.1	107.2	221.9	3.1-1	44.00	12.79
1957–	203.32	27.67	57.1	169.5	80.0	312.9	106.7	206.2	2.9-1	49.43	11.71

[1] INCOME STATISTICS (Million $) AND PER SHARE ($) DATA

[2] Year Ended Mar. 31	Net Sales	% Oper. Inc. of Sales	Oper. Inc.	Deprec.	Net Bef. Taxes	Net Inc.	Earns.	*Cash Generated	Divs. Paid	Price [3] Range	Price- Earns. Ratios HI LO
1968–	....	.....	.....	....	....	...	.....	....	....	77-1/4 - 65	.....
1967–	....	.....	.....	....	....	...	.....	....	2.40	81-3/4 - 65-1/4	.....
1966–	1,651.58	13.6	224.86	34.37	192.73	98.76	3.93	5.30	2.20	83 - 62-3/4	21-16
1965–	1,554.66	13.9	216.33	31.88	184.49	93.89	3.73	5.00	2.10	89-7/8 - 77-1/2	24-21
1964–	1,478.06	14.0	207.46	29.11	177.43	86.35	3.44	4.60	2.00	93-1/4 - 78-1/4	27-23
1963–	1,338.04	15.3	204.49	25.91	178.95	83.53	3.33	4.36	2.00	90-1/2 - 77-5/8	27-23
1962–	1,216.22	15.9	193.01	24.31	170.29	78.58	3.14	4.11	1.80	96 - 57-3/4	31-18
1961–	1,189.48	14.7	174.47	21.34	155.88	72.24	2.90	3.76	1.60	107-3/4 - 68-5/8	37-24
1960–	1,160.18	13.3	154.40	18.36	138.17	66.82	2.69	3.42	1.40	75-1/2 - 49	28-18
1959–	1,087.08	13.1	141.96	15.42	129.62	61.07	2.48	3.11	1.30	53-7/8 - 37-1/8	22-15
1958–	1,052.96	12.1	127.67	13.88	115.30	54.15	2.21	2.78	1.15	39 ¾ - 24	18-11
1957–	1,008.90	11.4	115.32	11.29	105.02	48.40	1.99	2.45	1.00	25-1/8 - 20	13-10

A giant packaged foods company with strong representation in a number of areas. Fiscal 1967 was the sixteenth consecutive year of record sales and earnings.

Maxwell House coffee is one of its many popular food items. Still further sales gains appear in prospect, aided by the acquisition of Burger Chef Systems. Sales and profit potentials should continue to benefit from research and product development and from increased emphasis on overseas growth.

HAT CORPORATION OF AMERICA

INCOME STATISTICS (Million $) AND PER SHARE ($) DATA

Year Ended Oct. 31	Net Sales	% Op. of Sales	Oper. Inc.	Deprec.	Net Bef. Taxes	[4]Net Inc.	5$2.50 Pfd. Earns.	[4]Earns.	Divs Decl.	[1]Price Range 5$2.50 Pfd.	[2]Common	Price-Earns. Ratios HI LO
1968–	---	---	---	---	---	---	----	----	0.10	-----------	-----------	-----
1967–	37.5	2.8	1.04	0.41	0.40	0.23	5.65	0.14	0.40	42 - 36	12-3/8 - 7-7/8	86-56
1966–	36.9	6.1	2.25	0.36	1.84	0.96	24.00	1.00	0.40	45 - 36	13-5/8 - 7-1/4	14- 7
1965–	36.6	5.9	2.17	0.35	1.71	0.92	23.08	0.96	0.40	45-5/8 - 41	10 - 7	10- 7
1964–	33.3	4.6	1.54	0.35	1.31	0.74	18.48	0.71	0.40	44 - 40-7/8	8-3/8 - 6-7/8	12-10
1963–	33.1	5.6	1.84	0.33	1.67	0.90	22.59	0.90	0.40	44-1/4 - 40-1/2	9 - 6-3/4	10- 8
1962–	34.2	5.1	1.73	0.30	1.65	0.84	21.12	0.83	[3]....	42 - 38-3/8	9-3/8 - 5-7/8	11- 7
1961–	28.7	5.3	1.52	0.30	1.24	0.63	15.75	0.60	[3]....	43-3/8 - 37-1/2	12-1/8 - 7-5/8	20-13
1960–	27.5	9.1	2.50	0.26	2.31	1.16	28.89	1.20	[3]....	38-1/2 - 35	9-5/8 - 6-5/8	8- 6
1959–	25.1	9.4	2.35	0.24	2.20	1.11	27.77	1.19	[3]....	39-1/2 - 35-1/2	9-7/8 - 5-7/8	8- 5
1958–	21.0	9.7	2.04	0.26	1.80	0.90	22.62	0.95	Nil	38 - 28-1/4	7-1/4 - 3	8- 3

PERTINENT BALANCE SHEET STATISTICS (Million $)

Oct. 31	Gross Prop.	Capital Expend.	Cash Items	Inven- tories	Receiv- ables	Current Assets	Current Liabs.	Net Workg. Cap.	Cur. Ratio Assets to Liabs.	Long Term Debt	[2]($) Book Val. Com. Sh.
1967–	10.61	0.74	1.46	9.92	6.64	18.03	6.73	11.29	2.7-1	0.43	14.88
1966–	8.98	0.34	1.35	8.61	6.30	16.26	4.52	11.74	3.6-1	Nil	15.14
1965–	8.74	0.37	1.36	8.50	6.12	15.98	5.12	10.87	3.1-1	Nil	14.73
1964–	8.39	0.42	1.40	7.89	5.93	15.21	4.64	10.57	3.3-1	Nil	13.68
1963–	8.47	0.61	1.55	8.26	5.50	15.31	4.84	10.47	3.2-1	Nil	13.37
1962–	7.91	0.64	2.13	7.52	5.44	15.09	4.36	10.73	3.5-1	Nil	13.45
1961–	7.43	0.36	2.52	6.29	5.78	14.59	3.28	11.31	4.4-1	1.07	12.46
1960–	5.10	0.32	1.14	5.57	5.63	12.34	2.77	9.57	4.5-1	Nil	11.13
1959–	4.79	0.24	1.48	5.60	4.85	11.93	3.45	8.47	3.5-1	0.33	9.84
1958–	4.56	0.23	1.99	4.66	4.34	10.99	3.19	7.81	4.1-1	0.59	8.66

[1]Cal. yrs. [2]Adj. for stk. divds. of 4% in 1962 & 8% each in 1959 thru 1961. [3]Pd. stk. as indicated in footnote 2. [4]Bef. spec. crs. of $0.31 a sh. in 1962, $0.12 in 1963 & $0.23 in 1965 & bef. spec. chge. of $0.18 in 1966. [5]Divds. pd. regularly.

This company manufactures quality hats for men and through a 1967 acquisition entered the men's wear and shirt field.

Its products include such well known brands as Knox, Dobbs, and Cavanaugh. Sales growth could be augmented by further acquisition in the apparel field as well as by expansion of hat activities in foreign countries.

LATROBE STEEL

INCOME STATISTICS (Million $) AND PER SHARE ($) DATA

Year Ended Dec. 31	Net Sales	% Oper. Inc. of Sales	Oper. Inc.	Depr. & Amort.	Net bef. Taxes	Net. Inc.	--[2]Common Share ($) Data-- Earns	Divs. Paid	Price Range	Price-Earns. Ratios HI LO
1968–	---	---	---	---	---	---	---	0.30	33 –23-1/4	---
1967–	50.70	12.4	6.28	1.23	4.72	2.43	2.06	0.60	35 –16-1/8	17– 8
1966–	51.98	13.9	7.20	1.33	5.84	3.08	2.64	0.75	20-7/8–13-3/4	8– 5
1965–	42.99	12.8	5.48	1.20	4.03	2.15	1.84	0.60	20-1/4–13-7/8	11– 8
1964–	34.91	10.6	3.69	1.20	2.27	1.53	1.33	0.60	20-1/2–12	15– 9
1963–	32.31	13.8	4.46	0.88	3.55	1.77	1.53	0.60	20-1/2–13	13– 8
1962–	32.20	15.4	4.97	0.70	4.30	1.97	1.73	0.50	14-1/4–10	8– 6
1961–	25.57	8.2	2.11	0.56	1.53	0.72	0.64	0.40	18 –12-3/4	28–20
1960–	24.79	10.6	2.63	0.53	2.07	1.11	0.98	1.00	21 –14-1/4	21–14
1959–	28.51	17.4	4.95	0.46	4.44	2.05	1.92	0.77	19 –10-1/8	10– 5
1958–	17.94	8.8	1.58	0.46	1.07	0.46	0.49	0.30	11 – 8-3/4	22–18

PERTINENT BALANCE SHEET STATISTICS (Million $)

Dec. 31	[1]Gross Prop.	Capital Expend.	Cash Items	Inven-tories	Receiv-ables	---Current-- Assets	Liabs.	Net Workg. Cap.	Cur. Ratio Assets to Liabs.	Long Term Debt	[2]($) Book Val. Com. Sh.
1967–	29.80	5.17	3.09	11.85	4.81	19.75	7.69	12.06	2.6–1	7.95	20.32
1966–	25.25	1.76	3.82	11.32	5.57	20.71	9.56	11.15	2.2–1	5.01	18.89
1965–	23.92	1.48	2.46	9.27	5.32	17.05	7.27	9.78	2.3–1	5.65	17.00
1964–	22.71	2.82	1.59	8.74	3.44	14.36	4.69	9.66	3.1–1	6.29	15.84
1963–	20.33	5.14	3.42	8.59	3.84	16.35	4.87	11.47	3.4–1	6.63	15.11
1962–	15.27	2.18	2.13	8.15	3.61	14.32	4.90	9.42	2.9–1	1.60	14.22
1961–	13.23	1.47	2.49	7.31	2.99	13.16	3.60	9.57	3.7–1	1.82	12.99
1960–	5.85	1.19	1.84	8.36	2.94	13.47	3.17	10.30	4.2–1	2.03	12.75
1959–	5.08	0.75	2.85	7.87	3.58	14.58	4.21	10.37	3.5–1	2.20	12.59
1958–	4.65	0.67	2.21	6.09	2.21	10.51	2.91	7.60	3.6–1	1.76	12.42

[1]Net prop. pr. to 1961. [2]Adj. for 2-for-one split in 1960 & stk. divds. of 3% in 1958 & 5% in 1960.

While small in comparison to the tonnage steelmakers, the company is a leading producer of high-priced tool and die steels and of special alloys used primarily in aero-space applications.

Sales prospects are enhanced by widening uses of special alloys in aero-space and other industries; tool steel demand should continue to increase. Finishing capacity will be expanded significantly by 1969.

LOUISVILLE & NASHVILLE

[2]FINANCIAL AND OPERATING STATISTICS (Million $) AND PER SHARE ($) DATA

Ended Dec. 31	Funded Debt	[1]Cash Items	Working Cap.	Freight Revs.	Total Oper. Revs.	Total Oper. Exps.	Fed. Income Taxes	Net Ry. Oper. Inc.	[3]--Carry-thru-- All Class 1 Roads	This Road	---Ratios (%)--- Revenues Absorbed By: Maint.	Transp.	Oper.
1967-	417.6	32.7	29.6	267.5	285.4	231.2	cr 1.6	31.4	11.7	10.4	34.4	38.6	81.0
1966-	411.0	41.9	35.4	269.0	292.2	222.6	5.6	38.2	11.6	15.0	31.2	37.6	76.2
1965-	386.6	41.4	39.3	250.8	274.6	215.0	3.0	34.7	11.0	13.7	32.7	37.9	78.3
1964-	390.1	43.6	46.7	235.6	259.5	208.9	cr 3.6	30.1	9.7	9.0	31.4	39.9	80.5
1963-	348.3	54.4	48.2	227.1	251.3	199.0	1.2	27.5	10.1	11.4	31.4	40.2	79.2
1962-	361.0	62.5	58.6	215.1	240.2	189.3	1.0	31.4	9.3	13.5	31.3	39.6	78.8
1961-	337.8	57.4	53.2	203.2	228.1	175.8	12.2	23.7	8.5	15.7	28.9	40.2	77.1
1960-	330.1	52.1	64.8	201.3	227.0	185.9	8.4	17.7	8.3	11.8	34.1	40.0	81.9
1959-	315.6	36.9	48.8	203.5	229.7	182.9	14.2	19.0	10.4	14.5	33.1	39.2	79.6
1958-	304.6	42.5	59.6	201.9	227.9	188.8	10.8	18.8	10.5	13.0	34.9	40.3	82.8
1957-	289.7	37.8	55.7	216.4	245.3	204.1	12.2	23.8	11.9	14.7	36.8	39.6	83.2

Year Ended Dec. 31	Net Equip. & Jt. Fac. Rental Ch.	Other Income	----Fixed Charges---- Amount Available	Total	Times Earned	[4]Net Income	-----Per Share ($) Data----- [4]Earns.	Divs.	Price Range	Price-Earns. Ratios HI LO
1968-	--	--	---	--	----	---	---	2.00	80-3/8-72-1/4	----
1967-	2.6	7.5	38.3	18.4	2.08	19.9	8.03	5.00	100-1/4-75-1/2	13-10
1966-	5.0	8.3	45.5	17.0	2.68	28.5	11.51	6.00	102-1/2-73-3/4	9- 6
1965-	2.4	8.1	41.6	16.1	2.58	25.5	10.30	5.00	92-1/2-66-1/2	9- 6
1964-	5.0	6.9	35.6	15.2	2.34	20.4	8.26	4.00	94-3/4-74	11- 9
1963-	4.0	8.4	35.3	14.4	2.45	20.9	8.48	4.00	91-1/2-59-3/4	11- 7
1962-	Nil	5.9	36.3	13.4	2.71	22.9	9.36	3.25	64 -50	7- 5
1961-	cr2.0	5.6	27.5	13.4	2.06	14.1	5.77	3.25	63 -49-1/4	11- 9
1960-	cr5.1	6.3	23.0	12.5	1.84	10.5	4.28	4.50	78-3/4-47-1/4	18-11
1959-	cr 6.1	6.7	25.3	11.9	2.13	13.4	5.50	5.00	88 -69	16-13
1958-	cr9.0	6.6	24.7	11.4	2.16	13.2	5.44	5.00	81 -55-1/2	15-10
1957-	cr15.0	5.5	29.2	10.6	2.76	18.6	7.63	5.00	93-3/4-54-5/8	12- 7

[1]Excl. special deposits. [2]Consol. [3]% of gross retained as pretax operating net. [4]As reported to ICC; excl. reserves for deferred taxes. cr Credit.

The railroad's lines tap extensive bituminous coal mining regions, as well as growing commercial and industrial centers in the South.

The company's future should benefit from further computerization of its operations. Prospects hinge on its ability to absorb rising costs, on industrial growth of territory served, and on greater utilization of new equipment.

McKEE (ARTHUR G.)

[5]INCOME STATISTICS (Million $) AND PER SHARE ($) DATA

Year Ended Dec.31	[1]Gross Inc. Fr. Contrcs.	% Oper. Inc. Of. Gr. Inc.	Oper. Inc.	Deprec.	Net Bef. Taxes	Net Inc.	[2]Common Share ($) Data			Price-Earns. Ratios HI LO
							Earns	Divs. Paid	Price Range	
1968-	---	---	---	---	---	---	---	0.75	46 -35	----
1967-	190.94	2.8	5.33	0.93	6.34	3.36	2.99	1.50	48-1/4-21-3/8	16- 7
1966-	147.06	1.9	2.79	0.93	4.52	2.34	2.15	1.50	35 5/8-19-1/8	17- 9
1965-	146.81	1.7	2.50	0.99	3.96	2.46	2.30	1.40	33 -24-7/8	14-11
1964-	63.12	4.6	2.90	0.40	3.55	1.95	1.84	1.00	29 -16-1/4	16- 9
1963-	63.00	7.8	4.94	0.33	4.73	2.04	1.94	0.72½	18-1/8-10-7/8	10- 6
1962-	57.59	5.3	3.08	0.23	3.02	1.36	1.29	0.50	23-3/4- 9-1/2	18- 7
1961-	80.58	1.9	1.55	0.25	1.29	0.55	0.52	1.50	34-1/2-21	66-40
1960-	60.58	8.2	4.97	0.12	5.21	2.44	2.33	1.50	35 7/8-24-3/4	15-11
1959-	52.21	13.5	7.05	0.13	7.51	3.68	3.52	1.37½ 36	-25-1/2	10- 7
1958-	83.62	9.1	7.62	0.13	7.63	3.68	3.55	1.25	32-3/8-16-1/2	9- 5

[5]PERTINENT BALANCE SHEET STATISTICS (Million $)

Dec. 31	Total Assets	Gross Prop.	Cash Items	[3]Contract Wk. In Progr.	Receivables	Current Assets	[4]Liabs.	Net Workg Cap.	Cur. Ratio Assets to Liabs.	Long Term Debt	[2]$ Book Val. Com. Sh.
1967-	62.52	10.51	6.96	17.00	23.18	50.73	34.72	16.01	1.5-1	Nil	22.21
1966-	50.05	9.52	6.08	12.83	18.12	40.23	24.71	15.51	1.6-1	Nil	20.73
1965-	41.97	8.28	9.02	12.05	11.20	34.80	19.19	15.60	1.8-1	Nil	20.04
1964-	30.24	5.79	6.38	4.26	11.18	23.01	8.53	14.48	2.7-1	Nil	19.14
1963-	28.86	5.38	7.42	5.43	7.82	21.53	8.13	13.40	2.6-1	Nil	18.23
1962-	25.67	4.42	5.02	4.42	8.82	19.41	6.22	13.19	3.1-1	Nil	16.95
1961-	29.04	5.55	4.92	5.48	10.34	22.07	10.40	11.68	2.1-1	0.02	16.14
1960-	27.18	4.67	9.21	4.74	8.53	22.68	7.60	15.08	3.0-1	Nil	18.64
1959-	27.45	4.60	14.66	3.68	4.47	23.00	8.84	14.17	2.6-1	Nil	17.83
1958-	31.07	4.86	13.82	6.34	6.26	26.62	14.82	11.79	1.8-1	Nil	15.68

[1]As reported to SEC prior to 1958. [2]Adj. for 2-for-1 split in 1959. [3]Less billings. [4]Aft. Deduct. U.S. Treasury tax notes. [5]Inc. all wholly owned subs. aft. 1964. [6]Preliminary.

McKee provides engineering and construction services for the iron, steel, petroleum, and chemical industries, as well as the non-ferrous metals and minerals industries and the food packaging industries; it also produces equipment and systems for a wide variety of industrial markets.

Profits for the most part reflect swings in capital spending by major customer industries and varying profitability on individual contracts.

MERCK & COMPANY

[1]INCOME STATISTICS (Million $) AND PER SHARE ($) DATA

Year Ended Dec. 31	Net Sales	% Oper. Inc. of Sales	Depr. & Obsol.	Net Bef. Taxes	Net Inc.	Earns.	[3]Common Share ($) Data *Cash Generated	Divs.	Price Range		Price-- Earns. Ratios HI	LO
1968--	---	---	---	---	---	---	---	0.80	89	−73-3/4	---	
1967--	528.13	33.0	19.82	162.28	89.31	2.51	3.06	1.60	94	−73-7/8	37	− 29
1966--	488.62	33.6	17.11	153.58	82.59	2.32	2.80	1.40	81-7/8−64-5/8		35	− 28
1965--	348.70	34.3	13.85	110.83	60.96	1.88	2.31	1.20	75	−48-1/2	41	− 26
1964--	286.70	31.7	12.70	84.77	44.87	1.39	1.78	0.94-1/3	51-3/8−34-3/8		37	− 25
1963--	264.60	28.7	12.33	68.73	35.83	1.11	1.50	0.66-2/3	36-5/8−25-7/8		33	− 23
1962--	240.52	26.9	12.55	54.94	29.24	0.90	1.30	0.60	31-5/8−20		35	− 22
1961--	228.56	26.3	10.08	53.89	27.19	0.83	1.15	0.53-1/3	31-7/8−24-5/8		38	− 30
1960--	218.14	25.1	9.95	49.21	27.81	0.86	1.17	0.53-1/3	32-1/8−23-1/4		38	− 28
1959--	216.91	26.4	9.17	53.59	29.99	0.93	1.21	0.53-1/3	30-5/8−22-3/8		33	− 24
1958--	206.64	27.4	8.13	55.22	27.72	0.84	1.10	0.46-2/3	28	−12-1/4	33	− 15

[1]PERTINENT BALANCE SHEET STATISTICS (Million $)

Dec. 31	Gross. Prop.	Capital Expend.	Cash Items	Inventories	Receivables	Current Assets	Liabs.	Net Working Cap.	Cur. Ratio Assets to Liabs.	Long Term Debt.	[3]($) Book Val. Com. Sh.
1967--	299.78	42.98	41.14	66.05	42.93	272.34	92.27	180.06	3.0−1	10.50	9.41
1966--	262.41	34.71	54.03	60.17	40.08	262.10	100.45	161.65	2.6−1	1.00	8.41
1965--	209.24	20.70	59.37	43.29	30.43	225.21	87.68	137.53	2.6−1	Nil	7.46
1964--	180.46	11.50	48.15	40.97	25.18	204.48	62.63	141.86	3.3−1	Nil	6.74
1963--	173-47	13.50	46.04	41.21	22.81	173.12	46.63	126.49	3.7−1	0.46	6.35
1962--	177.67	17.20	39.71	42.39	22.66	155.04	43.75	111.30	3.5−1	0.49	5.96
1961--	163.47	14.70	50.18	40.34	21.58	154.77	40.56	114.21	3.8−1	0.52	5.74
1960--	151.79	9.40	40.55	44.03	19.05	141.83	33.36	108.48	4.3−1	0.55	5.44
1959--	144.89	10.90	34.63	41.02	19.04	130.90	34.90	96.00	3.8−1	0.58	5.10
1958--	136.96	16.70	27.77	40.71	19.91	121.03	36.83	84.19	3.3−1	0.61	4.71

[1]Consol,; inc. all active wholly owned subsidiaries in all years & all majority-owned subs. aft. 1964; incl. Calgon aft. 1965.
[2]Divs. paid regularly. [3]Adj. for 3-for-1 split in 1964. *As computed by Standard & Poor's.

Merck is one of the world's largest ethical drug houses, producing a broad line of both bulk and packaged fine and medicinal chemicals.

The acquisition of Calgon Corporation, a producer of water treatment chemicals, should improve sales and earnings. In addition, the introduction of new products, including Mumpsvax, a live virus mumps vaccine, and T-1-Gammagee, a prophylactic tetanus agent, is expected to bolster volume. Sales are aided substantially by the company's extensive research program, the largest in the drug industry.

NEWMONT MINING

INCOME STATISTICS (Million $) AND PER SHARE ($) DATA

Ended Dec. 31	3Gross Rev	Divs. Recd.	Int. & Service Inc.	Net Profits on Sec. Sales	Inc. Taxes	Net Inc.	—²Common Share ($) Data—— Earns.	Paid	Range	Price-Earns. Ratios HI LO
1968—	. . . . .	. . . .	. . .	. . . .	. . .	. . .	. . .	1.10	66-3/4 –55-1/8	. . . . .
1967—	55.13	52.45	2.68	9.75	7.60	50.74	5.33	2.20	70-3/8 –44-5/8	13– 8
1966—	51.55	47.85	3.70	11.13	8.70	48.22	5.15	1.87	63-7/8 –35-5/8	12– 7
1965—	38.68	36.51	2.16	2.22	5.78	31.36	3.43	1.36½	56-1/4 –39-7/8	16–12
1964—	23.25	21.56	1.68	4.02	4.05	19.95	2.23	1.13½	43-1/8 –32-3/8	19–15
1963—	18.42	17.26	1.16	0.75	2.90	13.76	1.46	0.93	33-1/4 –22-3/8	23–15
1962—	12.89	11.68	1.21	2.31	2.27	10.39	1.15	0.87	31-1/4 –18-7/8	27–16
1961—	15.02	13.52	1.51	2.95	0.69	14.90	1.92	0.87	27-3/4 –23-1/8	15–12
1960—	17.66	16.36	1.31	1.29	1.52	12.31	1.58	0.87	29 –20	18–13
1959—	14.12	13.06	1.06	0.58	1.33	11.18	1.45	0.76½	39-1/4 –24-3/4	27–17
1958—	11.17	10.08	1.09	2.82	1.13	10.61	1.37	0.73	39-1/2 –24-1/2	29–18

PERTINENT BALANCE SHEET STATISTICS (Million $)

Dec. 31	Total Assets	in New Ventures	Cash Items	Marketable Securs. Cost	At Mkt.	Oth. Invest. & Loans	—¹Net Asset Value— Total	²Per Sh. ($)
1967————————	272.5	48.56	18.58	145.4	588.1	106.99	712.4	74.74
1966————————	245.3	12.71	41.08	133.9	537.9	69.60	641.1	68.14
1965————————	212.4	13.23	21.71	124.5	514.7	65.92	596.7	65.31
1964————————	191.1	11.30	12.30	119.5	372.6	58.93	440.5	48.61
1963————————	179.7	7.13	6.98	121.0	300.6	51.29	357.5	38.34
1962———·————	174.9	7.93	3.97	118.3	237.3	51.53	292.2	30.04
1961————————	113.0	7.96	10.66	55.2	203.4	46.98	260.3	33.51
1960————————	107.6	5.79	11.48	55.3	171.2	40.60	219.7	28.29
1959————————	101.4	8.00	9.19	50.8	188.2	41.14	234.4	30.35
1958————————	92.9	9.96	9.22	43.4	189.7	40.15	294.6	38.13

¹At mkt., except invest. with no quoted mkt. val. at cost aft. 1958. ²Adj. for 2½-for-1 split in 1963 & stk. div. of 10% in 1966. ³Incl. profits & losses on securities, etc.

Investments of this holding company are principally in non-ferrous metals (mainly copper), oil, and gas. United States and Canadian firms now account for about half of net dividend income, and two South African mining companies are important contributors.

Future additions to the earnings base are expected to come from expansion of the Southern Peru copper operation, the Granduc copper property in Canada, and possibly Atlantic Cement, as well as from developments resulting from the company's extensive explorations.

PACIFIC PETROLEUMS

[3]INCOME STATISTICS (Million $) AND PER SHARE ($) DATA

[1]Year Ended Dec. 31	Sales	Oper. Inc.	Other Inc. Net	[4]Depr. &Depl	Net Inc.	Earns.	*Cash Generated	Divs. Paid	[2]Price Range	HI LO
1968—	----	----	----	----	----	----	----	----	18 3/4—14 5/8	----
1967—	71.55	33.01	0.73	15.23	11.01	0.53	1.27	0.15	19 1/2—10	37—19
1966—	61.56	27.70	0.44	13.65	6.83	0.33	1.00	Nil	14 5/8— 8 5/8	48—26
1965—	54.73	25.07	0.61	12.86	5.46	0.26	0.91	Nil	11 5/8— 8 7/8	45—34
1964—	42.44	22.44	0.29	12.49	4.42	0.21	0.85	Nil	14 1/8—10 1/8	67—48
1963—	33.51	20.08	0.23	12.41	3.68	0.18	0.81	Nil	14 1/2—10 1/4	80—57
1962—	27.90	17.30	0.27	10.77	3.04	0.80	0.80	Nil	17 1/4— 9	101—52
1961—	20.20	10.71	0.35	8.37	1.02	0.07	0.57	Nil	14 7/8— 9 3/4	----
1960—	18.59	9.97	0.39	9.47	d2.48	d0.17	0.49	Nil	13 7/8— 8	----
1959—	10.95	6.34	0.36	7.88	d3.92	d0.48	0.46	Nil	19 1/8—11 3/8	----
1958—	9.49	4.93	0.33	7.05	d4.28	d0.55	0.30	Nil	22 3/8—16 1/4	----

[3]PERTINENT BALANCE SHEET STATISTICS (Million $)

Dec. 31	Gross Prop.	Cash Items	Inven-tories	Receiv-ables	Current Assets	Current Liabs.	Net Workg. Cap.	Cur. Ratio Assets to Liabs.	Long Term Debt	($) Book Val Com. Sh.
1967	450.27	2.50	6.53	15.69	24.73	16.05	8.68	1.5—1	132.90	11.55
1966	414.47	0.90	5.10	15.99	21.98	13.67	8.32	1.7—1	116.48	11.15
1965	386.59	10.15	4.09	13.09	27.32	10.37	16.96	2.6—1	117.38	10.80
1964	368.10	2.70	4.40	14.84	21.95	18.24	3.71	1.2—1	84.45	10.69
1963	339.90	3.06	2.88	10.53	16.47	13.08	3.39	1.3—1	68.78	10.49
1962	225.59	3.60	2.71	6.74	13.19	9.86	3.32	1.3—1	44.25	10.05
1961	193.67	2.56	2.30	5.20	10.22	8.57	1.65	1.2—1	47.80	9.10
1960	192.12	1.20	3.85	5.65	10.87	9.51	1.37	1.1—1	53.62	8.94
1959	105.92	2.36	1.62	3.34	7.36	5.48	1.88	1.3—1	50.00	7.40
1958	93.67	3.12	2.23	4.69	10.10	4.16	5.94	2.4—1	52.45	7.72

[1]Yrs. ended Feb. 28 of foll. cal. yr. in 1960 & prior yrs. [2]10 mos. [3]All dollar figures in Canadian currency, except price ranges. [4]Incl. all property charges. d Deficit.
*As computed by Standard & Poor's.

Some 45 percent controlled by Phillips Petroleum, Pacific is an integrated western Canadian oil company.

Expansion of operations in several areas—crude oil and gas production, refined product marketing, and gas liquids processing —has favorable implications. The Canadian exploration activities also add to potential.

PHELPS DODGE

INCOME STATISTICS (Million $) AND PER SHARE ($) DATA

Year Ended Dec. 31	Net Sales	% Oper. Inc. of Sales	Depr.	Net Bef. Taxes & Depl.	Net Inc.-- Bef. Depl.	Net Inc.-- Aft. Depl.	Capital Share ($) Data Earns-- Bef. Depl.	Earns Aft. Depl.	*Cash Generated	Divs. Paid	Price Range	Price-Earns. Ratios HI LO
1968--	--	---	----	----	----	----	---	---	---	1.70	72 1/2-59 1/2	-----
1967--	509.8	14.7	11.46	77.00	50.80	50.41	5.04	5.00	6.18	3.40	80 -62 1/2	16- 13
1966--	554.0	24.7	12.82	139.35	82.85	82.17	8.17	8.10	9.43	4.25	83 -54 1/4	10- 7
1965--	460.0	24.4	12.45	107.75	67.75	66.65	6.68	6.57	7.91	4.00	78 1/2-66 1/2	12-10
1964--	389.4	22.2	9.75	84.28	56.28	55.14	5.55	5.44	6.51	3.10	78 -61 1/4	14-11
1963--	327.2	20.5	10.80	60.93	39.93	38.87	3.94	3.83	5.11	3.00	63 1/4-52 3/4	16-13
1962--	317.9	20.8	10.58	61.40	39.73	38.70	3.92	3.82	4.96	3.00	62 3/8-44 5/8	16-11
1961--	312.3	21.3	9.94	61.40	39.20	38.12	3.86	3.76	4.85	3.00	65 1/4-46 5/8	17-12
1960--	286.7	21.8	8.57	58.41	37.31	36.05	3.68	3.55	4.52	3.00	57 5/8-43 1/2	16-12
1959--	285.6	20.1	7.93	54.72	34.57	33.46	3.41	3.30	4.19	3.00	70 1/2-54 1/4	21-16
1958--	269.9	23.9	8.16	60.61	38.01	36.48	3.75	3.60	4.55	3.00	64 1/4-37	17-10

PERTINENT BALANCE SHEET STATISTICS (Million $)

Dec. 31	Gross Prop.	¹Capital Expend.	Cash Items	Inven-tories	Receiv-ables	Current Assets	Current Liabs.	Net Workg. Cap.	Cur. Ratio Assets to Liabs.	Long Term Debt	($) Book Value Cap. Sh.
1967--	604.46	66.64	78.0	100.4	60.4	242.2	79.4	162.8	3.1-1	Nil	50.79
1966--	548.00	32.39	147.6	93.5	53.3	296.8	81.6	215.2	3.6-1	Nil	49.31
1965--	517.58	21.58	129.4	79.5	51.6	262.9	64.4	198.5	4.1-1	Nil	45.45
1964--	496.70	31.97	121.9	74.8	40.1	238.9	49.8	189.1	4.8-1	Nil	42.88
1963--	464.50	19.88	147.9	70.8	30.7	251.1	44.2	206.9	5.7-1	Nil	40.55
1962--	444.82	8.87	139.3	69.9	29.6	241.0	43.1	197.9	5.6-1	Nil	39.72
1961--	435.20	10.32	127.8	64.7	26.8	221.4	42.0	179.4	5.3-1	Nil	38.90
1960--	427.14	7.77	107.6	71.7	30.6	211.7	40.1	171.5	5.3-1	Nil	38.14
1959--	449.14	7.33	115.4	58.7	23.6	200.0	35.8	164.2	5.6-1	Nil	37.59
1958--	443.65	16.39	131.2	55.1	23.3	211.0	47.5	163.4	4.4-1	Nil	37.29

¹Excl. $25.8 million invested in Southern Peru Copper Corp. in 1957-9. ²Based on earns. bef. depl. *As computed by Standard & Poor's.

The second largest domestic copper producer, this company is a relatively low-cost operator which fabricates most of its copper into wire, cable, and tubing. The company is also an important custom smelter-refiner and has a 16 percent stake in Southern Peru Copper.

As a *domestic* producer, the company has less risk than most others. Mine output of copper, the prime determinant of earnings, should rise about 20 percent in the next 3 years. The small aluminium program could eventually be more important.

PHILLIPS PETROLEUM

[1] INCOME STATISTICS (Million $) AND PER SHARE ($) DATA

Year Ended Dec. 31	[4]Gross Oper. Inc.	%Op. Inc.of Gross	Oper. Inc.	[2]Depr. & Depl.	Net Bef. Taxes	[3]Net Inc.	[3]Earns	*Cash Generated	Divs. Paid	Price Range	Price-Earns. Ratios HI LO
1968–	—	—	—	—	—	—	—	—	1.25	66-5/8—53-1/8	—
1967–	1,981.6	20.7	410.2	170.1	227.77	164.02	4.74	9.62	2.35	67-1/8—49	14—10
1966–	1,760.3	21.0	369.6	158.1	203.60	138.40	4.14	8.85	2.20-1/3	58-7/8—44-1/8	14—11
1965–	1,450.7	21.2	307.8	140.9	165.88	127.72	3.83	8.05	2.05	60-5/8—49-1/2	16—13
1964–	1,341.5	20.7	277.4	125.8	152.20	115.02	3.44	7.20	2.00	56-1/2—47	16—14
1963–	1,335.1	21.6	288.1	132.8	166.23	108.09	3.15	7.03	1.97-1/2	55-7/8—47	16—14
1962–	1,244.6	22.6	281.8	129.4	158.32	106.96	3.11	6.88	1.85	59-7/8—42	19—14
1961–	1,220.6	24.3	297.2	131.1	165.85	113.78	3.31	7.12	1.70	64-1/2—51-1/2	19—16
1960–	1,200.2	24.1	289.4	139.5	166.93	112.93	3.29	7.35	1.70	54 —41-1/8	16—12
1959–	1,163.0	23.9	277.9	122.5	159.64	104.64	3.05	6.61	1.70	52-3/4—41	17—13
1958–	1.066.6	22.5	240.1	127.7	105.24	84.24	2.45	6.17	1.70	49-1/4—36-3/8	20—15

[1] PERTINENT BALANCE SHEET STATISTICS (Million $)

Dec. 31	Gross Prop.	Capital Expend.	Cash Items	Oil Inventories	Receivables	Current Assets	Current Liabs.	Net Workg. Cap.	Cur. Ratio Assets to Liabs.	Long Term Debt	($) Book Val. Com. Sh.
1967–	3,268.0	279.80	147.1	228.2	351.5	757.6	429.7	327.9	1.8—1	690.0	43.69
1966–	3,145.3	579.70	176.2	218.2	303.2	729.1	571.8	157.3	1.3—1	660.3	41.05
1965–	2,524.1	232.40	93.9	152.0	219.4	490.8	243.6	247.2	2.0—1	333.7	39.54
1964–	2,409.0	195.00	89.7	144.9	192.6	449.2	224.8	224.4	2.0—1	260.6	37.79
1963–	2,289.1	156.50	113.4	140.5	183.2	460.3	241.3	218.9	1.9—1	201.5	36.71
1962–	2,177.0	156.30	87.2	123.8	171.8	405.3	200.7	204.6	2.0—1	223.0	35.52
1961–	2,084.4	131.91	108.4	120.7	162.9	418.9	199.2	219.8	2.1—1	242.9	34.18
1960–	2,013.5	180.65	78.8	128.5	154.7	390.5	194.8	195.7	2.0—1	261.8	32.67
1959–	1,946.9	120.81	110.2	115.8	145.7	404.0	184.1	219.9	2.2—1	280.2	31.09
1958–	1,893.7	132.82	92.5	114.0	131.8	368.3	151.2	217.1	2.4—1	302.3	29.70

[1]Consol; incl. all cos. in which more than 50% interest is held aft. 1965 and incl. Sealright Oswego Falls aft. 1962. [2]Incl. all prop. charges. [3]Incl. $0.23 a sh. non-recurring inc. in 1959, $0.41 in 1960, & $0.10 in 1961; bef. spec. crs. of $0.25 in 1963 & $0.21 in 1966. [4]Excl. excise taxes.
*As computed by Standard & Poor's.

This leading domestic oil company with closely allied products is also significantly involved in natural gas and gas liquids, petrochemicals, and plastics. As mentioned above, the company holds a 45 percent interest in Pacific Petroleums; other major holdings are in the Middle East, North Africa, and Venezuela.

On March 25, 1968, Phillips and its associates announced award of a contract for a gas treating plant * to handle ultimately one billion cubic feet of gas per day. Completion was scheduled for the second quarter of 1969. The company has approved plans for an additional $40,000,000 of new plant construction at its Puerto Rico petrochemical complex, bringing total committed outlays to $175,000,000 for projects under construction or planned in Puerto Rico.

* Cleans impurities in gas.

RICHARDSON-MERRELL

INCOME STATISTICS (Million $) AND PER SHARE ($) DATA

Year Ended June 30	Net Sales	% Oper. Inc. of Sales	Oper. Inc.	Depr. & Amort.	Net Bef. Taxes	Net Inc.	Earns.	−2Common Share ($) Data−			Price-Earns. Ratios HI LO
								*Cash Generated	Divs. Paid	Price 1Range	
1968−	− − −	− − −	− − −	− − −	− − −	− − −	− − −	− − −	1.30	90 −72-1/2	− − −
1967−	269.0	20.3	54.49	5.27	48.92	25.05	4.38	5.30	1.30	103-1/4−66	24−15
1966−	247.8	21.1	52.34	4.37	48.07	24.16	4.20	4.96	1.15	87-3/4−59-5/8	21−16
1965−	213.4	21.5	45.78	3.89	42.36	20.42	3.54	4.22	1.00	85 −55-1/2	22−16
1964−	180.3	21.1	38.04	3.01	36.40	17.80	3.08	3.60	1.00	60-1/4−39-3/4	19−13
1963−	169.9	21.6	36.62	2.59	36.30	17.51	3.01	3.45	1.00	65-3/4−46	22−15
1962−	161.9	22.8	36.97	2.30	36.45	17.26	2.90	3.29	1.00	102 −40	35−14
1961−	151.5	23.1	35.01	1.98	35.31	17.03	2.86	3.19	0.93-3/4	111-3/4−78-1/2	39−27
1960−	132.3	22.5	29.78	1.93	30.25	14.38	2.42	2.74	0.71-1/4	93-3/8−57	39−24
1959−	115.2	21.7	25.04	1.81	24.39	12.16	2.03	2.33	0.60	72-1/4−31-1/2	36−16
1958−	107.0	20.6	22.04	1.60	21.88	10.07	1.88	2.18	0.60	36-3/8−17	19− 9

PERTINENT BALANCE SHEET STATISTICS (Million $)

June 30	Gross Prop.	Capital Expend.	Cash Items	Inven-tories	Receiv-ables	−−Current−− Assets	Liabs.	Net Workg. Cap.	Cur. Ratio Assets to Liabs.	Long Term Debt	2($) Book Val. Com. Sh.
1967−	103.90	15.42	23.0	53.6	44.88	129.68	57.56	72.13	2.3−1	Nil	20.05
1966−	83.08	11.49	24.3	50.5	35.33	116.00	41.88	74.12	2.8−1	Nil	19.44
1965−	52.29	7.85	21.2	30.7	14.38	68.86	19.22	49.64	3.6−1	Nil	17.78
1964−	48.98	8.84	16.4	26.5	11.96	57.21	16.21	41.01	3.5−1	Nil	15.49
1963−	44.72	7.27	18.9	26.0	11.23	58.34	10.19	48.15	5.7−1	Nil	15.52
1962−	38.96	5.01	29.3	23.9	9.24	64.47	15.39	49.08	4.2−1	Nil	14.75
1961−	35.70	4.89	25.5	23.3	10.42	60.61	7.59	53.02	8.0−1	Nil	12.95
1960−	32.28	2.30	25.7	21.0	9.72	57.85	10.97	46.88	5.3−1	Nil	11.08
1959−	30.59	2.19	29.0	18.7	8.52	57.47	6.78	50.69	8.5−1	Nil	11.32
1958−	27.89	3.41	20.0	18.7	7.78	47.76	6.12	41.64	7.8−1	Nil	10.66

1Cal. yrs.   2Adj. for splits of 4-for-3 in 1960 & 2-for1 in 1959.
*As computed by Standard & Poor's.

This company is a well-established producer of proprietary, ethical and veterinary drugs.

Future growth is anticipated through a combination of internal research, acquisitions, and aggressive marketing both in the United States and abroad.

SCHERING CORPORATION

[2] INCOME STATISTICS (Million $) AND PER SHARE ($) DATA

Year Ended Dec. 31	Net Sales	% Oper. Inc. of Sales	Oper. Inc.	Deprec.	Net Bef. Taxes	Net Inc.	[1] Common Share ($) Data				Price-Earns. Ratios HI LO
							Earns.	*Cash Generated	Divs. Paid	Price Range	
1968--	---	---	---	---	---	---	---	---	0.60	70 −56-1/2	---
1967--	150.66	21.2	31.89	3.69	36.60	19.03	2.39	2.85	1.15	72-7/8−53-1/2	31−22
1966--	135.77	20.1	27.28	3.38	32.18	16.73	2.12	2.55	0.97½	57 −38-1/4	27−18
1965--	117.56	19.9	23.40	3.15	27.54	14.32	1.82	2.22	0.85	46-7/8−28	26−15
1964--	102.63	20.7	21.23	3.25	23.85	11.95	1.50	1.92	0.77	29-3/4−20-3/4	20−14
1963--	92.60	21.0	19.41	3.26	20.47	10.52	1.29	1.70	0.75	23-1/2−17-5/8	18−14
1962--	87.55	20.8	18.23	3.29	19.24	10.24	1.24	1.65	0.75	30-1/4−15-3/8	24−12
1961--	82.92	20.2	16.76	2.94	17.98	10.03	1.20	1.56	0.75	35 −23-1/4	29−19
1960--	84.23	19.0	15.99	2.84	17.41	9.87	1.18	1.53	0.70	40-3/4−21-1/4	35−18
1959--	80.56	23.5	18.92	2.33	20.44	11.86	1.43	1.72	0.70	41 −26-3/8	29−18
1958--	75.18	29.1	21.86	1.88	22.96	12.45	1.53	1.76	0.60	30-3/4−16-3/8	20−11

[2] PERTINENT BALANCE SHEET STATISTICS (Million $)

Dec. 31	Gross Prop.	Capital Expend.	Cash Items	Inven-tories	Receiv-ables	Current		Net Working Capital	Cur. Ratio Assets to Liabs.	Long Term Debt	[1] ($) Book Val. Com. Sh.
						Assets	Liabs.				
1967--	65.22	6.85	29.38	24.71	28.89	92.45	34.97	57.48	2.6−1	0.80	11.29
1966--	58.50	5.62	34.42	22.24	25.06	89.95	35.40	54.55	2.5−1	0.21	10.23
1965--	52.56	5.37	32.42	18.14	20.60	76.86	31.29	45.52	2.5−1	Nil	10.07
1964--	49.53	3.25	33.52	15.06	20.62	70.01	27.04	42.97	2.6−1	Nil	9.12
1963--	47.60	3.74	34.72	13.41	18.55	67.45	21.88	45.57	3.1−1	Nil	8.45
1962--	44.80	4.32	37.63	13.85	13.68	65.82	20.23	45.59	3.3−1	Nil	8.26
1961--	42.18	7.08	37.07	12.01	13.02	62.74	18.75	44.00	3.3−1	Nil	7.97
1960--	36.24	6.61	32.18	13.91	12.44	59.46	15.14	44.31	3.9−1	0.09	7.50
1959--	30.85	5.16	31.76	14.48	11.51	58.68	15.69	42.99	3.7−1	0.10	7.00
1958--	25.86	5.27	33.49	12.38	8.53	55.21	16.10	39.11	3.4−1	0.11	6.17

[1] Adj. for 2-for-1 Split in 1966. [2] Consol.; inc. Brazilian subs. from 1966. *As computed by Standard & Poor's.

This drug company has been strong on research and acquisitions. The result is a better balanced product line as well as development of foreign business.

Valisone, a drug for treating allergic and inflammatory skin disorder, and several other new drugs should bolster sales of established lines. A number of research developments have considerably strengthened the product line in recent years. Acquisitions and expansion of foreign operations are other favorable factors.

SOUTHEASTERN DRILLING

INCOME STATISTICS (Million $) AND PER SHARE ($) DATA

Year Ended Dec. 31	[3]Gross Rev.	Divs. Recd.	Int. & Service Inc.	Net Profits on Sec. Sales	Inc. Taxes	Net Inc.	—[2]Common Share ($) Data—			Price-Earns. Ratios HI LO
							Earns.	Divs. Paid	Price Range	
1968—	- - - - - -	- - - - -	- - - - -	- - - - - - - -	- - - -	- - -	- - - -	1.10	66-3/4 - 55-1/8	- - - - - -
1967—	55.13	52.45	2.68	9.75	7.60	50.74	5.33	2.20	70-3/8 - 44-5/8	13- 8
1966—	51.55	47.85	3.70	11.13	8.70	48.22	5.15	1.87	63-7/8 - 35-5/8	12- 7
1965—	38.68	36.51	2.16	2.22	5.78	31.36	3.43	1.36½	56-1/4 - 39 7/8	16-12
1964—	23.25	21.56	1.68	4.02	4.05	19.95	2.23	1.13½	43-1/8 - 32-3/8	19-15
1963—	18.42	17.26	1.16	0.75	2.90	13.76	1.46	0.93	33-1/4 - 22-3/8	23-15
1962—	12.89	11.68	1.21	2.31	2.27	10.39	1.15	0.87	31-1/2 - 18-7/8	27-16
1961—	15.02	13.52	1.51	2.95	0.69	14.90	1.92	0.87	27-3/4 - 23-1/8	15-12
1960—	17.66	16.36	1.31	1.29	1.52	12.31	1.58	0.87	29 - 20	18-13
1959—	14.12	13.06	1.06	0.58	1.33	11.18	1.45	0.76½	39-1/4 - 24-3/4	27-17
1958—	11.17	10.08	1.09	2.82	1.13	10.61	1.37	0.73	39-1/2 - 24-1/2	29-18

PERTINENT BALANCE SHEET STATISTICS (Million $)

Dec. 31	Total Assets	Expend. in New Ventures	Cash Items	Marketable Securs. Cost	At Mkt.	Oth. Invest. & Loans	—[1]Net Asset Value—	
							Total	[2]Per Sh. ($)
1967———————	272.5	48.56	18.58	145.4	588.1	106.99	712.4	74.74
1966———————	245.3	12.71	41.08	133.9	537.9	69.60	641.1	68.14
1965———————	212.4	13.23	21.71	124.5	514.7	65.92	596.7	65.31
1964———————	191.1	11.30	12.30	119.5	372.6	58.93	440.5	48.61
1963———————	179.7	7.13	6.98	121.0	300.6	51.29	357.5	38.34
1962———————	174.9	7.93	3.97	118.3	237.3	51.53	292.2	30.04
1961———————	113.0	7.96	10.66	55.2	203.4	46.98	260.3	33.51
1960———————	107.6	5.79	11.48	55.3	171.2	40.60	219.7	28.29
1959———————	101.4	8.00	9.19	50.8	188.2	41.14	234.4	30.35
1958———————	92.9	9.96	9.22	43.4	189.7	40.15	294.6	38.13

This company is engaged primarily in contract drilling operations for major oil companies, with particular emphasis on offshore and foreign work.

Growth in offshore activities was spurred by use of Sedco-135 specially designed semi-submersible drilling barges, which can drill in water up to 600 feet in depth.

SYBON CORPORATION (formerly Ritter Pfaudler Corp.)

[1]INCOME STATISTICS (Million $) AND PER SHARE ($) DATA

Year Ended Dec. 31	Net Sales	[2]% Oper. Inc. of Sales	[2]Oper. Inc.	Depr. & Amort.	Net bef. Taxes	[3]Net Inc.	[3]Earns.	Divs. Paid	Price Range	[4]Common Share ($) Data	Price-Earns. Ratios HI LO
1968–	- - - -	- - - -	- - - -	- - - - -	- - - - -	- - - -	- - - - - -	0.15	44-1/2–31-1/4		- - - - - -
1967–	187.30	13.2	24.69	3.24	23.56	12.38	[5]1.45	0.55	42-3/8–22-1/8		29–15
1966–	175.16	13.1	22.92	2.96	21.47	11.48	[5]1.36	0.50	26-3/8–17		19–13
1965–	147.89	12.9	19.04	2.62	17.78	9.06	1.14	0.21½	20-3/4–18-1/2		18–16
1964–	119.34	9.4	12.19	2.34	12.10	6.11	0.89	- - -	- - - - - - - - - - - -		- - - - - -
1963–	109.84	7.8	8.53	N.A.	9.41	4.90	0.72	- - -	- - - - - - - - - - - -		- - - - - -
1962–	102.74	7.2	7.39	N.A.	8.35	4.41	0.65	- - -	- - - - - - - - - - - -		- - - - - -
1961–	98.83	6.0	5.97	N.A.	7.31	3.49	0.51	- - -	- - - - - - - - - - - -		- - - - - -
1960–	103.58	8.7	9.04	N.A.	10.06	4.82	0.71	- - -	- - - - - - - - - - - -		- - - - - -

[1]PERTINENT BALANCE SHEET STATISTICS (Million $)

Dec. 31	Gross Prop.	Capital Expend.	Cash Items	Inventories	Receivables	Current Assets	Current Liabs.	Net Workg. Cap.	Cur. Ratio Assets to Liabs.	Long Term Debt	[4]($) Book Val. Com. Sh.
1967–	63.91	7.81	7.85	45.18	43.38	97.74	31.57	66.17	3.1–1	20.51	9.47
1966–	56.78	5.32	8.86	41.41	41.36	92.89	37.09	55.81	2.5–1	13.71	8.73
1965–	50.11	3.45	8.88	37.34	35.80	83.25	34.40	48.85	2.4–1	11.82	8.02
1964–	44.43	- - - -	6.95	31.82	31.22	70.87	26.87	44.00	2.6–1	13.83	7.79

[1]In 1964 & prior yrs. represents pro forma comb. oper. results of Ritter Corp. & subs. & Pfaudler Permutit Inc. & subs; restated in subsequent yrs. for pooling of interests acquisitions. [5]Assuming conv. of debs. & exercise of options, earns. would be $1.41 in 1967 & $1.32 in 1966. [2]Aft. depr. & amort. in 1960–63. [3]Bef. spec. credit of $0.04 a sh. in 1964 and spec. charges of $0.09 in 1962 & $0.10 in 1961. [4]Adj. for 2-for-1 split in 1967. N.A.–Not available.

A leader in the field of dental and medical equipment, the company is putting increasing emphasis on industrial * and water treatment and on the introduction of new products.

Growth potentials in the five major divisions are favorable, reflecting advanced industrial technologies, a growing health consciousness, and mounting interest in pollution and waste control.

* Water cleansing

WESTERN UNION TELEGRAPH

INCOME STATISTICS (Million $) AND PER SHARE ($) DATA

Year Ended Dec. 31	-----Gross Oper. Revs.----- Message Service	Other Revs.	Total	% of Gross Revs. Depr. & Maint.	Taxes	[3] Oper. Ratio	Fxd. Chgs. Tms. Earn.	[2] Net Inc.	[2] Earns.	Divs. Paid	Price Range	Price-Earns. Ratios HI LO
1968-	----	----	----	----	----	---	------	---	----	0.70	48½-31	----
1967-	156.0	180.8	336.8	27.8	4.2	94.2	2.99	17.54[4]	1.61	1.40	46 5/8-30	29-19
1966-	162.3	158.1	320.4	27.1	4.1	93.2	4.10	21.89	2.46	1.40	58¼-28½	24-12
1965-	160.8	144.9	305.7	27.3	3.6	93.4	3.54	17.83	2.30	1.40	53½-30	23-13
1964-	163.2	136.2	299.4	27.3	3.4	92.7	3.50	17.16	2.29	1.40	37 -29	16-13
1963-	164.4	132.7	297.1	25.3	2.3	93.8	5.25	16.87	2.25	1.40	35 -25	16-11
1962-	180.7	96.8	277.5	23.2	3.0	96.6	22.68	10.61	1.42	1.40	41¾-21½	29-15
1961-	187.3	91.2	278.5	22.5	4.9	96.4	10.70	12.23	1.63	1.40	55 -38	34-23
1960-	189.6	86.5	276.1	21.7	5.7	95.9	7.51	11.02	1.72	1.40	57 -38¼	33-22
1959-	194.2	82.0	276.2	20.0	7.9	94.1	12.01	16.69	2.62	1.20	53¾-29¾	21-11
1958-	185.1	70.0	255.1	20.1	5.7	95.4	8.81	12.66	2.01	1.20	34¾-15	17- 8

PERTINENT BALANCE SHEET STATISTICS (Million $)

Dec. 31	Gross Prop.	Capital Expend.	[1] Depr. Res.	% Earn on Net Prop.	Funded Debt.	Net Prop.	----% Funded Debt of---- Gross Revs.	Invest. Cap.	Total Invest. Cap.	% Earn. on Inv. Cap.	($) Bk. Val. Com. Sh.
1967-	885.1	152.97	281.2	3.3	225.1	37.3	66.8	34.2	657.3	4.0	41.11
1966-	789.5	148.78	263.3	4.1	200.4	38.1	62.5	34.8	576.2	5.0	40.29
1965-	693.3	96.99	243.0	4.5	193.0	42.9	60.2	38.2	524.3	4.7	39.40
1964-	638.9	72.90	221.8	5.3	167.5	40.1	55.9	36.5	458.3	5.2	38.53
1963-	600.2	92.25	198.9	4.6	168.6	42.0	56.7	37.2	452.8	4.6	37.69
1962-	582.1	139.57	203.5	2.7	145.7	39.0	52.5	38.5	433.3	2.6	38.11
1961-	476.1	64.54	197.8	3.5	33.0	11.9	11.8	9.7	318.3	3.5	38.11
1960-	437.4	41.07	188.1	4.8	31.9	12.8	11.5	11.4	278.8	4.8	37.45
1959-	417.9	38.43	176.4	6.4	33.0	13.7	11.9	12.1	273.0	6.6	37.18
1958-	401.3	39.95	168.3	5.0	34.1	14.6	13.4	12.9	265.3	5.1	36.04

[1] Incl. reserve for devel. [2] Bef. spec. cr. of $0.79 a sh. in 1967 & bef. sp. chgs. of $0.03 a sh. in 1964 & $1.26 in 1963; aft. crs. of $0.12 in 1958, $0.03 in 1959, & $0.32 in 1961; aft. charge of $0.08 in 1960. [3] Aft. depr. & taxes. [4] Pro forma assuming conv. of pfd. stk. & exer. of options earns. would have been $1.55 a sh.

The company is now concentrating on the development of specialized communications services, such as the new Broadband Exchange Service, Telex, and private data networks for government and industry.

COMPANIES WHOSE NAMES NO LONGER
PROPERLY DESCRIBE OPERATIONS

It is interesting to note the misleading names of many companies, RCA for example, owns Hertz computer operations, Random House and Saint Regis Paper. CBS owns the New York Yankees. International Telephone owns Avis, No. 2 in the car rental field, as well as a real estate company. Pullman no longer operates Pullman cars. Bath Industries, formerly known as Bath Iron Works, makers of ships, is now a larger producer of floor coverings. Loew's Theatres is now a hotel company and recently purchased Lorillard Tobacco.

American Broadcasting

75% radio and TV
15% theatre operations
10% merchandise sales, publishing, and other income.

American Machine & Foundry

36% Industrial products
26% Government sales
20% recreation
18% bowling (including rentals and equipment sales).

American News

In addition to the newsstands, the company operates Savarin Restaurants and has a food service management division serving industries, plants, hospitals, schools, etc.

American Standard

With the acquisition of Mosler Safe in mid-1967, and the recently acquired Westinghouse Air Brake, AST has moved out of the construction industry to a significant degree. The company now operates in the security and office-products field, aviation, defense and aerospace, rapid transit, and mining. Currently, approximately 33 percent of total sales of $905 million are realized from non-construction items.

American Tobacco

Over 25 percent of revenues now comes from liquors, crackers, and snack foods.

Boise Cascade

Boise is most noted as a large lumber and paper company. However, this company over the last eighteen months has become the largest factor in the single family housing market. Furthermore, with the acquisition of Divco-Wayne, Boise became the largest factor in the mobile home industry. Currently, nearly 30 percent of total annual sales of approximately $900 million is derived from home construction, land development and mobile homes.

Campbell Soup

Aside from the well-known soup line, the company produces Swanson TV Dinners, V-8, Pepperidge Farm Fresh and Frozen Baked Goods, and Franco-American canned spaghetti and macaroni. In addition, the company is now thinking of going into pet foods and has obtained the right to use the name Lassie.

Chris-Craft Industries

60% pleasure boats
16% television revenues
13% carpet and foam rubber products (primarily for the auto-industry)

| | 8% chemical products including DDT |
| | 3% plastic products. |

Coca-Cola

Aside from the well-known Coca-Cola, the company produces a broad line of soft drinks and is a major factor in the coffee business—both consumer and institutional. It also has Minute Maid which, among the brand names, is the biggest selling frozen orange juice on the market.

Columbia Broadcasting System

65% broadcasting
25% phonograph records and musical instruments
10% textbooks.

Cook Coffee

Almost all of the revenue comes from the operations of supermarkets and discount department stores.

Electric & Musical Industries

50% phonograph records
30% electronic capital goods
20% household appliances

Hamilton Watch Co.

46% clocks and watches
19% silverware
35% military and industrial products.

International Silver Co.

46% silverware
12% bottle caps
11% auto parts and wire products
9% cosmetic cases and custom finishing of metal products
5% non-ferrous rolling mills
17% publishing and others.

National Can

National Can has taken some giant steps in the last year to lessen its reliance on the metal can business. In the last year, National has acquired six canning companies and a dog food company (Laddie Boy). For calendar 1968, these acquisitions contributed approximately $40 million to total sales or 16 percent. The company's long-range planning program has as its target a $600 million sales level by 1972 of which no more than 50 percent of the total will be from the metal can industry.

Outboard Marine

70% marine products
14% vehicles including snow mobiles
16% power mowers, garden implements, chain saws, and others.

Storer Broadcasting

Has acquired an 86 percent interest in Northeast Airlines, Inc.

SOURCE NOTES

Eccles,	*Beckoning Frontiers,* Knopf
Gardner,	*Pricing Power and the Public Interest,* Harper & Row
Garver & Hansen,	*Principles of Economics,* Ginn
Granville,	*Granville's New Key to Stock Market Profits,* Prentice-Hall
———,	*Strategy of Daily Market Timing for Maximum Profit,* Prentice-Hall
———,	*Committee on Finance and Industry Report,* London H.M. Stationery Office
Keynes,	*Essays in Persuasion,* London, Macmillan
Kuznets,	*Economic Growth and Structure,* Norton
Markstein,	*How to Chart Your Way to Stock Market Profits,* Prentice-Hall
———,	*First National City Bank,* Monthly News Letter, Ferbuary, 1965
Plotnick & McCrane,	*Fundamentals for Profit in Undervalued Stocks,* Prentice-Hall
Samuelson,	*The Modern Scene,* M.I.T. Press
Schultz,	*Bear Markets: How to Survive and Make Money in Them,* Prentice-Hall
Smith,	*Rockefeller Brothers Fund: Prospect for America,* Doubleday
———,	*Inquiry into the Nature and Causes of the Wealth of Nations,* Modern Library
Wyckoff,	*The Dictionary of Stock Market Terms,* Prentice-Hall
———,	*The Psychology of Stock Market Timing,* Prentice-Hall

The following institutions provided source material:

THE NEW YORK STOCK EXCHANGE
THE AMERICAN STOCK EXCHANGE
THE NATIONAL ASSOCIATION OF SECURITIES DEALERS

Index

189

332.6
Jarvis, N. Leonard
A woman's guide to Wall Street.

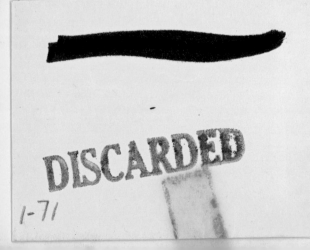

DISCARDED

1-71